BOLIVIA:
GATE OF THE SUN

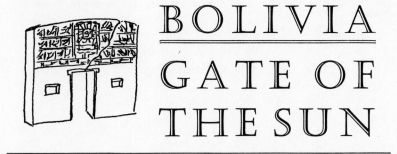

BOLIVIA
GATE OF
THE SUN

MARGARET JOAN ANSTEE

Paul S. Eriksson, INC.
New York

First American Edition 1970

Published in Great Britain in 1970 by
Longman Group Ltd London

© Copyright 1970 by **Margaret Joan Anstee**

Library of Congress Catalog Card Number 70-131239

SBN Number 8397-1068-2

Printed in Great Britain

For the late Professor J. B. Trend,
who first opened my eyes to Latin America and
for my parents, who made it all possible.

'This Bolivian Republic has a special
enchantment for me. The more I think
about the destiny of the country, the
more it seems to me a tiny marvel.'
Simon Bolívar to José Antonio Sucre

 CONTENTS

ILLUSTRATIONS

ix

ACKNOWLEDGEMENTS

Grateful acknowledgement is made to the following for
permission to use photographs:

Toni Hagen; 2, 8, 11, 14, 15, 17, 23, 25, 31, 32, 37,
39, 40, 41
International Labour Organization: 18, 19, 20, 21, 38
Arthur Karasz: 42
Wolf Lackschewitz: 3, 5, 6, 7, 9, 10, 12, 13, 33, 34, 44, 45
Alberto Tardío: 4, 28, 29, 30, 35, 36
United Nations: 1, 22, 26, 27
Manuel Ares: 24

The maps are by John Flower

PREFACE

I first thought of writing this book one day in August 1964 when I was bumping in a jeep on my way to meet some of the United Nations and Bolivian geologists working on a mineral survey in the lonely hills behind Uncía.

A long journey at the best of times, it was prolonged, as so often in Bolivia, by the need for repairs to the jeep, which were carried out in a blacksmith's shop at Llallagua, in the heart of Bolivian mining country. During those seven or eight hours there was plenty of time for contemplation of that hallucinating landscape known as the *altiplano*—the high plateau of the Andes—stretching into apparently limitless distances, and monotonous only to those unable to perceive its subtle and infinite variations of form and colour, its rare intensity of light; of the Aymara Indians, trudging to market along the dusty highway with their laden donkeys and llamas or toiling in stony fields, at the end of the long, dry, highland winter; of wayside fairs, crowded with animals and people, in unkempt villages where the adobe cottages huddle in the lee of the church; of, finally, the stark and bitter contours of the slag-heaps of Catavi and Siglo Veinte, and the miners, the mainstay of the fragile Bolivian economy, plodding out into the bleak light of a fading Saturday afternoon.

My impressions were heightened because I had only a few months left in this country where I had spent nearly six years.

I felt the need—almost a compulsion—to try to capture the essence of this experience, partly for myself and partly in an attempt to communicate it to others.

With the added perspective of time and distance my Bolivian experience crystallized and the form in which it might best be represented gradually evolved. I have tried to distil, from my own knowledge and experience, a composite impression of the country and its people. I wanted to convey not only the visual grandeur of the high *cordillera* and the precipitous valleys sweeping away into the Amazon, but also the feel of the country, the shape and texture of everyday life, the characteristics of the people, and the forces that for the last 140 years have striven to create a coherent nationhood.

In adopting this approach I had also very much in mind that Bolivia is a misunderstood and often maligned country. That this should be so among my own countrymen is not perhaps surprising, in view of their general—and mistaken—dearth of interest in Latin America. Harold Osborne, at the beginning of his informative book on Bolivia, convincingly interprets as an allegory of the average Englishman's ignorance of Bolivia the doubtless apocryphal story of Queen Victoria ordering the navy to that land-locked country when her Minister Plenipotentiary was ignominiously bundled out of La Paz on an ass, and then expunging the offending country from the map.

What is perhaps less explicable is the lack of comprehension shown towards their fellow-nation by other Latin American countries, many of whom have historical, political and cultural features in common. Again Harold Osborne has pinpointed the stock formula for Bolivia among its neighbouring states—*un pobre país*—a poor country—that biting phrase in which the mere transposition of the adjective in Spanish transforms the compassion for honourable poverty, inherent in the words *un país pobre*, into a whiplash of contempt dismissing the land as unworthy of further consideration.

Such negative opinions have been fostered by some well-known Bolivian writers and thinkers. Alcides Arguedas entitled his withering attack on his own country, published in 1910,

Pueblo Enfermo-A Sick People—and declared that the drama of
Bolivia arose from the contrast between the grandiose character
of its natural surroundings and the puniness of man: 'everything
is immense save man himself'. He went so far as to say that
Bolivia was the living exemplification of Bolivar's gloomy
prophecy on his deathbed that 'America is ungovernable and
those who have served the revolution have ploughed the sea'.

Since my years in Bolivia were among the happiest and most
interesting of my life, I would like to try in some small way to
put the record straight. No apologia of Bolivia is intended, but
rather an interpretation of that elusive quality *bolivianidad*—the
quality of Bolivian nationhood—as observed by a foreigner who
made her home there and was unusually privileged to see many
sides of life, good and bad.

I realized from the outset that the task was not easy, just as I
am now conscious of the inevitable shortcomings of the finished
work. I know also that many of my Bolivian friends will dis-
agree with much of what I say, for a love of polemic is not the
least endearing of their national qualities. I can only ask them to
bear with me in the knowledge that what is written here comes
from the heart as well as the head and is inspired by an enduring
love of their country and people. Others, echoing the opinion
of the Spanish writer, Carlos Badia Malagrida, that Bolivia is a
geographical absurdity, lacking any unity of its own and constantly being pulled into the orbit of the surrounding countries,
will contend that the theme of Bolivian nationality is a contradiction in terms. While I believe that even the most ardent
Bolivian nationalist will admit that no ineluctable historical
imperative demanded the creation of the Bolivian state in 1825,
within the frontiers traced at that time and no others, no one
who knows the country well can dispute that, during the troubled
course of the intervening 140 years, a national link has been
forged that could not easily be sundered. Bolivian nationhood
may still be in the process of formation but it is a force to be
reckoned with: as when, in 1959, an infuriated crowd attacked
the United States Embassy in La Paz in protest against the
article in *Time* reporting a suggestion that Bolivia should be

split up and partitioned among its more powerful neighbours. But the phenomenon is not merely a defensive one: it is also a creative and continuing experience and I hope that some echo of it may be heard in these pages.

There are many people without whose help this book would never have been completed. I think particularly of my friends, Latin American, English and African, who read early versions of the manuscript and encouraged me to finish something which had not originally been intended for publication. They are too numerous to mention by name, but I would like to express my warm thanks to Mary Gibson, Mr Robert Gardiner and Professor David Joslin, for their helpful suggestions on the first draft; to Sir Robert Jackson for his unfailing assistance, advice and support in the preparation of the final version; and to my father for his tireless and meticulous proof-reading and for making the index. A special debt of gratitude is due to my secretary, Bérénice Mack, who uncomplainingly typed and retyped a near-illegible manuscript in various parts of the world.

My friends responded so generously to my request for illustrations that it has, alas, proved impossible to include even some of the best photographs because of their numbers. Another cause for regret is that none of the photographs could be reproduced in the original colour, which would have done more justice to the beauty and variety of the landscape. It is, however, a great satisfaction to me that most of the photographs in the book were taken by friends who share my love of Bolivia: Arthur Karasz, who, long ago in Uruguay, incited my enthusiasm to go there; Alberto Tardío, a talented Bolivian photographer, whom I met almost immediately after my arrival; Wolf Lackschewitz, who was with me on that grim journey into the mountains in search of the crashed Swedish plane; Toni Hagen, who was one of my companions during the night we were stranded on the banks of the Yapacaní and who combines a marvellous gift for photography with exceptional qualities as a geologist—he himself will be publishing a book of his photographs on Bolivia in the near future.

Very special thanks go to Myriam Bono who, quite spontaneously, sent me the line drawings of Tihuanacu and Bolivian folklore motifs which decorate each chapter.

Finally, I am grateful to the United Nations for permission to publish this book and particularly to the Secretary-General, U Thant, to Dr Rolz-Bennett, Under-Secretary-General for Special Political Affairs, and to Mr David Owen, Deputy Administrator of the United Nations Development Programme, for making the necessary arrangements. None of the opinions expressed in the book in any way reflect the official views of the United Nations, however, but are personal to the author.

Geneva, December 1968

Author's Note

The political scene in Bolivia has changed considerably since this book went to press. On 27 April 1969 the President, General René Barrientos Ortuño, was killed in a plane crash. The Vice-President, Dr Luis Adolfo Siles Salinas, assumed the presidency for the remaining period until the next elections, due in 1970. However, he was deposed by a bloodless *coup* on 26 September 1969, and a Military Junta took over the government under the presidency of the Commander-in-Chief of the Army, General Alfredo Ovando Candia. The first official acts of the new government were to revoke the Petroleum Code of 1954, which may well have repercussions on foreign oil interests, and to promise better conditions for workers, especially the miners.

September 1969   MJA

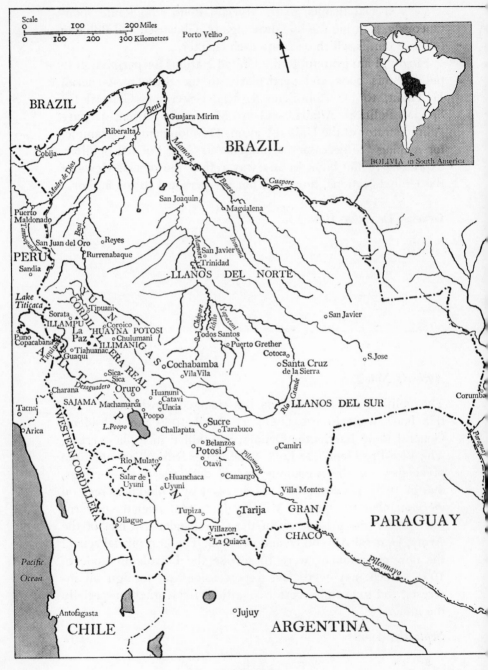

BOLIVIA

BOLIVIA: Roads and Railways

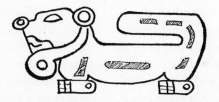

1   IT IS hard to understand why Bolivia should be so little
known and so often misrepresented abroad. It is not a small
country. Even its truncated frontiers of today contain an
area of some 420,000 square miles, larger than France and
Spain combined, although this is less than half its extent at the
time of independence nearly a century and a half ago. On the
Latin American continent it ranks fifth in size, following on its
neighbours, Brazil, Argentina and Peru, and on Colombia
lying farther to the north.

It is also a marvellously beautiful country. Land-locked
since the loss of its Pacific coastline to Chile after a disastrous
war nearly a hundred years ago, Bolivia is the heartland of the
continent, straddling the central range of the Andes which
forms the backbone of South America. Two main ranges of the
Andes cut through the western part of its territory: the Western
Cordillera running along the frontier with Chile and draining
towards the Pacific; and the Eastern, or Royal, Cordillera
dropping away to the rain forests and jungles and the broad
tropical savannahs of eastern Bolivia, which merge almost
imperceptibly into Brazil. For although Bolivia is thought of
primarily as a mountainous country, and possesses some of the
most magnificent mountain scenery in the world, over half of
its area is tropical lowland.

Nearly a century and a half ago the French explorer, Alcide

1

d'Orbigny, described it as 'a microcosm of the universe'. And so it is: a vertical microcosm, cascading down from dizzy snow-peaks that mock the tropical sky, through the steep gorges and high valleys which furrow the eastern side of the *cordillera*, and so away to the deep forests and wide tropical plains which sweep more gently towards the Atlantic ocean. You can choose any climate you have a mind for: the clear snows and biting crystal-line air of the uplands at between ten and twenty thousand feet; the gentle, slumbrous warmth of the temperate valleys between five and eight thousand feet; or the steaming jungles and torrid plains in the north and east, as little as 300 feet above sea-level.

It is a country with a fabled past, the centre of a succession of Andean civilizations, each superimposed on one another and culminating in the apex of the Inca Empire. But its earlier history is steeped in mystery and the descendants of the peoples who created those civilizations, the Aymaras and the Quechuas who till the harsh earth of the *altiplano* today, are ignorant of their remoter origins, which disappear in the mists of the legends and the mountains. Myth and speculation abound. Some say that the Garden of Eden was located somewhere on what is today the Bolivian *altiplano*, and that this was the cradle of the human race; others believe that the word Andes comes from *antis* and have detected a link with the lost continent of Atlantis; while others again trace descendence from Shem, the son of Noah, after the Biblical deluge.

There is still, today, an air of enigma about Bolivia, with-drawn behind the well-nigh impregnable wall of the Andes, locked at the heart of South America. Travel to the country is not easy, though the difficulties are becoming less now that the huge jets roar into La Paz, stopping with difficulty in the thin air. Perversely, one contemplates this advance with some ambivalence, recalling with nostalgia that once, not so many years ago, a cloud of dust was the sign that an aircraft had arrived and the signal for flocks of llamas and sheep to be hustled off the bumpy dirt landing strip.

I had always been fascinated by Bolivia since I first became interested in Latin America at Cambridge and during my years in the Foreign Office I had become familiar with the names of places and personalities. Later I joined the field staff of the United Nations Technical Assistance Board and when I was transferred from Colombia to Montevideo to head the small United Nations mission in Uruguay in 1957 I seized the opportunity of spending a couple of days in La Paz.

Because of its central location there are many ways of reaching La Paz, but each one of them involves scaling the towering, cloud-capped peaks of the Andes to reach the world's highest seat of government. Since that first visit I have taken all the best-known routes at one time or another, with the exception of the railroad from Brazil, which crosses the frontier at Corumbá and stops abruptly at Santa Cruz de la Sierra, still in the tropical eastern lowlands. This is a lasting regret, for I would like to see for myself whether there is any truth in the legend that passengers on that five-day journey are from time to time required to cut down trees at the side of the track to refuel the engine.

The story may be apocryphal but it is typical of the kind of difficulties besetting the traveller who tries to make the journey overland, as I did later. Driving up from Mollendo, the Peruvian port, through Arequipa and then up to Puno, on Lake Titicaca, and so to the Bolivian frontier is a bone-shaking experience, as hard on the nerves as on the springs of one's vehicle. The first part, as far as Arequipa, is deceptively easy, a black metalled snake smoothly insinuating itself among the blank folds of the desert. Afterwards, however, the road which zigzags laboriously up the steep eastern escarpment of the Andes is at times little more than a narrow cart-track, littered with stones and coated with thick loose dust at which the wheels scrabble impotently, while still struggling to climb upwards at what seem increasingly impossible angles.

And when the top is finally, amazingly, reached; after the highest point, at a bleak and windswept 15,000 feet, has been passed, one travels for hours across a harsh, uninhabited landscape whose only features are the outcrops of stony hills. It is a lonely road, and I remember feeling relief on passing three

3

lorries being convoyed up to Bolivia. It was comforting to know that they were lumbering doggedly along behind for there was no other traffic, and very few other signs of life to be seen, from dawn until dusk.

Those wild uplands seem very remote and alien. The traveller crossing them is sharply conscious of the nearness of the sky, as if the land had somehow merged into those blue unbounded distances or had itself become impregnated with them. The utter other-worldliness of this landscape attunes the eye and prepares the spirit for an experience out of the common run. After this the dazzling blue of Lake Titicaca—the elusive skyworld at last pinioned to earth—bursts upon the outer and inner vision of the beholder like a revelation and the densely populated world of the *altiplano* round the lake, little changed since the times of the Inca, can be observed and absorbed with the appropriate degree of detachment from the normal world.

The road from the Chilean port of Arica, through Tacna on the Peruvian frontier and then over the Andes to the Lake, is equally forbidding. I remember being begged, in 1962, by no less an authority (one would have thought) than the Bolivian consul in Arica, to desist from the foolhardy enterprise of driving into Bolivia by this route which, if it existed at all (and he implied that this was open to legitimate doubt) did so in such a marginal sense as hardly to merit the term. 'Road' was indeed a misleading description, but a perfectly passable track did wind up into the high ridges of the Andes and across another barren plateau, broken by a few spectacular snow-capped pyramids and steeped in the same ethereal atmosphere.

Before 1964, when the construction of a new runway permitted jets to land at El Alto airport above La Paz, even the air passenger received very much the same kind of impression, though less forcefully. This was how I myself first saw Bolivia in 1957, flying in on a DC–4. From the air the coastal strip of the Peruvian desert seemed to mark the frontier between the civilized, sophisticated life of Lima, which we had lately left, and this strange, uncharted world towards which the aircraft strained, its engines climbing at full throttle. We seemed barely

4

to clear the jagged summits which speared the sky, and barred the horizon in an apparently impenetrable phalanx.

It was May, the season of dry, cold, sunny weather in the Andean highlands and the outlines of this bare, lunar landscape were limned with crystalline clarity against a cobalt sky. Then, suddenly, Lake Titicaca appeared below us, penetrated by long fingers of land and ruffled into a myriad shades of blue by the wind. Harvest time was approaching and the usually subdued hues of the *altiplano* were mottled with warmer patches of yellow and bronze. In contrast the drab, adobe walls of the homesteads scattered over the terraced slopes around the lake seemed to blend indistinguishably into the earth from which they had been built.

The singularity of this compact island of life, after those vast distances where geography seemed to have eliminated man, was accentuated by the first breathtaking sight of the Cordillera Real (the Royal Cordillera) which borders the eastern edge of the Bolivian *altiplano,* and outvies the majesty of its own name. From the grandiose, tumbled peaks of the Illampu at the northern end a fretwork of silvery pinnacles stretches for over a hundred miles and guards the approach to La Paz, where the Illimani stands sentinel over the city. Both the Illampu and the Illimani tower to over 21,000 feet and the chain which links the two nowhere averages less than 18,000.

Unreality was heightened as the aircraft landed. One felt that there must be some mistake. For there was no sign of any town, not even of an airport, but only the flat, desert-like expanse of the *altiplano,* stretching as far as the eye could see and broken only by a few small huts. Unlikely as it seemed, the nearest of these turned out to be the next best thing to an airport, for, in keeping with the sturdy sense of individualism which one soon discovers infuses all aspects of Bolivian life, each company had its own miniature terminal into which the passengers were herded.

This is the moment, according to popular legend, when new arrivals collapse, overcome by *sorojche,* the notorious mountain sickness, sometimes even as they descend the steps of the aeroplane, and are carried off on stretchers to be resuscitated with oxygen masks. Such stories lend a touch of drama not often borne out by events in my experience, though many people suffer acute discomfort on first arrival, largely induced, one suspects, by the hair-raising prophecies made to them beforehand. But it is true that the stamina of even the most valiant traveller is severely tested. We were bundled, with dozens of others, into a small room already seething with customs and immigration officials and boys throwing luggage around, and where the sparse oxygen content of the air was still further diminished by the claims of all those competing to use it in such a confined space. From the start the newcomer is left in no doubt that the dominating life principle is the survival of the fittest against tremendous odds, and that the sooner he adjusts to this the better.

However, rewards awaited those of us, like myself, who managed to emerge breathless but unscathed. After a short drive between the squat adobe huts and stores near the airport, we suddenly came upon the missing city. The earth fell away abruptly, as if one had reached the end of the world itself, careening down into a deep ravine where, hundreds of feet below, the blue and red roofs of the centre of La Paz shone in crisp sunlight. The town straggled down the whole length of this narrow defile cleft between the mountains, disappearing at the bottom among the rounded hills of the lower reaches of the Choqueyapu river, while just below us untidy lines of adobe huts, roofed with corrugated iron, pushed encroaching tentacles up into the folds of the steep escarpment marking the end of the *altiplano*. This in itself was imposing enough as a panorama. But it was thrown into relief, given depth and magnificence by the Illimani, brooding with folded wings on the skyline like the legendary white condor of the Andes.

There is a vertiginous quality about the descent into La Paz. It is only partly the effect of the narrow road twisting tortuously back on itself as it edges its way down the mountainside. It is only partly, too, the almost hallucinatory quality of the rare mountain air which stretches the nerves in taut expectancy, heightens perceptions and gives a new dimension to vision. Mostly, or so it seemed to me on that first occasion, it was the commotion along the wayside: on the outskirts donkeys and sheep were being hustled along; lorries, piled improbably high with *campesinos*—country-folk—from the villages on the *altiplano*, and produce for market, rocked perilously down the road; lower down the passers-by picked their way between the *cholitas* who squatted in long lines, almost clinging to the steep surface of the street, their bowlers tilted at equally impossible angles as if in counter-equilibrium, as they offered their wares of vegetables and fruits, hot peppers, meat, trinkets and protective charms, tumbled together on the ground around them. It was a kaleidoscope of colour, synthesized in the swirling bell skirts of the women—brilliant reds and blues, oranges, pinks and mauves flaunting, as in some exotic ballet, against the background of sombre earth-coloured buildings and the unclouded winter sky.

In those days there were only two main hotels, modest but tolerable establishments, both situated on the main street, the Prado, which bisects the centre of the city and boasts a few stunted trees and flowers. The classic advice to the new arrival is to take a *maté de coca*—an infusion of the *coca* leaf supposed to relieve the effects of altitude—to eat and drink nothing else and to rest for at least twenty-four hours. I dutifully drank the bitter-tasting *maté* but rest proved impossible and after a while I walked up towards the top of the Prado.

Soon I came to the Calle Zagárnaga, a narrow cobbled street climbing steeply up the hill alongside the San Francisco church, and festooned with every conceivable kind of local merchandise: bright skirts and *aguayos* (the women's shawls) swinging like banners on poles projecting from the doorways; bowler hats nodding in serried ranks above; inside, counters piled with silverware of all kinds, old and new, and walls hung with the brightly-beaded blouses and hats worn by the Indian women on ceremonial occasions, and even flamboyant devil costumes and masks in the tradition of the Oruro carnival. There is nothing one cannot buy in the Calle Zagárnaga, down to magic potions

7

and the dried foetus of the llama which local superstition maintains must be buried for luck in the foundations of every new dwelling.

Yet it was the scene outside the San Francisco church which most enthralled me. Behind, the mellow walls of the old church seemed to glow against the deepening blue of a sky now shading into evening, and the magnificently carved façade of the main porch, with its Spanish baroque pattern translated in Indian motifs by the hands of local craftsmen, portrayed the intertwining of the two cultures which have combined to form this nation. In the foreground an aged merry-go-round, sounding a brash note of modernity despite its decrepitude, creaked and groaned bearing, on each one of its battered steeds, a *chola*, as the women of mixed blood are called, or an Indian woman. Round and round they gyrated, with immense dignity and solemnity, their russet faces impassive as the horses uncertainly rose and fell, their bowler hats tipped at the accepted, provocative angle, their babies still firmly trussed in the shawls on their backs, sleeping or gazing out at the bystanders with the same unwinking stare.

It was at that moment, I think, that I resolved to come back to live and work in Bolivia.

2 I SUPPOSE that the idea was always at the back of my mind during the next two years or so in Uruguay, but I was very busy, and when it came to the point there was nothing I could do about it. As it turned out no initiative of mine was necessary. The offer of a posting to La Paz was made to me out of the blue, almost as a joke, in an aircraft flying over Venezuela. To me it seemed as if the fates themselves had taken a hand and I accepted immediately, causing equal astonishment in return.

In January 1960 I set about the business of transporting my entire household from Montevideo to La Paz, including Montserrat, my Spanish maid, whose extreme efficiency and devotion were surpassed only by her highly emotional reactions to most situations. Profiting, as I thought, from some unfortunate earlier experiences over the transport of luggage in South America—the quickest way from Bogotá to Montevideo had proved to be via New York, and took six months—I decided that nothing should part me from my possessions. Besides, I wanted to see as much of the country as possible, though at that moment I happily had no inkling of just how much of the country I would see, or in what conditions. I decided to travel on the night steamer over to Buenos Aires, there to board the train which toils up into the Andes once or twice weekly and arrives in La Paz four days and four nights later.

At least that was the theory. Perhaps the difficulty encountered in making even the preliminary arrangements for this journey should have caused me a twinge of premonition, but this is an aspect of travelling in Latin America that I had learned to take in my stride: people love to make difficulties, to hint darkly at all kinds of unimaginable dangers in order to have the satisfaction of assuring you with an expansive wave of the hand, when all is arranged, as if they alone had been responsible for this minor miracle:

'You see! *¡No hay problema!* [No problem!].' All too frequently this soothing phrase proves to be over-optimistic or even a gross misrepresentation of the facts. Indeed, had I been less single-minded about the whole enterprise, the excessive use of such blandishments ought in itself to have put me on my guard.

As it was, we started off with fourteen crates and seventeen pieces of hand luggage, including a fur coat and a guitar. The initial stages went well and some apparently insuperable problems, such as the adamant refusal of the Argentine customs to inspect luggage on a Saturday morning or even allow it to be transported to the train for Bolivia, were eventually overcome after an anxious interlude spent disputing the validity of that most revered social conquest of the River Plate, so misleadingly named *el sábado inglés* (the English Saturday). We were, therefore, legitimately flushed with success when we finally clambered into our sleeper that Saturday evening and any qualms over the dilapidated state of the carriage, which bore the legend 'Made in England 1904', were dispelled in the excitement of departure.

And indeed, once we had settled down, things did not seem too bad. We had a compartment to ourselves, with an upper and lower bunk on which the sheets looked clean, and there was even a tap and a tiny basin. Later, a very reasonable dinner was served in the dining-car, which looked much newer than the rest. I felt ashamed that I had loaded myself up with enough provisions for an expedition, including two dozen hard-boiled eggs, when it was clear, as I looked round the spick and span white tables, that this was a perfectly normal journey, on which many normal people, including some extremely elegant Argentines, had confidently embarked.

The next morning found us in the middle of the Argentine *pampa*, green and flat and thickly populated with cattle. Shortly afterwards the train began to climb gently and we reached Córdoba, already in the foothills of the Andes. After that the landscape changed abruptly and became almost desert-like. The only vegetation was scrub and cacti among which goats and donkeys grazed instead of the cattle, sheep and horses abounding on the lower plains.

It was very hot and dusty and we began to discover that our accommodation was not all it seemed. The tap had already turned out to be merely an adornment, for not one drop of water did we manage to squeeze out of it during the whole journey. There was no way of folding back the top bunk during the day and a tall person like myself was faced with the choice either of lying down all the time or of sitting on the lower bunk with one's head pushed forward at an awkward angle and the edge of the top bunk wedged uncomfortably in the back of one's neck.

The train progressed erratically. It stopped at least an hour in every station—and there were many of them, some no more than wayside halts—and then tried to make up lost time by scuttling along at a desperate pace. During these bursts of energy the unfortunate passengers had the sensation of being in a small boat in a very high sea and were mercilessly buffeted from side to side. Then, just as suddenly the train would stop with a crisp hiccough while the passengers, taken unawares, momentarily continued at the same speed, until they too were brought to an abrupt halt by sharp and painful collision with the back of the seat.

By Monday the landscape had changed again, and with it the whole character of the train and its inmates. In Tucumán we were deprived of the company of the last sprucely tailored Argentines—most of them had left us in Córdoba—and the smart air-conditioned dining-car was replaced by a smaller,

11

older version more in keeping with the rest of the train. Outside a lush green landscape, subtropical in its profusion, had stolen a march on the desert and scrub of Santiago del Estero, and in the distance the skyline was already serrated by the erratic graph of the Andes.

The few passengers now left resembled the survivors of an expedition. Most were Bolivians returning from long or short stays in what they clearly considered to be the cultural oasis of the River Plate. One bedraggled, middle-aged couple took us into their confidence. As the frontier approached their conversation hovered increasingly around one theme: how would they manoeuvre through the customs the various hairdressing impedimenta they had bought in Buenos Aires for the beauty salon that their daughter had recently started in La Paz? Was it better to declare everything from the outset? Or should they declare part and hide the rest? Endlessly we discussed the pros and cons of the various solutions. Now and then they embarked on the only other subject that interested them—the abysmal decline of everything in Bolivia over the last few years as against the good life of an unspecified past; only then did their faces come to life and seem almost to glow with genteel middle-class indignation. Otherwise they scurried around dispiritedly, looking for suitable hiding places for their bulging bags of nets and rollers, defeat written large on their worn countenances— as much for the future of their country, one felt, as for the chances of getting their loot past the customs undetected and untaxed. It was only later that I discovered that contraband, on a large or small scale, counts among the more important national preoccupations. La Paz has a flourishing black market, openly referred to as such by its inhabitants, and the smugglers are organized to the extent of actually having their own trade union, which goes by the discreet name of 'The Syndicate of Frontier Merchants' and even stages demonstrations or strikes against the government whenever their members' privileges appear to be in danger.

Another of the group was a young girl returning to Tarija from her studies in Argentina. This was no casual visit home

12

for the summer vacation, however. Rosario—for that was what we came to call her—explained to us that she was a political exile because of her activities on behalf of an opposition party, and only now able to travel to see her family, after an absence of several years, through a recently declared political amnesty. I remember feeling merely surprised that someone so young should have been involved in politics to such an extent. Again, however, this was a typical insight into the Bolivian scene. Every Bolivian at heart is born an exile in his own country and many consider exile as an essential and inescapable part of life's experience. Politics is a sport, to which its *aficionados* are introduced young, and which is played with great intensity and seriousness, often until death, which may well come sooner than expected. Yet, if it is a cruel sport and one often practised without quarter, it is also mitigated by rules and principles: amnesty follows exile, while the right of asylum often, if not always, extenuates the terrors of revolution. According to the fortunes of the game there is a constant stream of Bolivians crossing and recrossing the country's many frontiers, on their way to and from exile, sometimes clandestinely, sometimes openly, with or without the protection of an amnesty, and sometimes even with the connivance of those in authority.

Even the guarantee of an amnesty did not prevent Rosario also from growing visibly more nervous as we drew nearer the frontier. It was, as a matter of fact, a very half-hearted advance, as if the train itself was reluctant to reach the border. At Güemes we shunted despondently back and forth for some time and found afterwards an even more decrepit dining-car. In Jujuy there were more couplings and uncouplings and it was a much diminished chain of two carriages, a dining-car, and a couple of goods-wagons which at last began in earnest the steep ascent up the mountains, leaving below a broad, arid valley, pocked with scattered stones and boulders where a river sometimes ran. One felt that the train wished to be as unobtrusive as possible so that it might merge into the lonely landscape and steal across the frontier unnoticed.

The frontier should have been crossed at midnight. Instead,

we stopped at yet another wayside station, above which the tall shadows of the overhanging hills could just be discerned in the night. It was well in the small hours when we creaked into motion again and five a.m. by the time we reached La Quiaca, the last village on the Argentine side of the border.

We had not been there long when anxieties over contraband and the fate of returning political exiles were swept from our minds by more immediate problems. The first shock came when we went along the corridor for breakfast to find that this time the dining-car had been removed completely! The train attendant delivered the second: the track on the Bolivian side had been cut in at least thirty places by the unusually heavy rainy season this year, he said, and the Bolivian railway refused to accept more trains. What was more, he added darkly, there were rumours of political trouble in the mining town of Huanuni further north—some even spoke of a miners' revolt—which made the continuation of the journey even more hazardous.

We were not allowed long in which to brood on our predicament. Outside a strident voice began to bawl:

'*¡Abajo, los pasajeros!*'

Suiting the action to the word, hefty porters leapt aboard and began hurling our precious hand luggage out through the window, disregarding our feeble protests and demands for information.

We were not even alongside a platform but had been abandoned on a siding a quarter of a mile before the station. When we had levered ourselves down from the train, I left Montserrat, forlornly standing guard over our belongings, now strewn all over the line, while I went to find the station-master and the goods-wagon with our fourteen crates, which had disappeared. Farther along I found the other half of the train, including the goods-wagon, equally abandoned, and the centre of a furious group of Bolivians, among them Rosario and the middle-aged couple. No self-respecting Bolivian will ever take things lying down, and these were no exception. They were almost forcibly resisting ejection and defending their right to keep at least the roof of the sleeping-car over their heads until alternative

14

accommodation or means of transport was arranged for them. It was a situation after their own hearts and the fun waxed fast and furious, while a harassed station official, the purity of whose lineage was by now the subject of vociferous and uncharitable speculation, tried vainly to hold his ground.

In the end, two or three people were left behind to guard the one carriage still occupied, and the rest formed a deputation to call on the station-master. I was conscripted into this band, who considered that the presence of a foreigner, and especially one with an official position, would strengthen their case.

The station-master had prudently withdrawn himself into some inner sanctum, and when he was finally run to earth would make no concessions. In vain angry passengers waved their tickets in his impassive face, claiming that the company was committed to taking them to their destination, another two days' and two nights' journey further on. It was not merely that the Bolivian railway would accept no more trains because of the broken track, he explained; the Argentine part of the railway was most certainly not going to let another train cross the frontier. With a suitably tragic expression he went on to tell, with ample statistical detail, how a large part of the Argentine rolling-stock had already disappeared without trace on the Bolivian *altiplano* and even went so far as to infer that the whole Argentine railway system was in danger of grinding to a halt. The train we had come in must return immediately to Jujuy and the south, and if the passengers would not alight of their own volition, then the police would be brought to eject them by force.

A somewhat deflated group trailed off to find the Bolivian consul, and persuade him to champion our cause. For people in our depressed state of mind La Quiaca hardly presented an inspiring spectacle, with its stumpy adobe houses lolling over the dusty road leading up the hill. Some of its timelessness and inertia seemed to have rubbed off on the Consul when we found him, no doubt as a result of many years of residence. He sat slumped in his chair and considered our position gloomily, then suddenly launched into a tirade against the railway company and the travel agencies in Buenos Aires to whom, he said, he had telegraphed days ago telling them to issue no further tickets to Bolivia.

'La Quiaca is already full of stranded Bolivians, hundreds of them,' he expostulated. 'Many of them are ill, most have no money, and what can I do?'

He spread his hands in an expansive gesture of despair and impotence which clearly included ourselves as well as all those poor unfortunates. Silently we left, realizing for the first time why so many people crowded the waiting-room outside.

Our Bolivian companions returned to their carriage to barricade themselves in for a long siege until the railway started working again. Resisting entreaties to join them, I decided to push on somehow, acting on the Stevensonian principle I have never yet found to fail that 'to travel hopefully is better than to arrive'. First I dealt with the heavy crates which we could not take with us. They were unloaded on to the platform and placed in the care of a porter whose assiduity I attempted to ensure with a large tip. He in turn promised to despatch them to La Paz by the first train. All the same, they looked rather forlorn, abandoned there at the tiny station, and it seemed improbable that one would see them again.

Next came the problem of reaching the Argentine frontier which was some way distant. In the end we simply wheeled our numerous bits and pieces there on two or three little wooden handcarts, assisted by two small boys. At the frontier post a young, handsome and very smart Argentine immigration official looked at our passports and then dubiously back at us:

'How on earth are you going to get to La Paz?' he enquired. I explained that we meant to enter Bolivia and then find whatever means of transport might be available. The officer shook his head:

'You do realize that your visas allow you only one entry into Argentina, and that if you leave you won't be able to re-enter by this frontier, for there is no one here who can issue you with a new one? If you take my advice, you will go back on the train to Jujuy, and then to Salta where you may perhaps be able to take a plane; if not, then you can always return to Buenos Aires and fly from there.'

The concern sounded genuine and made me hesitate a moment. But it seemed such an admission of defeat to retrace our steps that I shook my head. Nonetheless, the rubber stamp descended on our passports with ominous finality.

Outside a lorry waited, already piled high with merchandise and Indians. We were told that for a small fee this vehicle would transport us across the border to the Bolivian frontier post of Villazón and so we scrambled aboard with all our paraphernalia. In a few moments we reached the frontier. The efficiency of the guards at this remote outpost was remarkable, not least because they leapt smartly to attention on seeing the official visa in my passport; certainly they could have been for-given some scepticism at the signs of our dusty blue jeans and soiled shirts. Instead, full diplomatic honours were accorded. The officer in charge cordoned off one corner of the lorry and gave orders that the baggage was on no account to be opened. While the spirit behind this treatment was heart-warming, its practical effect (as I was so often to discover in the years that followed in Bolivia) left a good deal to be desired, for the frontier guards then fell upon the goods and packages of our unfortunate Indian companions and proceeded to examine them with minute precision. The whole investigation lasted nearly an hour during which diplomatically privileged and unprivi-leged alike sweated under the actinic rays of the mountain sun at the height of its power, and Montserrat's nose turned a bright and painful red.

Even when we at last bowled over the bridge into Villazón our troubles were not over, for we had to spend another hour in the police station where our credentials were again meticu-lously examined. At long last, after three hours of frenzied activity during which we had advanced about the same number of kilometres, the lorry desposited us at the door of the 'best' hotel in Villazón, grandiloquently called the Hotel Pan-americano.

By contrast with our new surroundings La Quiaca already

17

seemed an important metropolis, no doubt because of our growing realization that, although we had at last reached Bolivian soil, we were now on our own. Villazón was no more than an *altiplano* village whose sole claim to existence derived from its location at the frontier point on the main line connecting Bolivia and Argentina. It consisted of one wide, main street— if such a word can be used of a broad and uneven expanse of hard earth—bordered on either side by a row of one-storey cottages of untreated adobe. This drab khaki effect was heightened by the swirling ochre dust which enveloped everything within sight whenever a vehicle passed or a sudden eddy of the capricious highland wind whiffled along the street. Down the middle ran the single track of the international railway line, scarcely aesthetically pleasing, but bearing mute testimony to the village's *raison d'être* and encouraging stranded passengers with the reflection that where trains had once run they might yet pass again.

It was with this hopeful thought that, having installed ourselves in the hotel, we followed the tracks to the railway station in search of news. On the deserted platform a sign not only confirmed that we were in Villazón, Bolivia, but added the surprising information that the altitude was 3,500 metres (nearly 11,400 feet) above sea-level. Inadvertently, defying all the advice given to first arrivals in high altitude, we had indulged in much greater physical effort, heaving around heavy suitcases and pushing handcarts, than during a normal day at sea-level. Yet we felt no ill-effects. It was then that I first thought that many of the sufferings endured by people coming to the *altiplano* could well stem from psychological reactions inspired by the alarmist stories and warnings retailed to them before arrival.

We finally ran to earth a disconsolate and solitary character hunched over a glass of beer in the railway cafeteria which exuded the same air of forlorn abandonment as the rest of the station. This turned out to be the station-master who confirmed that the line was badly damaged in several places by landslides but offered a ray of hope by assuring us that work to clear them was going on apace. All the same he would make no guess as

18

to when we might be able to continue our journey. By this time it was early evening, and we were hungry, having had little food all day. We did the sensible thing, returned to the hotel and hoped for better luck next day.

The same sentiment recurred at the close of each of the succeeding days, but its bright hopefulness became increasingly tarnished as time passed with no progress to show. Our days were spent in feverish efforts to find some way out of the impasse. Helpful suggestions abounded and we could not complain of any lack of co-operation on the part of the local inhabitants. There were those who suggested that we might proceed by lorry to Potosí, but they were as quickly contradicted by others who pointed out that the heavy rains had washed out the roads as well as the railway, and that what was normally a one- or two-day journey was now taking three or four, if not more. Then the local military commander obligingly offered to fly us out in a small army plane which was due to bring in supplies of meat. We dubiously inspected the small bumpy field at the end of the village where it was supposed to land but were reassured by the commander:

'¡No hay problema!' he proclaimed cheerfully.

Nonetheless, the plane failed to make a landing there next day because the ground was water-logged and another possible solution was discarded. Every afternoon we toiled up to the station to enquire whether there were any new developments. Every afternoon we found the station-master still further steeped in alcohol and the melancholia which seemed to accompany it. The rains continued and every night heavy downpours washed out the repair work carried out the previous day and created new damage. It seemed a hopeless situation and we could not afford to wait on events much longer.

Boredom as well as frustration had set in. Villazón had little fascination to offer even at the best of times, when the clear mountain sunlight shone down from a burning blue sky and lent some sparkle to the otherwise drab scene; when, as often, the rain poured down and turned the main street into a morass of mud it was little short of miserable. Living conditions were also far from comfortable. The grandest thing about the Gran Hotel Panamericano, as can be well imagined, was its name. It consisted of five or six rooms round a central patio, each with a wooden door fastened outside with a padlock. (This made it impossible to lock the door from inside and Montserrat, with her nervous disposition, insisted every night on barricading the entrance with a pile of suitcases, though against what conceivable attacker I was never able to find out.) Still, it was cleaner than one might have expected and the innkeeper and his wife were helpful and genuinely concerned about our predicament.

The staff was small: there was a man of-all-work, Don Pancho, who was much in demand; indeed the patio incessantly rang with the cry of 'Don Pa - a - ancho' and Don Pancho was kept so constantly scurrying back and forth with a willing smile that he rarely got anything very effective done. The other main personage was a cook who prepared her confections over a wood fire in the windowless kitchen, resplendent in the brightly-hued skirt and swirling petticoats of the *chola* and sporting, at a purposive angle, a decaying bowler hat that she never seemed to take off, though there were moments when its imminent descent into the nearest cauldron seemed unavoidable. Yet the food she produced, thick *altiplano* soups and hotly-spiced meats, was tasty, if hardly varied.

There were few other guests; one or two were stranded like ourselves by the collapse of rail communications, but they did not engage local interest to the same degree as ourselves because we were the only foreigners. We had become something of an object of community concern and small groups gathered in the evenings to debate our problem and suggest solutions. So it was that on the fourth day a decision was taken. It was to a large degree precipitated by the afternoon's exchange with the station-master, by now so sunk in drunken inertia that it was almost impossible to converse with him at all but who, stung by our importunate questions, had suddenly roused himself to make one of those prescient statements common to the very inebriated.

'The next train,' he declared succinctly and with an oracular air, 'will leave in exactly one month's time.'

With that he relapsed into the stupor from which he would doubtless not emerge again until the first train steamed in. Money was also becoming a problem, for the funds which had been ample for a four-day train journey for two people, were by now sadly depleted. That afternoon, too, Rosario had suddenly appeared. Continued resistance in the besieged railway carriage at La Quiaca had soon proved pointless and she now proposed to press on next day to Tarija, some 200 kilometres across the mountains. There, too, was the nearest airstrip where we could pick up a Lloyd Aéreo Boliviano plane for Cochabamba and La Paz. She would arrange the hire of a truck which would take us and a few other people to Tarija next afternoon—four hours' journey at the most, she optimistically declared.

Next morning I managed to make radio communication with my office in La Paz, which by this time was worried about our whereabouts. It was arranged that they would pay our air-tickets to the Lloyd offices in the capital and would also forward some ready cash to me in Tarija through the airline office there. There was an exhilarating feeling in at last taking some definite action and getting on the move again.

Rosario had asked us to be ready after lunch and so, promptly at two o'clock, we took leave of our friends at the hotel, and waited outside with all our luggage heaped around us. Time passed but no truck appeared. The people to whom we had bidden farewell came out to see why we were still there. After an hour I could stand it no longer, and went to the market place to see if I could find Rosario and her vehicle. The search was fruitless but I did find a lorry also bound for Tarija and came to an agreement with the driver. The lorry was already piled high with sacks of fruit and vegetables, on top of which some twenty or more Indians were precariously perched. I clambered into the driver's cab, and we drove off to the hotel. As we were trying to wedge ourselves and our various packages into the already overloaded vehicle a smaller truck careered up behind us, klaxoning hysterically, and disgorged Rosario and a lot of other people. There was much confused explanation about the two-hour delay but the main fact to grasp was that we were leaving at once. Our belongings were hastily transferred, the bewildered driver of the lorry was recompensed and we were off at a fine pace.

We did not keep it up for long.

After turning several corners on two wheels we drew up smartly outside a house into which the driver and one of the passengers disappeared. A long interval ensued, during which it was explained to me that a tarpaulin was needed to protect the outside passengers against the strong sun (there were six of us with the driver: Rosario, ourselves, and a couple with a small son, and we took it in turns to share the driver's cab). The tarpaulin that was eventually produced proved too small, and by the time we had located a larger one somewhere else the sun was sinking perceptibly lower. Any hopes of an immediate departure were soon dashed, however, as it transpired that permits were needed from the customs authorities and the police. I was beginning to understand the dread significance of the word *trámites*, for in each case there were lengthy delays. Nor was I much reassured by the driver's indomitable optimism. When he finally swung himself into the cab a few minutes after five o'clock, he declared with a smile of triumph:

'And now, all we need is petrol.'

We stopped at a small, windowless store. In the dark interior I glimpsed a barrel and a hose but the barrel turned out to be empty.

'*¡No se preocupen!*' 'Do not preoccupy yourselves!' cried the driver, laughing uproariously at my worried expression. 'There's another shop.'

There was, but it too had run out of supplies. Even this did not shake the incurable buoyancy of our driver.

'No problem!' he assured us, smirking a little at the ease with which he was vanquishing this self-imposed obstacle race 'YPFB (the state oil company) has its depot a little way along the Tarija road, so we'll stop on the way.'

That information was also correct but of little help to us, as the depot was hermetically shut.

'But, of course, they close at five p.m.' said our driver, for the first time looking a little crestfallen.

He began to shout, and bang the gate and blow his horn, making such a din that finally someone appeared. After much argument, conducted with skill and enthusiasm by both sides, this individual finally agreed to fill the tank of the truck. Emerging victorious from this encounter our driver turned to us with shining eyes, inviting our praise and admiration. It seemed churlish to point out that a great deal of time and trouble would have been saved had the petrol been bought first, before the establishment closed, and I bit back the words that sprang to my lips. Even so, it was hard to keep silent a moment later when the driver crashed into gear, his old spirit now quite restored, and enquired confidentially of the world at large, in a tone judiciously edged with doubt:

'Who knows whether the tank holds enough petrol to get us to Tarija?'

What really forestalled all retort, I think, was the sudden understanding that he regarded this as a pleasurable challenge.

At six p.m., the hour confidently predicted for our arrival in Tarija, we had only just left the precincts of Villazón. The scenery was magnificent but the road outmatched it in impressiveness, a narrow dirt-trail twisting and twining along the rim of the mountains and the tortuous contours of the river valleys, with dizzy precipices plummeting down on one side or the other. The swaying movement of the truck soon took its toll: Montserrat began to feel sick and the small boy deposited the remains of his lunch in my lap. Night fell fast and drew a merciful curtain over the giddy drops but relief was short-lived for the truck's headlights were not working. For what seemed an eternity we edged our way along the track at a snail's pace until at last, at about eight p.m., we stopped at a dilapidated tavern.

Except for the lorries outside one might have been entering a Cervantine hostelry straight out of *Don Quixote*. There was only one room, poorly lit by flickering lamps and packed tight with travellers, for there was nowhere else along the road where refreshment could be obtained. The lamplight glimmered on the dark faces of Indians and *cholos*, some of them huddled in homespun blankets on the beaten earth floor, others crowded together at the crudely hewn benches and tables laid out along the crumbling adobe walls, where they consumed plates of steaming peppery stew and kept up a high babble of conversation, suspended only for a moment to inspect the new arrivals with curiosity. By this time coffee—hot, black and gritty—was all that we could face, and we sat down to wait until the driver managed to repair the lights.

An hour later we set off again. The road continued to coil round the mountainside and now climbed quite steeply. Soon we ran into a new hazard—a swirling mountain fog which obliterated everything more than a few yards ahead of us. It became possible to advance only if I leant over the precipice side and shouted instructions to the driver, for the road was narrow and the slightest deviation meant disaster. At last we emerged from the clouds and a more heartening sight met our eyes: there, far below us, but visible and almost within reach, a cluster of lights beckoned.

'There is Tarija!' exclaimed the driver, pointing dramatically.

Memory may have telescoped the sequence of events in that dreadful journey, but it does seem to me that the loud explosion followed immediately on that joyful cry, as if in punctuation. There was no doubt as to what had happened: one of the back tyres had burst. Nothing, however, could shake the indestructible faith of the chauffeur.

'Do not preoccupy yourselves, no problem!' he rattled off, 'I have a jack.'

At that moment I failed to appreciate the significance of the air of pride which accompanied this announcement. We had indeed got a jack, but it certainly did not belong to this vehicle but must have come from a very small car. After a great deal of energetic effort the side of the lorry was levered up only to collapse immediately, almost pinning the driver underneath. Unabashed, he promised us that someone else would be passing soon and would be able to help. Sure enough, after another half-an-hour's wait lights began to sweep round the ridge behind us, and a lorry soon drew up on the patch of flat grass beside us, for we were occupying the whole of the road. We were not in luck, however; the driver seemed taken aback by the very idea that he should carry such an implement, and after expressing his sympathy at our plight, drove on.

'Do not preoccupy yourselves!' the driver admonished us once again. 'Perhaps the next one will have a jack.'

But there wasn't a next one. Instead there was another explosion, this time that of a thunderclap which resounded through the mountains and was followed immediately by more lightning and a torrential downpour. It was just after one a.m. We huddled under the tarpaulin alone with the mountain, the night, the bitter cold and the rain, at something like 12,000 feet up.

The night that followed does not bear description. The tarpaulin so assiduously sought the previous afternoon to protect us against the ravages of the sun proved signally inadequate against the relentless drumming of the rain. Runnels of water trickled down into every crevice, the cold and damp seeped into our bones and our limbs seized up with cramp. More than once I was reminded of the old *gaucho* refrain which Alcide d'Orbigny had quoted incessantly to himself during a similarly drenching night:

'*¡Una mala noche se pasa como se quiere!*'—'One passes a bad night as best one can.'

One also despaired of the dawn but at last it came, pallid and grey as our faces.

And then, at six-thirty, came also the welcome noise of an engine somewhere behind us. The shape of a small pick-up gradually emerged through the damp mist clinging to the sides of the mountain and slithered to a stop in the mud to which the trail had now been reduced. But our hopes were short-lived. The driver looked as surprised as the earlier one, and replied with the patient courtesy reserved for those who make unreasonable demands that it was not his habit to carry a jack with him.

(Such an omission on these rough mountain roads seemed to me, in turn, quite incomprehensible; I could only conclude that to come prepared for what was, after all, the most likely eventuality, was despised as a dilution of the spirit of adventure, and perhaps even as a reduction of a man's stature in his own eyes, according to the concept of *machismo*—the image of virility—so dear to Latin American male hearts.) He did, however, promise to send back help from Tarija as soon as he got there.

With this he put the car into gear and made to drive past us through the patch of grass as the other lorry had done the previous night. Alas, seven hours of rain had reduced it to a quagmire and after two or three yards the pick-up was sinking rapidly, axle deep in mud. Seeing our hope of rescue disappear before our very eyes we all of us rushed to push it out, galvanized into frantic activity despite the cold and our empty stomachs. Stones and grass were stuffed under the wheels, we all heaved mightily, and the wheels whirred round spattering our clothes and faces with sludge. But the pick-up refused to move. In the end, now covered with mud as well as soaked to the skin, we gave up.

Even our driver had lost his perennial optimism and with it all his driving energy. Perversely, I longed to hear the reassuring clichés that had earlier irritated me so much. Instead, he confided that, with this rain, it was very unlikely that any lorries would leave either Tarija or Villazón that day, or even for two or three days more, for fear of landslides. I asked whether there was not something else we could do, but all his natural inventiveness seemed now to have deserted him and he sat glumly hunched over the wheel contemplating the chilly drizzle which had followed the rain.

Still I insisted: 'How far is it from here to Tarija?'

'Fifteen kilometres, twenty, twenty-five . . . who knows?' he demanded dejectedly of all and sundry.

'Then I shall walk there to get help,' I declared firmly, hoping by these means to shame one or two of the men into taking some action. I should have known better. The argument was tossed desultorily back and forth, every possible hypothesis was examined minutely, but the last thing anyone really wanted to do was to take any action. Two hours later they were still discussing our situation and by this time I had finally decided that I would set out.

Just then, however, help arrived out of the blue. A whole convoy of four or five lorries came chugging up the road and round the bend towards us. Surely it was reasonable to hope that one of them might have defied tradition so far as to carry a jack? Happily, this prayer was answered. Moreover, it was a good solid jack, and within twenty minutes our problems were miraculously solved: the wheel was changed, and the stranded pick-up lifted almost bodily out of the mud by the numerous passengers travelling on the lorries. In no time at all we were bowling down the mountainside towards Tarija.

Suddenly life seemed good and hopeful again. As if catching my mood Rosario asked:

'How would you like to stay in a really luxurious hotel in Tarija?'

Rhetorical question indeed! Visions of hot baths, soft, warm beds and appetizing food flitted before our eyes as Rosario painted the delights of the Social Club. As we descended farther, the sun came out and it became perceptibly warmer. Neatly tended fields replaced the barren wastes of the mountains, flowering hedges bordered the road, and people in gaily coloured clothes greeted us cheerfully as we passed. Tarija seemed a smiling town.

The building before which we drew up in the main *plaza* certainly bore an imposing aspect, reminiscent of solid Victorian architecture in England. Inside it looked less promising. Paint was peeling off the walls of the broad halls and corridors and grime was visible everywhere. Once upstairs our hearts sank even lower. In the gloomy room into which we were shown the beds sagged dispiritedly under covers which seemed uniformly grey with age and dirt. Bathrooms there were, and indeed they bore all the signs of past magnificences, for the baths were long and high and fitted with fine brass taps, the water-closets decorously perched on a small eminence in the corner. But it was all encrusted with rust and dirt and did not seem to have been used for a very long time. The reason was not difficult to find for when, with difficulty, we turned the taps nothing happened for a moment and then, after much gurgling and other sounds of travail within, a pathetic trickle of very brown, very cold, liquid spattered out.

As if this were not enough, on opening our saturated suitcases we found the contents, including bed-linen and new dresses specially made before we left Montevideo, not only wet but indelibly marked with leather stains. The guitar which Montserrat had loyally hugged to her during the night was also spoilt beyond repair. This was too much for Montserrat who started to weep.

I too was near the end of my tether and the sight of her tears dropping onto our sodden garments was the last straw. I said, more crossly than I had intended, 'There's already quite enough water about without your adding to it. As the sun is shining, I suggest you lay the things out to dry on the roof, while I go and find out when and how we can fly out to La Paz.'

I sped to the local office of Lloyd Aéreo Boliviano (LAB), without waiting to change or wash. Apart from the fact that time seemed vital, I had at that moment nothing to change into or with which to wash.

The clerk at the Lloyd office was not encouraging.

'We have only two flights a week and they are fully booked for the next fifteen days.'

Tactfully I pointed out that I was travelling to La Paz to occupy an official position of some importance, that the Government were expecting me, and that my office had arranged with the Lloyd head office that my companion and I should be given priority. This kind of approach is always embarrassing to make but on this occasion it was more so because I became increasingly aware of an ill-suppressed glint of amusement in the clerk's eye, which finally he could no longer prevent from burgeoning into a great gust of laughter. It dawned on me that he didn't believe a word of what I was saying. Suddenly aware of my

above: Vista of La Paz with the Illimani in the background.
left: The façade of the San Francisco church in La Paz on a feast-day.
below: Street market in La Paz.

above: Puerta de Kallasasaya, Tihuanacu.
left: Aymara child in precolonial Tihuanacu.
below: The central motif of the Gate of the Sun, Tihuanacu.
bottom: Colonial Tihuanacu.

mud-spattered face, my dank hair straggling from under a saturated kerchief, my filthy jeans and muddy shoes and socks, I understood why. At that moment I felt very near to tears myself. The clerk saw this and being, like most Bolivians, a kindly man, took pity on me.

'You are a foreigner?'

I admitted as much.

'Have you ever been in Bolivia before?'

'I've been in La Paz a couple of times but never very far outside. I don't know this part of the country at all and haven't even a map.'

'Then I will help you to find the quickest way to La Paz. If you leave this office and turn right, then left, then left again, you will come to a little square. There you will see a row of lorries loading up. For a small sum you can arrange for yourself, the other señorita and your luggage to be transported to a place two hundred kilometres from here—only four or five hours' journey—where you can get a train to La Paz.'

The clerk spread his hands almost as if in blessing, well pleased with himself for having thus solved my problems. But an awful doubt had struck me.

'Would that place of which you speak by any chance be called Villazón?'

'Yes, but how on earth did you know?'

I managed to gulp: 'My dear sir, if you see me in the state I am in now, it is because I have spent sixteen hours, including all of last night, trying to get here from Villazón. For your information, the next train is expected to leave there in a month's time.' And fled.

The rest of that day was discouragingly reminiscent of Villazón. The military authorities said that a military plane would be going to La Paz next day but that there was space for only one passenger and none for the luggage, while the local highway service would not be drawn about the state of the road to Potosí. After another radio conversation with the office in La Paz, during which they assured me that Lloyd

Aéreo Boliviano had been approached at the highest level, I went to the house of the Manager. I discovered that he had received instructions from his head office and after long negotiation he promised first one seat, and then two, on a plane leaving for Cochabamba on the next afternoon, Saturday. We should have to spend Saturday and Sunday nights there, but on Monday morning early could fly to La Paz. Even money had arrived by this time, and we congratulated ourselves that we had only one night to spend in Tarija's luxury hotel.

We were up betimes next morning and as soon as the airline office opened at nine o'clock I went there to check the final details. Unexpectedly good news greeted me:

'If you come here, immediately, with all your luggage we can send you on a special plane leaving at ten o'clock instead of this afternoon. Hurry, please, for there is no time to be lost.'

My feet hardly touched the ground as I dashed back to the Social Club. We finished packing our bags in record time and in less than fifteen minutes were back at the office, breathless but happy, with a trail of small boys behind us bearing our paraphernalia.

Unhappily, the situation had changed in the interim. There would be *information* about the special plane at ten o'clock. Ten o'clock came but no news. The deadline was postponed until eleven, then twelve, then two. Disheartened, we went off to lunch. Afterwards news was again promised for three o'clock and then four. At half-past four it was finally admitted that both the special plane and the regular flight had been cancelled owing to bad weather. Hopes, to which we dared not attach too much importance, were held out for the next morning and we must report at seven a.m.

By this time we had almost become fixtures in the airline office but we obviously had to find somewhere else to spend the night and we were determined that that place would not be the Social Club. At lunchtime we had seen a modest little whitewashed *pensión* with a pleasant patio and there we were lucky enough to find a room. It was an unpretentious place—there was no bathroom—but it was clean, the landlady was kind and the food wholesome. We had discovered that there was a cinema in Tarija and cheered ourselves with the prospect of a gay night out.

Even that was to be denied us for, as we were putting on our coats after supper, the lights wavered and then expired. The landlady felt obliged to apologize to us on the behalf of Tarija, assuring us that this was the first time in years that such a thing had happened there. It was scant consolation, for the lights remained obstinately out for the rest of the night. We morosely consumed the remains of a bottle of brandy by the light of a guttering candle and crept to bed.

And then, next day, things suddenly came miraculously right after all. The special plane came early. True, it was a C–47, intended for cargo, and without seats or safety belts or other refinements. The only thing that really mattered was that it flew, and that we were on it.

At Cochabamba more surprises awaited us. We were met by no less a person than the local Lloyd manager and given VIP treatment. After the experiences of the previous nine days it seemed to our suspicious minds that there must be some catch. On the contrary, the manager told us that, although there was no regular Sunday flight between Cochabamba and La Paz, it so happened that the Government had sent a plane specially down to Cochabamba on official business and this was now waiting to take us back. And so, true to the tradition of unpredictability which was later to inform all my Bolivian travels, we completed the last lap of our journey in some style as the only passengers on a DC–4, with the whole company of stewards and air hostesses dancing attendance on us.

Oddly enough we experienced a sensation almost of anti-climax, heightened when, on reaching La Paz airport, we found a large company gathered to greet us, for somehow the office had managed to find out how and when we were arriving. It seemed a renewed contact with reality when we reached the house I had temporarily rented and found that the water-heater was broken so that the hot bath and shampoo for which we had been longing had still to be postponed.

Two days later the same DC–4 in which we had flown the last lap of our journey crashed with an almost full complement of passengers and crew on a regular flight from Cochabamba. There were no survivors. The vicissitudes of our journey suddenly seemed very insignificant.

One month later to the day, the first train streamed into La Paz station from the Argentine frontier and vindicated the prognostication of our station-master friend. Incredibly, it contained our fourteen crates, all intact.

3 HAD WE been able to complete our journey from the Argentine frontier by train we should have spent the last two days crossing the *altiplano*, an immense, high plateau which stretches 500 miles from north to south between the eastern and western arms of the Cordillera de los Andes in Bolivia and southern Peru. Sometimes as much as 150 miles wide, it averages between eleven and thirteen thousand feet above sea-level and you cannot travel north, west or southwards from La Paz without traversing some part of it.

In my many journeyings to visit development projects it became my constant travelling companion, for the *altiplano* has a presence of its own which even the towering peaks that so often dominate its horizons cannot diminish. This springs partly from the sense of measureless distance engendered by its vast size and by the startling clarity with which the eye, aided by the thinness and diaphanous quality of the air, encompasses a panorama far beyond the range of normal human sight.

The effect is not restricted to physical vision. This is no small and intimate world where a man can comfortably measure the stature of his being. That faraway skyline taunts as well as beckons and the onlooker cannot remain aloof but finds himself imperceptibly absorbed into this forbidding yet strangely luminous world. No compromise can be brooked; the choice is between total rejection or total acceptance.

The Indian over yonder, trudging apparently towards the edge of the world, is barely distinguishable from the land around him. His dun-coloured, weatherworn face and homespuns blend into the dun-coloured, weatherworn landscape. It is as if he himself were made of earth, and differentiated from it only by the fact of his moving upon it. And where is he bound? The traveller scans those desolate reaches of barren, stone-pocked land and does not find an answer. At last a keen eye descries, far away, the brown huddle of an adobe homestead, itself made of earth and cowering close to the ground as if seeking protection from the wild elements that roam untrammelled across these upland wastes. Even the vividly-coloured skirts—scarlet and purple, yellow and orange—of the women who watch their flocks of puny sheep near the road are no more, in their flaunting challenge of the drab surroundings, than inverse recognition of the ultimate futility of revolt against nature of the *altiplano*, a brief flaring of antithesis which fades into insignificance as one's gaze travels on to the immensity of distance beyond.

Yet traditionally, and almost paradoxically, people have chosen to live on this inhospitable plateau in preference to the high valleys or the tropical lowlands lying to the east. One may be chary of accepting the claim put forward by some enthusiastic Bolivian writers that this was the cradle of the universe but certainly the Bolivian *altiplano* and the Peruvian *puna* nurtured some of the most remarkable prehistoric civilizations of the continent.

The Aymara and Quechua Indians who still survive as two distinct races, each with its own language, were by no means the first inhabitants, but earlier peoples are perpetuated only in the dwindling groups of the Urus and the ancient tribe of the Chipayas, whose languages, probably dialects of Puquina, bear no relation to Aymara or Quechua. The Urus were already an oppressed and backward people at the time of the Spanish conquest and were described in contemptuous terms by several sixteenth-century chroniclers as little better than animals. They were still then quite numerous, living mainly round Lake Poopó, south of the present-day town of Oruro, which is

34

in fact a corruption of Uru-Uru, meaning 'much Uru'. Other groups eked out a miserable existence on floating rafts of *totora* reed on Lake Titicaca, eating roots and raw fish and, according to one anthropologist, the last of these died out in 1960. A small group of Chipayas remains in the south of the *altiplano*, still using the mode of dress imposed upon them by Spanish missionaries four centuries ago.

An insuperable difficulty in reconstructing the early history of the Andean peoples is the lack of any written records until the arrival of the Spanish *Conquistadores* in the sixteenth century. Some of their chroniclers wrote down not only what they themselves saw of the magnificent empire of the Incas which came to an end with their invasion—and was indeed largely destroyed by it—but also what they managed to glean from local people of what had gone before. This was not a great deal, for while there was a fairly clear outline of what had happened during Inca times, what had preceded them was shrouded in mystery. Although the art of writing as such was unknown to the Incas, they had the mnemonic device of the *quipu*, a system of recording statistical information by a complicated combination of knots worked in different coloured cords, and developed to such an ingenious degree that it could record a considerable amount of historical information. Many of these vital records were destroyed by the Spanish invaders, but even had they all survived until today they would be of little use without an interpreter who had learnt the key by heart; inevitably the professional 'rememberers' trained to decipher these knot-string records gradually died out when the system fell into disuse. These are not the only difficulties. It is also known that the official Inca history was extremely selective and devised to obliterate the memory of past peoples and cultures so that the Incas would figure as the unchallenged originators of civilization in the high Andes. Archaeological investigation has revealed, however, the layers of Andean cultures which preceded them.

Of the many theories put forward about the origin of the Andean peoples probably the most credible is the immigration thesis. Even this has many variants, ranging from a migration, for reasons unknown, from the tropical valleys and lowlands on the eastern side of the *cordillera* up into the *altiplano*, to more ambitious movements of peoples from places as far afield as Africa, Asia, Europe or Oceania. Perhaps the most convincing version, though it, too, suffers from inconsistencies, is that the immigrants crossed the Behring Straits from Asia and flowed down into what is now South America, at the end of the Ice Age; and this certainly would help to explain the marked mongoloid cast of feature to be seen in both Aymaras and Quechuas.

The people themselves have no tradition of immigration, however, but have inherited legendary associations which equate their origins both with the region they now inhabit, and with the creation of the world. That Lake Titicaca should play a central part in all of these myths comes as no surprise to the traveller dazzled by the first glimpse of that cerulean vision, an oasis of light and colour amid the aridity and sub-dued half-tones of the surrounding high plateau. Neither does it seem strange that the region near the lake should have seen the mysterious rise and equally mysterious decline of a great and powerful civilization that preceded the Incas, for this is the most fertile area and enjoys the most benign climate to be found in all those bleak uplands.

Thirteen miles from the southern shores of the lake, and at an altitude of nearly 13,000 feet, present-day Aymaras graze their sheep and llamas among the ravaged but still imposing remains of the megalithic stone monuments of Tihuanacu, relics of a bygone civilization of which no recollection, oral or imita-tive, has come down to its modern descendants.

The significance of the surviving monuments—the Gate of the Sun, beautifully carved and chiselled out of a solid piece of rock by people who knew neither the wheel nor the use of iron, its companion arch known as the Gate of the Moon, the huge megalithic stairway, the crumbling terraces of the pyramid which forms the largest unit, and the fallen, monolithic idols— is still unfathomed. Was it a centre for religious ceremonial, a political metropolis or an important market, as the modern village of Tihuanacu still is today? Or was it perhaps a combination of all three? Its antiquity is equally uncertain. Posnansky, who spent most of his life trying to unravel the mysteries of Tihuanacu, claimed immense age for it and believed it to be the birthplace of all American, and perhaps even of all world, civilization. Some think that a great empire, known as the Megalithic Empire of the Andes, became prominent around the middle of the first Christian millennium, while others again believe that it was primarily a religious cult, supported only by a very loose political organization. Two clearly distinguished building techniques have been identified. What natural or man-incurred disaster brought the first Tihuanacan period to an end remains, like the causes of the final fall of the civilization some time in the ninth century, as steeped in mystery as the influences which inspired its apogee.

In its heyday the bounds of Tihuanacu's influence must have been cast as widely as those of the Inca Empire which followed, for traces of Tihuanacu culture have been found as far away as Colombia in the north, Argentina and Chile to the south and the Peruvian coastlands to the west. Many of the contemporary cultures and, later, the Incas, adopted their symbol of the Sun-God, which wept condor's-head tears and snake's-head tears, and the totem figures of the condor, the puma and the llama recur on pottery throughout the region. The condor was supposed to be the messenger of the sun, because its immense wing-span allowed it alone to fly high enough to approach the deity; even today one is told that condors are frequently seen near the Gate of the Sun at Tihuanacu, bent presumably on the business of ancient gods, though I cannot say that I ever caught sight of one there.

When you see these immense ruins of basalt and sandstone, their great stone slabs dressed and polished and minutely fitted together, you realize that the civilization of Tihuanacu had not only attained a high degree of cultural development but also possessed the complex social and political structure essential for such a vast undertaking. Were these artistically talented

37

and highly organized people the forebears of the Aymara peasant whose days, in the twentieth century, are circumscribed by the narrow limits of his fragmented patches of land, where he scratches out a bare subsistence in much the same way as his ancestors must have done in Inca times, except for the assistance of draught animals and ploughs introduced by the Spaniards? If so, they have retained no vestige of their heritage. Even when the Spanish chronicler, Pedro Cieza de León, visited Tihuanacu in 1549 no one could explain the origin of these ancient buildings except in superstitious terms. Yet, if the suggested chronology is roughly correct, the period which had elapsed since the empire was at the height of its powers, five or six centuries, was not long in terms of historical perspective.

'I asked the natives,' says Cieza de León '. . . if these buildings had been built in the time of the Incas, and they laughed at the question, repeating what I had said, that they were built before they reigned, but that they could not state or affirm who built them. However, they had from their forefathers that all that are there appeared overnight.'

But the question marks which encircle most of the pre-colonial period for us do not tantalize the imagination of the Aymara. For him it is enough to know that the world began with Virajocha—and even he is an anonymous god for the term is a title, meaning 'Creator Lord', and not a name—rising from the centre of Lake Titicaca. There is a close link with the legends woven round the enigmatic stones of Tihuanacu. According to one of these Virajocha first created men of enormous size in a world which lacked either sun or warmth. These, however, in some way incurred his displeasure and so he destroyed them by a flood, and created a new world, with sun, moon and stars as we know them today, and peopled by a new race of men. A variation on this, according to some Aymara traditions, is that the giant human statuaries at Tihuanacu are made in the image of the first race of large-size men, whom Virajocha in his anger turned into stone. Yet another version affirms that these images were fashioned by Virajocha himself, as a kind of grand design of the humanity he wished to create, and then served as proto-

38

types for his disciples who, on his instructions, went forth and called the various peoples and tribes into being from rocks and caverns, rivers and streams.

With the upsurge and consolidation of the Inca Empire the focus of power in the Andes swung away from what is now modern Bolivia to the lower and more fertile valley of Cuzco in the heart of the Peruvian *sierra*. Here, around AD 1200, was founded the dynasty that was to carry the political and cultural development of the whole Andean region to the zenith of its achievements in pre-Colombian times and to cause even the rough Spanish soldiery, who burst upon this closed mountain world in 1532, to marvel at the complexity of its institutions and at the magnificence of its wealth, which surpassed their most covetous imaginings.

Once again the traditions relating the origins of this comparatively recent civilization intertwine remembered events with myth and fable and take many forms. The sixteenth-century chronicler Garcilaso Inca de la Vega, recalling in Spain, in his old age, the tales he had heard as a child among the surviving members of the Inca family, to whom he was related on his mother's side, has handed down the legend that the Inca dynasty also had supernatural origins springing from the sacred lake. There, it is said, on the island of Titicaca (which means 'jaguar rock', the feline motif that became the symbol of the Incas, but which is now called the Island of the Sun—*Isla del sol*) the Sun God brought forth his son and daughter, Manco Capac and Mama Ojllo, to spread the arts of civilization among the races of mankind who, at this time, were debased in ignorance and barbarism—a reference perhaps to the chaos which had succeeded the overthrow of Tihuanacu. They were told to go forth and travel on until they reached the place where the golden staff carried by Manco Capac would sink into the ground of its own accord. The miracle took place at Cuzco and it was there that the royal pair, following the behest of the Sun God, their father, established the seat of their new empire.

No one quite knows when this small mountain state in the valley of Cuzco began to expand into a vast empire embracing the major part of the western half of the continent. What is certain is that, at the time of the Spanish conquest in the sixteenth century, their dominions stretched over an area of 380,000 square miles, from the north of Ecuador to central Chile, a linear distance of 3,000 miles. All of these vast domains were welded into a complex administrative whole and inter-connected by a network of all-weather roads. Communications were carried from one end of the Empire to the other with unbelievable swiftness by a system of relay runners, or *chasquis*, often in less time than it takes an airmail letter to cover the same distance today.

By the middle of the fourteenth century what is now highland Bolivia had been incorporated into the Four Quarters of the World, as the empire was called, as part of the Province of Kollasuyu, which also embraced the Titicaca basin, including that area which is now in Peru, as well as the northern parts of Chile, and Argentina. Still today the inhabitants of La Paz and the surrounding highlands are known as *kollas*. The Inca road in this region ran southwards from Cuzco, bifurcated round both sides of Lake Titicaca to join, at the southern end of the lake, into a single track which cut through the southern part of modern Bolivia, and went on to Tucumán in the north of Argentina.

The rise of Inca power marked also the ascendancy of the Quechua culture over that of the Aymaras. It is not known whether the Incas themselves were Quechuas or indeed whether they originally spoke Quechua, but they made it the universal language of the Empire as well as the language of the adminis-tration. Its extension to the outermost corners of the Inca dominions, as well as the unification of the lands and peoples which they comprised, was fostered by their strategy of trans-planting peaceful populations, already assimilated into the imperial framework, into the newly-conquered lands lying on the frontiers of the Empire. The southern and eastern parts of the Bolivian *altiplano* are today largely populated by Quechuas who as likely as not were settled there under Inca rule. The process of harmonization was interrupted, however, by the internal strife which marred the later years of the Inca Empire and by the arrival of the Spaniards so that, even today, the Quechuas and Aymaras are completely distinct peoples, although at some point in the dim origins of their history they must have shared a common heritage.

The organization of Inca society was strictly hierarchical, assigning to each one his appointed place and functions, according to the circumstances of his birth. The lot of the highland Indian then, as now, was hard, and the soil of the Andes as stony and barren as it is today. Yet the Incas developed an agricultural system which not only provided day-to-day sustenance but also produced a surplus. Each *ayllú*, or group of extended families, had its own lands which it tilled communally for its own maintenance. In addition, they were expected to work on the lands belonging to the Inca—the State lands. This was a form of tribute and the produce of these lands supported all the privileged classes, the Inca and his family and their courtiers, the nobles, the religious orders and government officials. Part of it was also used to stock granaries of foodstuffs which were kept as reserves against emergencies such as war or famine. If the harvest failed in any district supplies were distributed from these stores to save the affected *ayllú* from starvation.

Thus, although the common peasant had to work hard and was obliged to contribute to the State, the services rendered were not one-sided for he knew that in time of need the state would also succour him. Moreover, the Indian had an accepted and recognizable place in the structure of society. That place might be rather lowly, and there might be no prospect of social mobility, however hard he worked, or whatever his personal merits might be. All the same, the Indian was integrated into the Inca hierarchy whereas under the Spanish rule soon to come, and the kind of social organization which followed in its wake until long after independence, he was merely oppressed. He was still regarded as the lowest of the low, and still required to work under conditions of slavery, but now everything was extorted from him and he was deemed to have no rights in return. This was part of the cruel contradiction at the very heart

41

of the Renaissance; and Spain, characteristically, provides an extreme example. The expansion of the intellectual horizons in the sixteenth century, which at one level meant the flowering of the individual and the burgeoning of new forms of artistic expression, at another was transformed into an expansion of the physical horizons of the world, and this was largely destructive in its effects, signifying the death or subjection of many proud races and the wanton devastation of cultures whose exquisite achievements we are now laboriously trying to piece together again.

The change came here in 1532 when Francisco Pizarro landed in Peru and at Cajamarca captured the Inca Atahuallpa, who had only just vanquished his rival brother Huáscar in civil war. Although Atahuallpa was ransomed by a quantity of gold sufficient to fill a room to the height of a man's upstretched hand—gold brought by flocks of llamas which converged on Cajamarca from the four quarters of the Empire—he was nonetheless cruelly garrotted and burnt at the stake in the following year. Despite the sporadic resurgence of other indigenous leaders, Inca power had to all intents and purposes been crushed.

This did not mean a return to order. The struggle for power was engaged between the Pizarros and the Almagros, and later between Gonzalo Pizarro, brother of Francisco, who had been assassinated, and the Spanish Crown. In staking their rival claims for territory the contendents undertook vast journeys of exploration and in a surprisingly short space of time most of the area that now forms the highlands and valley areas of Bolivia, as well as present-day Chile, had been traversed by the predatory, conquering armies.

Once again the centre of power changed its location. By 1537 the Conquerors held Cuzco firmly in their power, and the city of Lima had been founded. For the next two centuries and more Lima was to be the centre of Spanish power in the southern part of the American continent as the seat of the great Viceroyalty of Peru. But the area to be governed was so immense as to require some regional devolution of authority and the axis of the central Andean region switched from Cuzco to what is today Bolivian territory. This area had early excited the greed of the European invaders because of the famed silver mines of Porco, in the present Department of Potosí, which were already being exploited by the Incas. In 1538 the city of Chuquisaca, the famous city of four names—Chuquisaca, Charcas, La Plata and Sucre—which is still the legal capital of Bolivia, was founded in a benign and fertile valley lying in the eastern folds of the cordillera. Twenty-one years later, Chuquisaca became, by Imperial Decree, the centre of the Audiencia of Charcas, within the Viceroyalty of Lima. It held sway over a vast region comprising most of modern Bolivia, southern Peru as far north as Cuzco, and the administrative districts of Buenos Aires, Tucumán and Paraguay, as well as the Atacama region on what is now the Chilean coast.

By the end of the century a network of towns had sprung up within the Audiencia. Their location was determined by mining considerations for the extraction of mineral wealth and the imposition of the Catholic religion were the twin precepts of the Spanish conquest of the Americas. Everything else, the welfare of the original inhabitants, the development of agriculture, was ruthlessly subjected to the pursuit of those two overriding aims. Even measures intended to restrict abuses in the end served only to foment them; the *encomiendas*, devised to protect the Indians by entrusting them to supposedly deserving Spaniards, who would care for their physical and spiritual well-being in return for their labour, merely hastened the reduction of the original inhabitants to conditions that can only be described as slavery. All the land, in units of ever-increasing size, came to be concentrated in the hands of the foreign conqueror, and the semi-feudalism of sixteenth-century Spain was transmitted to her colonies. But not only were the Indians debased into serfdom on what had been their own communal lands but they were also forced to provide labour for the mines under a system known as *mita*, the far crueller refinement of an Inca precedent. Even the Church, which attributed greater importance to the spiritual welfare of the Indian than to his

43

physical well-being, was at least indirectly guilty of fostering such practices and was not averse to acquiring great wealth for itself: the ecclesiastical foundations and the clergy became the greatest landowners of all.

Yet it was the friars and the missionaries who first recognized the Indian of the New World as a sentient human being, rather than a mere unit of labour or a somewhat hypothetical immortal soul. Many individual priests tried to protect the Indian by drawing the attention of the Crown to the malpractices of which they were victims, and Fray Bartolomé de las Casas wrote eloquently in their defence. Probably the Order of the Jesuits provided the most effective assistance. Working in remote areas such as Mojos, Chiquitos and the Beni in the tropical lowlands of what is now eastern Bolivia, and in Paraguay, they alone tried to introduce craftsmanship and better methods of husbandry designed to improve the lot of the local inhabitants, whom they converted from semi-nomadic tribesmen into settled and relatively prosperous agriculturists. This was one of the few small patches of light on a canvas that was otherwise almost unrelievedly dark, but it too was extinguished with the expulsion of the Jesuits from Spain and its dominions in 1767.

Historians differ in their estimations of the size of the population in South America before the Spanish conquest, but though the figures vary there is now fairly wide agreement that a catastrophic decline set in after the conquest, some say as much as 90–95% within several decades or a century. In part this was due to the maltreatment of the Indians and to the social disruption caused by the conquest, but the spread of European diseases hitherto unknown was probably also responsible for much of the demographic tragedy. In the span of a few years these previously isolated regions had to contend with a series of new bacteria and viruses that had taken millennia to infiltrate Europe.

Black as the judgment of Spanish domination must be when given with the hindsight of an age that has suddenly come alive to the iniquities of colonialism, one must also concede that their record does not compare unfavourably with the colonial prac-

Llamas in the *cerdillera*.

above: The road to Copacabana, with Lake Titicaca and the Cordillera Real in the background.
below, left: Balsas on Lake Titicaca.
below, right: View of Lake Titicaca.
bottom: The Cordillera Real seen from the Isla del Sol.

tices of the day. True, the Spaniard enthralled and exploited the hapless Indian who had no redress, but seen from the long view of history can his conduct be judged more reprehensible than that of his Anglo-Saxon counterparts who built their peaceful farm colonies in the temperate zones to the north, on lands which they wrested from the Indians by the simple process of exterminating their natural owners? The Andean Indian race has at least survived, even if this survival has been precarious and secured only in cruelly adverse circumstances. Then, too, the Spaniard did not simply conquer and dominate. Because these were exploitation rather than settlement colonies, the Spaniards who controlled them were mostly adventurers who brought no wife or family to these harsh, new lands and the consequent inter-mingling of peninsular and Amerindian blood led to the genesis of a new *mestizo* race.

It was, however, a stormy mixture, and nowhere more so than on the central chain of the Andes later to be called Bolivia. Uprisings against Spanish rule broke out here sooner than anywhere else. Early in the seventeenth century there was a fierce clash in Potosí between the *peninsulares*, as the Spanish-born colonists were called, and the *criollos* Spaniards of pure blood who had been born in the colonies. Then in 1661, there were revolts in La Paz by the *mestizos* and again in Cochabamba in 1730. Perhaps the most interesting phenomenon, because it ran counter to the general pattern of the independence movements which finally achieved success early in the nineteenth century, was the series of Indian insurrections that reached a climax during the last quarter of the eighteenth century. Quechuas and Aymaras threw in their lot together, and though their complaints were more often against the injustices of colonial government, rather than a gesture of defiance against the Spanish Crown, the restoration of the lost glories of the Inca dynasty was a common theme. In 1780 the city of La Paz was itself besieged for several months by 80,000 rebellious Indians, but when the siege was finally broken the movement was also virtually at an end. Many of the names of the leaders, such as Tomás Catari, Tupac Amara, and Tupaj Catari, are still revered, but the standard under which they fought for the reinstatement of the Indian to his rightful place in society was not to be raised again until our own times.

The struggle against the Spanish Government at the beginning of the nineteenth century was about something quite different. By a strange paradox the first cry of revolt in Sucre on 25 May 1809 was one of loyalty to the captive Spanish king: '*¡Viva Fernando VII!*'; but by the time the challenge had been taken up by Pedro Domingo Murillo in La Paz on 16 July of the same year, secession from the rule of the Spanish monarchy had become the watchword. Murillo's 'Defensive Junta' was short-lived and he himself was put to death. The fight for independence was taken up in other parts of the continent, principally by Simón Bolívar in the north and by José de San Martín in the south. By what in retrospect seems almost an unfortunate precedent, often repeated since in different forms, the precursors of liberty in Alto Perú were almost the last to achieve their freedom. It was not until 1825 that the new Republic of Bolivia was established and named after the Liberator, who was elected its first President by the assembly of Upper Peru.

Despite the many advanced humanistic ideas contained in the first Constitution which Bolívar drew up for his 'favourite child', which conferred sovereignty on the people and abolished slavery, the practical effects of liberation did not go far down the social scale. Although enlightened ideas had inspired the first stirring calls for independence such notions held little appeal for the main bulk of the people, who had supported the revolution and fought to make it possible. These were not the Indians, but in the main the *criollos*, the American-born Spaniards who were jealous of the trade monopoly which favoured the merchants who stayed safely at home in Spain, and of the superior privileges accorded to the *peninsulares*, those born in metropolitan Spain. Their aim was not therefore to transform the fabric of society but to adapt it to their own advantage. Thus the lower échelons of that severely hierarchical society were unaffected by the change and many of the high-sounding ideals of the revolution were soon lost in oblivion. The Indian continued to be oppressed and exploited and Bolívar died in lonely disillusion in 1830.

No one gave the Indian more than a passing thought until nearly a century later. After the downfall in 1839 of the Confederation with Peru, the life's dream of Santa Cruz, who had been President of Bolivia since 1828, there followed an inglorious period of thirty or forty years which most Bolivians prefer to forget. A succession of brutal and mediocre dictators seized power one after another, civil strife was constant, and public life was marred by the most shameful excesses and abuses. The era culminated in the disastrous and totally mismanaged War of the Pacific which Bolivia and Peru waged against Chile from 1879–1883, and as a result of which Bolivia lost all her territories along the Pacific Coast, including valuable nitrate deposits. This was not the only territorial loss. In 1860 an ill-conceived treaty with Brazil ceded some 100,000 square kilometres of land in the rich rubber-growing areas of the Amazon basin and this was followed in 1903 by the further cession to Brazil of the region of Acre, after a frontier war.

Greater political stability reigned from 1880 until 1920, first under the conservatives and then under the liberals. However, although liberalism had strengthened the country both politically and economically, it had done so by creating a plutocracy which could not fail, in the long run, to produce further dissension and opposition. Economic power was concentrated in the hands of a few families—the Patiños, the Aramayos and the Súarez—who did not hesitate to use it for political purposes. Although continuity was outwardly maintained during the years 1920–32, there was a return to internal sedition and unrest, and to the fragmentation which has so bedevilled modern Bolivian political life.

One of the new minority groups formed took as its central theme the essential Indianness of Bolivia which one or two writers had already begun to explore. Not all of them thought of this as an exotic quality, much less a positive one. Alcides Arguedas, for instance, deplored the tendency of the majority

47

to forget that Bolivia was predominantly an Indian country, but made clear that he regarded this as a negative and retrograde element in national life. It was Franz Tamayo, the poet, writer, thinker and educationist, who made the apologia of the Indian, and became the leader and inspiration of a group which demanded the reinstatement of the Indian at the centre of Bolivian culture. Tamayo's approach was romantic and Rousseauesque, and at times almost mystical; he saw in the Indian the 'noble savage', the repository of all that was best and purest in the country's indigenous tradition. There was, however, a more practical side to his thesis: for him the Indian also represented 'an enormous concentration of internal energies' and was a man of action rather than an intellectual. Once and for all, Tamayo declared, Bolivia must lay the 'Spanish ghost'. These aspects of his teaching became the ideological corner-stone of various minority groups with a strong nationalist slant.

Perhaps they might have remained no more than a minority opinion had their views not been thrown into relief by the tragedy of the Chaco war against Paraguay in the 1930s. For the first time people of all social strata and different regions had fought together and the abnegation of the Indians was plain for all to see, because it was mainly they, ill-clothed and under-nourished, who died on those cruel sands, chewing stoically on their wads of coca.

The Chaco war had far-reaching political and economic consequences and has to a large extent determined the cause of political events over the last thirty years. An early exponent of a more nationalistic policy was Colonel Busch, President from 1937 to 1939, who was determined that the nation's natural wealth should be utilized for the benefit of the country as a whole. But when he died by his own hand, in mysterious circumstances, the country's policies were once again controlled by the large mining interests.

Then, in 1943, the tradition Busch had started was taken up by the combined military and civil adminstration of Colonel Gualberto Villaroel. It was under his leadership that the Nationalistic Revolutionary Movement—the MNR—which was to play such a significant role in the nineteen-fifties and early 'sixties first came to power. Several measures designed to protect the national economy and to improve the status of the lower classes, especially that of the Indians, were passed but these aroused the fear and opposition of the entrenched privileged classes. In 1946 there was another bloody revolution, but this time of a cruelty that has rarely been matched, even in the revolution-studded annals of Bolivian history. Villaroel himself was thrown from the balcony of his office in the Presidential Palace and then hanged from one of the lamp-posts in the main square below, the Plaza Murillo.

But the MNR had the support of the miners and the *campesinos*—the peasants—who form the mass of the population and are either of pure Indian or *mestizo* blood. Foiled of the fruits of an electoral victory in 1951 by a military Junta, the MNR came to power again through a successful revolution on 9 April 1952 and remained there until 1964. The new President, Víctor Paz Estenssoro, immediately undertook sweeping reforms, including the nationalization of the mines, an agrarian reform and a complete reorganization of the educational system.

The critics were loud in their condemnation of these measures. Paz has himself quoted the bitter remark made by a member of one of the ousted parties, who claimed that the crime committed by the MNR was 'to have placed the stinking hoof of the aborigine on Bolivian society'.

Probably no words attempting to justify the reforms could more clearly underline the need for them than that trenchant phrase. Naturally such far-reaching changes could not fail to cause an upheaval in a country whose structure was largely feudal and the next years saw many difficulties, both political and economic. But surely no one reflecting on the fact that only sixteen years ago the Bolivian peasant was bound like a serf to his master and his master's land under the iniquitous system of *pongueaje* can dispute that an attempt to integrate the Indians into the political, economic and social life of the country was long overdue.

4 WHEN you have travelled for hours, or even days, across the upland wastes of the *altiplano* you marvel that its inhabitants have been able, through the centuries, to vanquish such adverse conditions. Survival could only have been achieved through the development of a close relationship between man and his surroundings.

It was from these rocks and scanty pebbled streams that Virajocha called forth the progenitors of the Aymaras who today inhabit the plain around La Paz and it was from the jaguar rock in Lake Titicaca that Manco Capac and Mama Ojllo rose to found the Inca Empire of Cuzco. The sense of territory extends to the community, for the Aymaras also believe that each *ayllú* took its origin from some prominent natural feature of the district where it is situated. Such places are still regarded with superstitious awe as *huaca*—of religious and almost magical significance—and as the homes of ancestral spirits who must be worshipped and placated.

There cannot be many regions in the world where man's subjugation to his environment is greater than on the *altiplano*. The infertile, stony soil is watered only by a brief, torrential rainy season, furrowing the fields with gushing streams that erode as much as they irrigate. It is not only the landscape which dominates by its unlimited vistas. The ultimate arbiter of the fortunes of the Andean Indians is the Pachamama, the earth mother, whose ire has been appeased by constant worship since Inca times and before, a goddess who was not eclipsed by the advent of Catholic Christianity with the proselytizing Spaniards but who from time to time assumes the guise of the Virgin Mary. It is a guise she wears lightly, for the mask is as transparent as the clear highland air that blows above her and the Andean Indian, with his effortlessly synthetic interpretation of the world around him, finds no difficulty in looking beyond to the earthier and more compelling beliefs of his ancestors. Even a *mestizo* or *cholo*, that amalgam of Spanish and indigenous blood, who has long lived in the city, will not drink without propitiating the Pachamama by the age-old ceremony known as *ch'allar*; and by first sprinkling some drops of the beverage upon the ground he perpetuates the Inca practice of pouring libations upon the earth at sowing time.

This ancient identification of man with the soil he tills acquired a new and savage dimension when the Spaniards came and seized the lands previously apportioned among the different strata of Inca society. Countless thousands who had owned land communally with their peers were reduced to the level of serfs and bound to the land on which they served; in their condition of *pongos*, as they were called, they were not allowed to move from the estate without their master's permission but could be hired out as if they were animals. Arguedas has described how, early in this century, they were forced to carry the harvest from the farm to the owner's town house on their backs, at their own risk and cost, sometimes covering a distance of up to a hundred miles several times over; even though railways were by then in existence no landlord would think of using them to carry farm produce. Some Indian community lands remained but they were constantly encroached upon, bought out by the rich at ridiculous prices or taxed iniquitously, and became increasingly confined to the poorer and remoter areas.

The agrarian reform carried out after the 1952 revolution was therefore aimed at something more than social justice: it was the restoration of a heritage of which the Indians had been dispossessed four centuries since. This is why the return of their land has meant much more to the *campesinos* of the *altiplano* than the improvement of their material lot, although that was vital to people living so near to the starvation line. It has signified a return to human dignity and has had immeasurable psychological effects, restoring the individual's estimation of himself, and making him feel that he belongs to his country.

There is a special symbolism about the ceremony at which land titles are distributed. The new owner, having received the precious certificate of ownership, rolls over and over on the ground that is now his, still bound to the earth which gives him sustenance but in a new compact which affirms his self-respect. Afterwards, he contentedly swigs his beer, having, naturally, first rendered tribute to the Pachamama. The brilliantly coloured *aguayos*, or native shawls, twined over rustic triumphal arches, flutter like banners in the strong sunlight, and aged crones, grinning toothlessly, wreathe coloured streamers around the necks of distinguished visitors and rub confetti into the hair of all and sundry with such vigour that it is days before one sees the last of it. Then the village band canters on, well stocked with brass, a thunderous bass drum and a contingent of native flutes, and sets toes tapping and petticoats whirling with the repetitive but irresistible beat of a mountain *huayño*. And suddenly even the most detached observer is swept away into the dance and the infectious joy of the occasion.

The ritual of the agricultural year still plays out today the close kinship between man and his land. In Inca times the year was divided up into great festivals, or Raymis, which corresponded to the farming seasons, and agricultural work became endowed with a ceremonial incorporating the religious cults due to the sun and the moon and the Pachamama. These hallowed traditions were not supplanted by Catholicism but woven so closely into the new religion that it is difficult today to unravel the pagan threads from the Christian. In August, when the cold winds of winter at last begin to relinquish their icy hold, you may still see the oxen pairs plodding at the head of their ancient wooden ploughs, with bright red flags flying bravely from their yokes in salute to the coming of spring. The oxen are an innovation brought from Europe by the Spaniards but the sense of the ceremony itself, the honouring of the Pachamama, is as old as the first inhabitants of these inclement lands.

The *cordillera* is the constant backcloth for almost every view of the northern *altiplano*, remote and awe-inspiring, imposing itself upon the imagination. It too has its place in the cosmogony of the Aymara Indian and the solemn beauty of its myriad peaks, soaring into the sky like cathedral spires, fretted in ice, bespeaks the divinity with which he invests them as the origin of the universe and of his own race. Each summit is a god with special attributes, the *Achachila*, or ancestral spirit of the nearest valley or village. When an Aymara crosses the watershed into the next valley and sees another *Achachila* for the first time he will kneel down in worship, take off his hat, and make an offering of the coca he is chewing by throwing it to the ground. One of the reasons for the contempt in which the Urus are held is the belief that their *Achachila* is the mud of Lake Titicaca and that this is why they live on their *totora* reed rafts, contemplating their lowly progenitor.

The mountains are the lords of this landscape. The Illampu, a hulking mass bristling with peaks like a porcupine with spines, that glowers over the northern edge of the Royal Cordillera, and disputes with the Sajama, away to the west near the Chilean frontier, the honour of calling itself the highest mountain in Bolivia, bears the proud name of the Inca Storm-God. The rank of these deities varies according to their size, and the Illampu is probably the most awesome of all. When Sir Martin Conway started to climb it in 1898 the local Indians threatened to attack him because they feared that he would profane their god who would punish them; and he was in the end able to go only halfway up, because no Indian porters would accompany him.

Certainly the mountains can become menacing in a quite unpredictable way. I once set out with the young volunteer from the office and a friend of his to walk from Chacaltaya, the highest ski-run in the world, to the Cumbre de Yungas, the narrow pass leading to the eastern valleys. Chacaltaya lies under the Huayna Potosí, and the excursion was intended only as an energetic hike of about twenty-five kilometres through rough country just below the snowline, at a height averaging over 17,000 feet above sea-level.

When we reached the top of Chacaltaya, however, the scree bordering the snow looked very rough and we decided to strike higher up, across the top of three deceptively gentle hummocks of snow. All went well until we started to descend the third. Suddenly we found that the slope was steeper than it looked, and that it was almost impossible to get a grip on the packed, frozen snow, as we had no climbing equipment. We could neither scramble back the way we had come nor continue downwards and we could not see the bottom. For an hour we fought our way sideways across the slope towards a ridge of shale, kicking footholds with our boots and clinging desperately to the steep wall of snow, suspended above a desolate waste of moorlands where there was no sign of life or habitation. In that time I suppose we advanced about twenty yards. The shale looked as far off as ever and we were exhausted by the strenuous physical effort while our hands were numbed with cold in spite of the brilliant sunshine.

There was nothing for it but to let go and slide down the remaining two hundred feet or so on our backs. One went at such dizzying speed that it only took a moment or two. But it was a frightening and painful experience for the snow and ice lay thinly on corrugated rocks which bit into every vertebra of one's spine. Having for years suffered with a temperamental back I remember wondering with dreadful clarity as I ricocheted down how the boys would manage if I collapsed in the middle of this wilderness.

But the *Achachila* was kind for our landing was pillowed in a deep drift of snow and I found to my surprise that my spine was still articulating properly. From below we could see that our struggle across the snow-wall had saved us broken limbs and perhaps our lives: had we slid down at the point where we first got into difficulties we would have crashed over an ice wall on to a tangle of rocks. As it was the damage was slight. I lost several layers of skin from both arms as a result of my efforts to break my descent, and one of the boys had a frost-bitten finger which recovered in a day or two.

At the other end of the Cordillera, beside the Illimani, there is a curious, flat-topped mountain known as the Mururata, or headless one. According to Aymara mythology the luckless victim was a chieftain who was attacked by an Indian armed with a sling; so great was the blow that the head flew off and fell to earth many miles away to the west where it can now be seen as the pointed white cone of the Sajama, while the blood which spurted from the severed head fell to the ground in between and became the copper mines of Corocoro. The boundary between the life of ordinary men and that of the gods is never very precise. The gods are not always fearsome and omnipotent but often homely characters, jolly, boisterous fellows, going off to market together and rolling home drunk, or squabbling with one another, reflecting everyday life for the Aymara Indian on a larger scale, as a domestic drama played on a wide screen might do for a European.

But the cosy image does not last. Before long you feel yourself almost oppressed by the telluric force of the *altiplano*. The mountains are at once the bourne and the beginning of the known world which they have fashioned in their own image. Franz Tamayo caught the exact meaning of this landscape and those who dwell in it in his lines:

> *El alma de estos montes*
> *se hace hombre y piensa*

—'the soul of these mountains is transformed into man and thinks'. It finds its synthesis also in those gaunt megalithic statues of Tihuanacu which stare unseeingly into the mountains from which they came.

One can imagine how those of the Conquistadors whose eyes had become attuned to the harsh light and wide vistas of Castile must have descried here a magnified reflection of the bare meseta they had left so many wearying weeks beyond the sea. Here they were offered the same mortifications of the body and of the spirit but multiplied a hundredfold, in an arena that would allow full play to the cold passion of Spain, that passion which rejected the wan, ephemeral pleasures of this world and steered its course by the star of eternal salvation. But Spain has long been a paradox and another more earthly passion—the lust for gold—drove many of these intrepid conquerors. One can imagine, too, how the strange contours of this land must have beckoned them on until, when at last they stood on a crest of the surrounding hills and saw ridge upon ridge of mountains billowing away beyond them into the purple distance, the tales of El Dorado thundered in their ears with a new conviction. The chimerical quality of the high Andes, with its rarefied air and dizzying distances, seems peculiarly suited to the retreat from reality which began imperceptibly for the Spaniards in the sixteenth century and was carried to such tragic lengths in the next. One sees the Indian, ignorant and oppressed, playing Sancho Panza to the spurious Don Quixote of the conquistador and somehow, all these centuries later, managing to have the last word. It seems right that in 1960 their creator, Cervantes, should have been made Corregidor of La Paz, a city for which he harboured a particular affection although he never saw it.

Other parts of this landscape might have been invented by the poetic imagination of Góngora: the crystal frieze of the *cordillera* on the horizon; the frozen violence of the glaciers; the baroque, icicle-hung interiors of the snow caverns hidden high in the mountains; the gullies scattered with ashen rocks, like naked bones gnawed white by the scavenging wind of the *altiplano*.

The sense of strangeness and wonderment, of infinite perspectives and possibilities, deepens at Titicaca, the Sacred Lake of the Incas. As he winds his way along its tortuous peninsulas and inlets, the traveller is dazzled by scenes of flashing beauty where the petrified snows of the *cordillera* are mirrored in the diamantine blue waters below and so fixed twice upon the incredulous vision. Yet the approach to the lake, over some seventy kilometres of dusty road from La Paz, is not spectacular. At first one is scarcely conscious of the faint azure haze on the horizon which seems no more than the mist of distance.

Gradually, as the miles between lessen, the pallid line intensifies in hue and expands in size until the foreground is dominated by an immense sweep of deepest cobalt which blends indefinably with the sky.

The land has changed imperceptibly too. The earth here is more fertile and the sudden predominance of various shades of green strikes strongly on eyes accustomed to the more sombre and subtle tones of the *altiplano*. Small crofts wander down to the water's edge and people are busy in their fields. Some sit on the ground by the lakeside and weave coarse cloth from llama and alpaca wool on primitive looms. The cattle here are fatter and browse contentedly among the reeds with the water lapping their bellies. The *totora* reed is the great standby of the lake dweller, providing fodder for their cattle, thatch for their houses, and raw material for their *balsas*, the high-prowed coracles rocking gently in the wash of the shallows. Far out, where the fishermen are at work, they ride low in the water and would be almost indiscernible but for the white sails which have now largely replaced the reed sails of the traditional *balsa*. Otherwise, the *balsa* today differs little from that of Inca times, which Cieza de León described with wonderment and curiosity in the sixteenth century, or from the craft in which, nearly three hundred years later, Simón Bolívar crossed the lake from Peru when he made his triumphal entry into La Paz early in 1825. Its construction is a work of art, for the stiff reeds have to be woven together, coaxed into the sinuously elegant lines of the finished craft and then bound tightly to withstand the onslaughts of wind and water. The *balsa*-builder's craft is arduous and exacting but his product is short-lived, for the *balsa* after a few years becomes water-logged and many blackened, rotting hulls swing among the reeds alongside the shining straw and sculptured prows of new vessels. Yet, despite the increasing use of more modern boats in recent years, the *balsa* shows no signs of dying out.

It survives as a fishing craft, but no longer ferries the ordinary traveller across the lake. Yet the alternative means of transport are not as modern as you might think, even though the lake

57

lies across the only highway between Peru and Bolivia, straddling the frontier between the two countries. Three times a week elderly Scottish-built steamers—the first one was hauled up in pieces, on muleback over the mountains from the Pacific, before the turn of the century and assembled on the lake shore—chug through the night between Guaqui, the tiny port on the Bolivian side which is linked to La Paz by rail, and the bustling Quechua market town of Puno, high in the Peruvian *sierra*, whence one railway winds down to Arequipa and the Pacific and another threads its way across the backbone of the Andes to Cuzco.

If you follow the main road on from Guaqui, a rugged causeway hugging the lake shore, you come to Desaguadero, the only river draining out of Lake Titicaca, which is also the frontier between the two countries. There are villages on both sides of the river, squalid, frontier-type villages, bereft of the charm of the lakeside hamlets where the fishermen and the farmers dwell, and breathing the taint of contraband and suspicion in their sleazy adobe bars.

It is all sadly at variance with the romantic legend of how the Desaguadero river was created. It seems that in remote times the mythological Tunupa—not a god, but a miracleworker—appeared to the degenerate cyclopean people of Tihuanacu and warned them that if they did not return to their old way of life their realm would be devastated by flood. The people would not listen, but tied Tunupa on to a *balsa* and threw him out on to the lake in the middle of a terrible storm in which he was bound to perish. But the *balsa* floated to the shore which opened up miraculously in a long canal—now the Desaguadero —down which Tunupa travelled to Lake Poopó. Afraid that the natives there would also try to kill him he sank into the salt, but the Urus continued to revere him. Their hope that one day he would leave his hiding place was rewarded when he reappeared as a volcano near Poopó and the salt-flats of Uyuni.

According to another version Tunupa came from the north with a big wooden cross on his shoulder and followed by five disciples. The Indians did not listen to his teachings but one of his disciples fell in love with a local girl, converted her and asked Tunupa to baptize her. In revenge, the girl's father had all the disciples killed. Tunupa reproached the people and was tortured and flung upon the lake, escaping only by the magical appearance of the Desaguadero. His cross could not be destroyed and would not sink, so it was buried in a well from where, it is said, it was taken out in the sixteenth century.

Crossing the Desaguadero today requires much patience and perseverance. The formalities are intricate and require visits to at least three offices on each side—immigration, customs and police. They are not housed together, for that would deprive the achievement of translating oneself from one country to the other of all merit, but are tucked away in dwellings scattered at some distance from one another. Most of these look singularly unlikely from the outside and never bear any indication of their function. Moreover the offices have all to be visited in a certain order and to err in this is to be sent ignominiously back to the beginning to start all over again, as in a game of snakes and ladders. Even when you've thrown your dice correctly and arrived at the right spot, your onward progress is far from assured, for ten to one the office concerned is empty or padlocked and further sleuthing is required to track down the missing official gossiping over the bar in the next street, or sipping a cup of coffee at home with his feet up, business being hardly brisk. One would not really be surprised to hear that many weary wanderers give up the unequal struggle and creep quietly back the way they have come.

The game is well-spiced with emotion, for the frontier closes like a flower at sundown and so, as the various officials thumb their way stolidly through your passport and ask endless questions about your mother's maiden name and why you ever thought of coming here anyway—a question which has already sprung unbidden into your own mind—your eyes cannot help straying frequently to your watch, for the prospect of spending the night in either village is not enticing.

Nowadays, they are linked by a broad concrete bridge, erected by mutual agreement between the Peruvian and Bolivian governments, but until a year or two ago you had to cross the Desaguadero over a curious structure of odd-shaped pieces of scrap metal, riveted together into a kind of intricate jigsaw. Though the effect was bizarre, there was a certain grotesque ingenuity about it. The crumpled and rusty metal had an appearance of great antiquity which had been cleverly exploited by the designer—for he deserves the term—who had fancifully resorted to the Middle Ages for inspiration and adorned the patched metal gates at either end with a kind of portcullis roughly carved of the same metal strips and unevenly fanged with rusty-looking teeth. Perhaps he had been spurred on by the thought that no ordinary bridge would suffice here where, from pre-Inca times until at least a century ago, when the American archaeologist, E. G. Squier, photographed it, a most unusual and famous bridge, made of a rush road laid over *balsa*-reed pontoons, had existed without interruption, except for the renewal of the *balsas* every two years. This, like so many other wonders of the New World, had excited the interest of Cieza de León who wrote that ' . . . in the time of the Incas, there used to be guards to collect toll from those who crossed the bridge, which was made of sheaves of oats and constructed in such a way that men, horses and all else could pass over it.'

No toll was collected on the metal successor to this ancient bridge and it was certainly not true to say that every form of traffic could pass over it. If your car was broad in the beam, small boys had to run backwards ahead of it waving you on, for there would be a clearance of not more than a centimetre or two on each side, and I remember once having to negotiate a gaping hole almost as wide as the bridge itself. Lorries and buses could not be accommodated at all but had to take an altogether different route, across the straits of Tiquina.

Promptly at five o'clock, Peruvian time, which is six o'clock for the Bolivians (for the hour changes here, too, as a further trap for the unwary) the pseudo-mediaeval doors, hanging a little drunkenly on their creaking hinges, were simultaneously slammed shut with a ceremonial clang of great finality.

Not, of course, that anything is ever as final as all that in these parts. There is always some way round if you go the right way about it with the right person; as on one occasion when I scurried across the bridge at the last moment before the frontier closed only to find that, bemused by the plethora of formalities, I had forgotten my passport on the Peruvian side. It seemed for a moment an insoluble situation, at least until the next day, but it was not long before a small boy began daringly to swing himself along the outer skirts of the bridge and shortly afterwards returned with the missing document for a consideration. All this took place with the full connivance and approval of the frontier officers on both sides of the river some of whom observed his progress with interest and even shouted advice. They did not, however, consider that tolerance thus far exercised might be stretched a little more to include the opening of the gates for a few brief moments to enable the errand to be accomplished with less danger to life and limb. Meanwhile, underneath, heavily-loaded *balsas* plied busily between the banks without let or hindrance.

The new bridge seems sadly functional and impersonal compared with its two predecessors and must inevitably affect the crossing at Tiquina, previously the only place where heavy vehicles could cross the lake between Peru and Bolivia. At Tiquina, which lies a little to the east, one of the many tongues of land that protrude into the lake curls back upon itself to form a narrow strait. The vehicles are ferried over on clumsy-looking boats powered by enormous, ungainly sails and by ragged urchins who pole and paddle with a variety of roughly-hewn wooden implements. Here too there is an air of makeshift about everything. Ropes are frayed thin and knotted together, the mast creaks and bends ominously and the boom swings wildly. Manoeuvring a vehicle on to the boat through the square opening at the stern is a nightmare experience. The approach is littered with boulders and sharp flints which have to be kicked into position afresh for every crossing and which jerk the steering out of true at the crucial moment when the wheels have to be guided on to the narrow planks forming a flimsy nexus between dry land and the deck. Even worse is the repeat performance in reverse when the other side is reached. On both occasions conflicting instructions, encouragement and abuse are bellowed at the driver by the boatman and his crew, accompanied by a great demonstration of unco-ordinated pushing and shoving which eventually, and almost unbelievably, ends in the vehicle being loaded on or off.

The amateurish impression is misleading because great skill is required and once underway a zigzag course has to be steered according to the drift of the water and the wind. Huge lorries and buses are carried in this way, tilting a little tipsily as they plough ponderously across this alien element. Once I even saw a flock of llamas being ferried across, heads all pointing the same way, aristocratic noses high in the air, and on their faces a look of horrified disbelief.

The water is translucent and icily cold. Near the shore tall weeds wreathe mysterious garlands below the surface but the lake bed soon plummets out of sight beneath a shifting mosaic of jewel colours, as if aquamarines and sapphires, turquoises and emeralds were being tumbled together on a cloth of indigo velvet. It is so deep that the deeper-draught steamers between Guaqui and Puno can pass through the narrow centre channel.

In spite of the precarious craft and the cut-throat competition between rival boat owners, the safety record is surprisingly good. A few years ago a bus did plunge to the bottom but there was no loss of life as the passengers were on a separate boat. However, the property lost included all the documents for United Nations Day which an economy-conscious headquarters, more versed in thrift than geography, had decided to send by surface means.

The lake is not always a placid inland sea. There are dangerous currents and strong, sudden winds that whip its still surface into a boiling maelstrom in a matter of minutes. Such squalls are common at dusk, and for this reason the ferry ceases long before failing light curtails operations. Here too the traveller must beware lest he arrive too late and be forced to cool his heels till morning. Once, I did rush up in a flurry of dust to find the ferry had closed, but managed to persuade a boatman to take me over without my car, so that I could at least find a bed in the hotel on the farther side of the straits. It was a dreary barracks of a building, originally intended to encourage the tourist trade presumably, but so lacking in the most elemental comforts and facilities, and so bitingly cold, that it seemed to have been devised specially for the physical mortification and consequent spiritual regeneration of the numerous pilgrims who were the only other guests, and who roused me into shivering wakefulness in the early hours when they clumped righteously out on the last lap of their long trek to the sanctuary of the Virgin of Copacabana.

The rigours of the night were obliterated by the beauty of the early morning. The lake itself was very still, as yet uncluttered by sails, and the rising sun struck sparks of coruscating light from its smooth surface; every object stood out clearly defined in the crisp cold air; small dwellings, like doll's houses, marched resolutely up the steep escarpments overhanging the straits, trim in their neat coats of whitewash. It seemed a miniature world, a world of make-believe in which each object was small and neat and carved lovingly to scale, even to the smoothly rounded pebbles lying on the beach. At the other extreme, the dual image of the lonely white peak of the Illimani, piercing the sky in the remote distance, and floating upside down at the far end of the lake, only served to enhance the impression of a formal, sculptured beauty in which the generous but slap-dash hand of nature had had no share.

The land in the vicinity of the lake is an oasis in the midst of a vast upland desert. The rough stone causeways that twist around its shores are bordered by houses that bespeak a certain dignity, houses often two storeys high, with outside staircases running up to narrow wooden balconies, their tall, straight whitewashed walls pierced at regular intervals by discreet casement windows. Terraced fields sweep down to the shores of the lake following the precipitous contours of the valley. Accustomed to the unbroken vistas of the *altiplano* one is surprised to find trees, mostly eucalyptus, growing sometimes in great profusion where the hillside drops steeply into the lake, sometimes forming an avenue along a straight stretch of road, or standing like solitary sentinels against the sky. The blue of the water, the heightened shades of colour and contrast, the more variegated lines of a landscape broken by trees all contrive to give an impression of a softer, easier countryside and the proximity of the lake undoubtedly reduces the rigours of the climate.

If one strikes southwards from La Paz, the scene is very different. The long, straight dusty road stretches monotonously on, leading, it seems, to the very edge of the world. Even the *chullpas*, the crumbling adobe burial towers, become more numerous, their narrow openings all turned towards the east so that the Sun-God would be the first sight of their dead on resurrection; but most of them have long since been despoiled of their crouching mummies and the decaying remnants of their earthly possessions ceremonially heaped around them have been looted or have dissolved into dust.

Southwards the earth becomes perceptibly even more barren and desiccated. Stones are so numerous that many fields resemble the dried-up beds of rivers even though great cairns piled along their sides show that a diligent, if hopeless, effort has been made to remove them. Many of them have been built into rough, dry-stone walls which enclose fields and corrals, a crazy lacework of rock chinked with glimpses of the blue sky beyond. The tumbled remains of other walls can be seen high on dry, ochre hillsides which look as if they have never produced a blade of grass, and indeed the land lies fallow here for as much as seven years. It seems a colourless countryside compared to the vivid blues and greens around the lake, but during the long miles when there is scarcely a bend in the road, nor any change in the contours of the landscape, you discover it to be painted so skilfully from a palette of muted reds and browns and greys that the sepias merge into the buffs, grey rocks flush imperceptibly to soft pink and so to madder, and the distance becomes infused with warm apricot light. These uplands are unobstrusive in the modulations of their moods and the subtle shiftings of their tints. Only when the grain is young after the yearly rains is the earth spiked with an unambiguous green, while at harvest time nature allows herself a brief festival of colour when the millet-like grains of the indigenous *quinua* and *cañahua* glow vermilion and orange against the yellow stalks of the barley.

The most typical feature of this landscape is the bristly fans of the *ichú* grass, known in Spanish as *paja brava*; translated literally this means 'savage straw' and the term is well-earned as anyone who has walked unwarily into a clump of it will ruefully agree. As one gets nearer to Oruro the *paja brava* encroaches more and more on the tilled land and gives a tundra-like aspect. The llamas and alpacas, scarce near the lake, appear in flocks of ever larger numbers for the *paja brava* is their staple diet. The llama is the typical inhabitant of the *altiplano*, 'the frugal companion of the Aymara', as Gregorio Reynolds, the Bolivian poet, has movingly described in a sonnet whose Parnassian restraint is peculiarly suited to the llama's austere habitat. No prospect in these gaunt lands is complete without their tall, dignified forms, gazing with Olympian indifference at the unpromising horizon. Their wool provides the Aymaras with clothes and blankets and is woven into the sacks they carry on their backs; they are the traditional beasts of burden, although since Spanish times this task is shared with the donkey; their dung is used for fuel to warm the cheerless adobe huts and to cook food; and they provide milk and, eventually, meat.

As the hours pass and the land unfolds monotonously ahead, changing so indefinably as to seem remorselessly the same, the spirit is lulled into a dream-like state, at one remove from reality, as on a sea-voyage when one is for a time divorced from the normal trappings of life. Indeed, the *altiplano* resembles nothing so much as a vast ocean, billowing away into the infinite especially where, beyond Patacamaya, the vista stretches, unimpeded by any intervening bluff, right to the Sajama and the smaller twin snowcaps that stand guard over the Chilean frontier. One can plot the course of other travellers upon its well-worn routes by the curling spirals of dust, pluming up like smoke from companion steamers. Roadside villages heave into sight like glimpses of landfall over the rim of the horizon, dark shimmering blobs that resolve themselves with decreasing distance into islands of squat brown houses, dominated by the church as a lighthouse might loom over some minor port. At times the resemblance increases with closer inspection, for many churches are roughly-cast buildings of adobe, with rounded towers, daubed with whitewash, leaning a little uncertainly over the village square. Others, like the church at Sica-Sica, are more imposing and float into view like some proudly turreted battleship; Sica-Sica church was built of stone in colonial times and its intricate carved façade, in which the Indian and the Spanish traditions were inextricably intertwined, stands out in baroque contrast with the humble simplicity of the dwellings around it.

The wayside hamlets appear deserted, their padlocked doors flush on the street. Whole families are away working in the fields from dawn to dusk. Once a week, in places of any size, there is a market in the *plaza* where every conceivable object is sold: coca leaves, magic charms and potions, hot peppers and vegetables, local cloth, earthenware pots, reins, slings and ropes made from llama hide, wool for spinning and spindles to spin it on, and even a wide selection of musical instruments. In many regions, barter is still the preferred system of exchange and time no object, so that many hours are whiled away while the contendents, squatting on the ground, add and subtract from their minute piles of merchandise, against a chorus of vociferous argument. Often the best part of the morning may be spent in exchanging a handful of beans for some other commodity such as peppers or salt, and many long hours will be spent in trudging to and from market from some distant homestead. On such days the roads are thronged like a mediaeval thoroughfare with a great concourse of people and animals: donkeys and llamas (for horses and mules are rare) laden with wares for sale or recently purchased with hard haggling; women in their best and most brightly-coloured skirts, the inevitable baby's head bobbing inquisitively over their shoulders from an opening in the gaily-striped *aguayo* in which the rest of the child's anatomy is tightly bound to its mother's back; and behind follow their menfolk, as likely as not chivvying along a recalcitrant bull or pair of oxen.

The impression of a seascape increases as one approaches Oruro, for the land is flatter and the vegetation sparser. In places large areas are encrusted white with salt. The distances and the clear air create the effect of a mirage. Small hills float like atolls in pools of shimmering water; llamas and alpacas swim into sight like strange amphibians; Oruro itself hovers on the horizon in an opalescent haze like a secret city, an impression greatly at variance with the grim practicality and straight lines of that most frugal town. When the rains come, at the turn of the year, the water becomes reality and sometimes only the twin ribbons of the railway and the road remain unsubmerged on their protecting embankments. In exceptional years even they may be endangered for there is no drainage to speak of and then you may have the excitement, as I have, of battling through the mud and the rising floods in the last jeep to make the journey before communications between Oruro and the capital are broken for several days.

It is not a beautiful place, nor does it inspire easeful thoughts. I was the more astonished then, to see one day, the fleet silhouettes of three vicuñas, rarest and shyest of animals, bounding across the road ahead in a series of graceful arabesques. In this land of extremes it is the juxtaposition of beauty and harshness that live in the memory.

5 ONCE, when I had proudly taken home some clothes I had had made from llama and alpaca wool handwoven on the *altiplano*, Pancha, my *mestiza* cook, raised her hands in horror:

'*Pero, señorita - a - a -*'—and her voice tailed away in a gasp of sheer incredulity—'*!ésta es tela que llevan los* indios!'

What she meant was: 'How *can* you wear this? This is the kind of cloth that the *Indians* wear.'

No words can convey the withering contempt that she managed to inject into the name of that much-maligned race which, ironically enough, must have supplied at least seventy or eighty percent of the blood now surging so indignantly through her veins at the very thought that she should be even indirectly contaminated by them, through my ill-chosen apparel; for it goes without saying that I was letting her down as well as myself. Yet when I took those same despised garments to New York and London, friends could not conceal their envy.

'Hand-woven,' they exclaimed, covetously. 'But they must have cost the earth . . .' thereupon reeling off the names of a few notoriously expensive shops where I might conceivably have purchased these marvels.

Pancha's dismay was the typical reaction of the *cholo* so deeply impregnated with disdain for the Indian that he seeks to deny his own origins. She and her like may surely be excused when a long line of distinguished Bolivian writers favoured with an education described as liberal (as well as some supposedly well-informed foreign observers) have expressed themselves equally scathingly about this long oppressed people, and with more conviction because of their greater eloquence. Alcides Arguedas, one of the first writers to seek national themes, found little comfort in them. While recognizing the predominantly Indian character of the country, he considered it to be the root of all its problems.

'Were it not for the predominance of indigenous blood, the country would today be on the same level as many people more favoured by currents of immigration from the old continent,' he stated categorically. The Aymara he described as living on the *altiplano* 'wild and furtive like an animal in a wood; given over to his rites and the cultivation of the sterile soil where his race must surely soon come to an end.' The Aymara character is harsh, he has no finer feelings and is filled with rancour. 'He has no willpower or perseverance of spirit and feels a profound hatred of all that is different from him.' It is true that Arguedas was writing fifty years ago, and he does attribute these negative racial characteristics to the subjection and near-slavery in which the Indian was forced to live; but he also implies that the iron has driven so deeply into the Indian's soul that no recuperation is possible, even if conditions were improved.

Later, in his novel *Race of Bronze*, Arguedas pleads a more humanitarian thesis, favouring the Indian. But this earlier book, analysing national problems under the significant title *A Sick People*, helped to create what Fernando Diez de Medina has called the 'black legend', which still persists today despite the counter-movements, in literature, of the indigenist school under the leadership of the great Franz Tamayo; and, in government, of policies designed to restore the Indians' lost rights. Echoes of these doubts about the level of the Indians' natural intelligence and his capacity for development find their way into the works of writers as sympathetic and well-documented as Harold Osborne, though admittedly his book *Indians of the Andes* was written before the 1952 revolution had shown what the Indian might achieve in more propitious circumstances. One was hardly surprised therefore to hear much more disparaging terms used by foreigners in La Paz, and even some Bolivians—usually people who seldom ventured far out of La Paz, or if they did, had little to do with the *campesinos*.

I was fortunate to see the other side of the picture because my work involved frequent visits to outlying villages and many Indian families became my friends. But it was lonely walks taken for pleasure that brought me almost accidentally to the valley of Cristina and Juan.

If you take the long road from La Paz which winds down through the valley of the Choqueyapu you come first to Obrajes, once a separate village, with its prim Spanish-style square, and then to Calacoto, perhaps the only modern residential area in the city, inhabited mostly by Americans, whose neat villas contrast strangely with the tangled vermilion crags of the Sierra de Aranjuez which loom behind them. Beyond, the road begins to rise once more, the tarmac peters out, and a narrow stone-strewn track ascends the range of hills which hems in La Paz at the lower end of the valley. The bare fang of the *muela del diablo*, the devil's tooth, which is, besides the Illimani, the most spectacular landmark to be seen from the city, once more incises the sky on the right while ahead, behind the village of Ovejuyo, wind and water have cut such deep runnels down the sides of the hills that they resemble the pipes of some gigantic organ. The hollow below is more sheltered. In the dry season, spindly willows sigh over the waterless bed of the river; yellow broom and white ox-eye daisies splash the sparse hedgerows with colour; and the pungent smell of wild lupins catches the back of your throat.

There is little traffic on the road, except for lorries bound for a distant mine hidden away at the foot of the Illimani, and in the heavy rains these carve out deep ruts in the trail, making it impassable to smaller vehicles. But if you do reach the top of the watershed behind Ovejuyo, a strange and beautiful sight awaits. At first, there is little that seems spectacular: a small peaty lagoon reflecting the sky and the reeds that fringe it, a few broken wooden crosses and crumbling adobe tombstones marking a lonely, windswept burial ground at the highest point. This is La Sierra de las Animas, the hill of the Spirits.

And then you turn a corner and the glistening white summits of the Mururata and the Illimani leap out at you as if they were the guardian spirits of the landscape. The valley that lies below stretches right to the foot of the Illimani. Through the middle a river has gashed a deep channel, carving strange pillars and castellated forms of eroded earth and giving the landscape the stylized formality of a baroque painting.

Here, legend no longer seems fantasy. Once, resting on a rock above the river, I sensed a shadow pass over the sun and looked up to see the massive black shape of a condor hover for a moment and then soar away into the mountains as if he were indeed inspecting an intruder on behalf of the Sun-God. Andean mythology is rich in fables about condors. Not far from here, it is told, Suma Pangara, a shepherdess, was watching her flocks at the foot of the Illimani when a condor swooped down seeking a young lamb as his prey. Instead, he was enraptured by the girl's beauty and fell in love with her. After visiting her for several days he carried her across the mountains. Her parents searched desperately for her and at last found her lying at the bottom of a deep gorge, but when they had carried her home she died. Later, according to the legend, the condor was found dead on her tomb, his great wings spread over her grave and his beak impaled in the ground.

Not many people come here from the city, for the *paceño* is incurably urban, and the silence weighs like an unseen presence. One might think that it was an uninhabited land, were it not for the sudden lilt of a *quena*—the Andean-Indian flute—played by some solitary and unseen shepherd. There is a cold clarity about the sound that seems to enclose the spirit of this valley and the echo hangs in the air long after the sound of the music has ceased.

But few parts of the Bolivian uplands are uninhabited, except for those perpetually covered in snow. Wherever there is a

71

piece of land not too steep for a man to stand upright, you may be sure that it has been tilled, even if it is no larger than a pocket handkerchief. In this valley the road leads some miles further on to the sizeable village of Palca, hidden away in the deepest part of the valley where, they say, the rains, when they come, wash gold down the streets. But I used to take a footpath nearer at hand which crosses the river and leads after a few miles to a deserted *hacienda*, abandoned, presumably, since the agrarian reform, whose broken windows stare blindly at the Illimani and one of the most beautiful views in the world. Nowadays, it is the local headquarters of the peasants' syndicate and trespassers are not welcomed: when I wandered around it for the first time I was warned off by a churlish old man, flourishing an aged rifle. I had not been in Bolivia long and the incident seemed to bear out all I had heard about the dour unfriendliness and latent violence of the Andean-Indian.

And then I met Cristina and Juan. Cristina looked no more than seven or eight years old, though she may have been nine or ten at the time of which I speak, for children here are small. When I first saw her she was crouching on the ground, so absorbed in the game she was playing that she had forgotten the flock she was supposed to be watching and did not notice my approach. Like all little girls over two or three years old, she was already dressed as a woman, in a faded red *pollera*, or skirt, with the regulation three tucks running round the hem, and a tattered blouse and shawl. On her head was a weather-beaten bowler hat, green with age and evidently handed down, for it was still too large and descended almost to her eyes. She had picked some tiny green berries from a bush growing nearby, and by piercing their centres with stiff pieces of *paja brava*, no longer than a match, had fashioned some miniature tops which she was intently spinning on the dusty ground. No pampered child born in kinder circumstances could have shown more fascination with the latest mechanical toy. But when she looked up, tossing back her black pigtails, I could see the difference. It was not just her ragged clothes or her dirt-engrained cheeks, chafed red by the biting winds of the *altiplano*. Rather it was the expression in her eyes as she looked at me. They were beautiful eyes, large, dark and well-defined as you so often find in Andean-Indian women, but they were not a child's eyes. They looked at you warily, clouded with a responsibility acquired too young, born of the need to care, day after day, and often all alone, for a flock of sheep which had been hers to guard since she had been old enough to run after them and able to throw a stone with her sling to stop them from straying. Those eyes spoke too of the harshness of life, of the need to keep up an unremitting struggle for survival, a lesson learnt almost unconsciously as soon as she had become aware of the world around her. It was an expression that one learns to recognize on the anxious faces of all those children on the *altiplano* who dash to stop their animals from wandering in the path of passing vehicles.

Yet she was a gay child and was soon chattering away. She told me that her name was Cristina but was vague about her family. She lived with an 'aunt' in the hamlet over the hill and did not seem to know what had happened to her parents. She thought they might be in La Paz. Yes, she had been to school, but went no longer as she had to look after her sheep. No, she was not lonely, though she often saw no one all day, for she had the company of Juan. Juan, dragged along to meet me by one of his hindlegs, proved to be a black lamb, the smallest in the flock. He was evidently accustomed to his special status and submitted uncomplainingly to being cradled in Cristina's arms while she prattled to him in Aymara.

This was the first of many meetings for I used to walk in the valley on most Sundays when I could get away. Juan grew up fast, inevitably, but was still the inseparable companion of Cristina. To watch them together was to understand that the Andean-Indian child, undernourished and deprived, resembles any other child in its need for affection and companionship and in the wonderful imaginings with which it transforms the world around into a secret place of its own. Then, one day, there was no Cristina pasturing her flocks in the usual spot. I did not think anything of it, but the next time she was not there either. I never did see her again, but whenever I picture that broad and beautiful valley, stretching away to the towering white summits that seal it from the outside world, I hear the notes of the *quena* faintly in the breeze and see Cristina playing with Juan and her home-made spinning tops.

There were others to whom I must have become as familiar a sight as they to me: bell-skirted women treading water out of sodden, frost-blackened potatoes, spread out on the ground, and now to be dried in the sun to make *chuño*, the dehydrated potato which has been a staple food since Inca times; old crones toiling up to the hamlet, bent double under loads of *tola*, a twiggy shrub, which they use as fuel; young men who played football on an improvised pitch with great verve, defying the breathless thinness of the air; and an old man, with a burnished wrinkled face under the bright colours of his *lluchu* or woollen cap, bearing the legend 'La Paz 1964' blazoned across its ear-flaps, who inspected his minute fields of *quinua* and beans every Sunday, solemnly knitting some unrecognizeable garment in grey llama wool as he walked around.

But almost as memorable as Cristina and Juan was Pablo, a young boy of thirteen or fourteen who would come flying down from a corraled adobe homestead on a hillock near the spot at the end of the road where I left my car. It became something of a ritual. There was never any sign of him in the morning but when I returned from my walk in the late afternoon the opening of the car door would be a signal for him to emerge from the hut on the hill and come careering down brandishing a rusty tin alarm clock for me to wind. The clock was invariably stopped, or hours wrong and I came to the conclusion that I was the only one initiated into its mysteries. Perhaps it was some kind of esoteric status symbol, for it was difficult to explain in any other way this obsession with time in a timeless valley. The procedure never changed. After the clock-winding ceremony, carried out with great solemnity, as if we were checking the accuracy of Big Ben, I would give Pablo the rest of my picnic sandwiches and we would talk a little before I drove back over the Sierra de las Animas to La Paz. And then, one day, Pablo arrived at less speed than usual, carrying his alarm clock, but carefully cradling in his other hand an enormous duck's egg, which, he shyly explained, was a special present for me. It was a gesture typical of the kindness and dignity which I found in all the Andean-Indians I met, contrary to everything I had been told to expect.

Pablo's talks with me were always about education, about the mud-walled one-room school over in the next valley, where he had just learned to read and write, but which had now been closed for lack of a teacher. One could see that it was as if a light had been extinguished from his life. The revolution of 1952, with all the setbacks and errors almost inevitable in such a far-reaching upheaval of the established order, opened up a new life for the Indian peasant. It has not been an easy process, nor is it yet, to undo the injustices of over four centuries or to replace the traditions and attitudes which have become ingrained during that time. I can remember my distress when, as late as 1960, I accompanied a Minister on an official visit to a fairly remote *altiplano* village and a wrinkled old man knelt before me to kiss my hand presumably because, as a European, I resembled the old landowners, whose rule had extended over the greater part of his lifetime, and must therefore receive the same treatment as they had exacted.

Such incidents are happily becoming rarer and a new generation is growing up, conscious of their dignity and their rights as human beings. The agrarian reform has been far from perfect but ownership of his own land has still probably done more than anything else to restore to the *campesino* the self-respect that had been crushed by centuries of cruel repression. Yet at the same time he recognizes his own obligation towards the nation. Many is the time I have heard the leaders of rural communities saying to a minister, or other government representative, with a simple directness, enhanced by their quaintly antiquated Spanish which seems to have come straight out of the Golden Age: 'You see, Señor Ministro, we need this school [or road or clinic] and we need the help of the government in making a design for us and in providing the materials we can't get locally. For our part, we will provide, as a contribution from our community, all the labour required, the stone and the adobes.'

75

It was the firm negotiating position of men proudly aware of their own standing and all that it entailed.

I was able to follow this process at first hand through the Andean-Indian programme, a pilot operation in which the International Labour Organization and other United Nations Agencies were helping the Government to integrate the Indians into the economic, social and cultural life of the country, as fully-fledged citizens instead of the serfs they had been for so long. Not all the innovations required were easy to introduce but education was always the spearhead. Contrary to much that is written and spoken even today, most Indians, like Pablo, are thirsty for education and regard it as the pathway to a better life. Yet, as recently as 18 November 1966, a turnover article in *The Times* stated categorically: 'Centuries of oppression have made the underdog, be he Indian or mestizo, singularly slow of response to the argument that he can better himself through education.' This may be true of other parts of the Andes, where no real attempt has yet been made to emancipate the Indian, though in such places it is legitimate to wonder whether the argument has been put to him at all. Certainly such a statement does not accurately reflect the attitude of the Bolivian Indian over the last fifteen years. I cannot number the times when Indians have said to me 'We were exploited for centuries because we were too ignorant to defend ourselves. I want my son to be educated so that the same fate can never befall him again.'

This desire for education has not been merely passive. Whole communities have turned out all over the *altiplano* and the high valleys to build their own schools from adobe bricks they have made themselves, giving their labour free and unstintingly for the work of construction, and on occasion even collecting money amongst themselves for the purchase of items that cannot be produced locally. Sometimes when the building has been finished the villagers pay the salary of a teacher until such time as they can persuade the hard-pressed government to include an item in the budget. For years the grimy stairs of the Ministry of Peasant Affairs have groaned under the weight of Indians who have poured into La Paz from all over the country, by every conceivable means of locomotion, to present petitions of this kind. Through such communal efforts the number of rural children attending school increased over threefold in the twelve years from 1952–64, while the number of rural schools grew in proportion.

Few of the schools are well equipped. Scant resources cannot be stretched to provide furniture which is always expensive on the treeless *altiplano*, even if home-made, because of the high cost of wood. Inside you often find the children squatting on a mud floor chanting their tables, or perhaps using primitive desks and benches made out of rough hunks of adobe stuck to the ground, and there are never enough books or pencils to go round. The children are dirty and ragged, their bare feet calloused from the long walk across rough ground from their scattered cottages, their dark cheeks chapped and ruddy from the icy upland winds and the burning rays of the sun. Many of them left home early in the morning without breakfast and will still not have eaten when they return late in the afternoon. It is hard to imagine conditions more adverse to learning, but the fervour for education continues undiminished. *'Buenos días'* chorus the children as you enter—for Spanish, and not Aymara or Quechua, is the language of instruction—and timidly proffer grubby notebooks, covered with painstaking characters and drawings.

The Indian may want his son to be educated but he feels no such concern about his daughters. The proportion of girls being educated is small and decreases rapidly in the upper classes of the primary schools. This is due partly to an innate sexual prejudice and partly to economic factors: most small girls, like Cristina, and some small boys, are needed to tend the flocks which represent the family's capital, while older relations carry out the more skilled jobs. That the prejudice is also there, however, was made very clear one day which I spent visiting six or seven schools with a French woman social worker. In the last of these we found, for the first time, one solitary girl in the sixth, and highest, primary grade. We both converged upon her to give her, as we thought, some much-needed encouragement in her lonely position. Hardly had we begun to look at her notebook than the schoolmaster rushed up in some dismay to bear us off to another pupil, apologizing that her work was not up to the standard of the rest and adding artlessly, by way of exoneration:

'But what can you expect? She's a woman, after all!'

Then as it slowly dawned on him that this was perhaps not the most tactful remark to make to two visitors of the opposite sex, he hastened to retrieve the situation by saying, not without undertones of scarcely-concealed doubt:

'Of course, it *may* be different in your countries, but that's how it is here!'

I was reminded of my first official visit to Potosí with two of my staff when there were difficulties about return reservations on the train. We applied for help to the Prefect who most obligingly dashed off a note which, to the embarrassment of my colleagues and my own amusement, enjoined the station-master to give the gentlemen the first-class sleeping compartment usually reserved for the Prefectura and added, with ample subjunctives and future conditionals to underline the unlikelihood of the whole proposition: 'and if there *should* by chance be another bed available it should be given to the señorita.'

The virtual exclusion of women from such educational benefits as now exist in rural areas is serious not only because they are responsible for bringing up the next generation but also because, according to local tradition, they carry out important agricultural functions, especially in caring for animals. One cannot be surprised that the woman constitutes a very conservative element in rural Andean-Indian society. Even so, there are signs that the old order is changing here too. Under the guidance of rural development centres women's clubs are growing up which give training in the care of home and children and on matters of wider interest. Often the obstacles are very great. Windows, for example, are resisted as loopholes for evil spirits and thieves, or, at best, the cold, and yet gradually the one smoke-filled room of the traditional hut, where whole

78

families live, sleep, cook and eat, is being transformed. The oven is relegated to an outhouse, the bare mud walls are papered with discarded newspapers and magazines and there may even be a wooden bed, a table and some chairs.

Some years ago I attended the inauguration of a women's club at Sora, near Oruro. A more unprepossessing place would be difficult to find. The community hall was set in the middle of saline flats on the shores of the new lake that has formed behind Oruro from the overflow of the Desaguadero river, which drains Lake Titicaca but can find no outlet for itself. The lake is getting larger every year and is invading more and more arable land, never renowned for its fertility. On this quasi-desert, in the cold, dry month of June, there was scarcely a blade of grass to be seen. Yet enthusiasm was undaunted. The bright skirts and shawls of the women could be seen converging on the hall from miles away until thirty or forty of them must have gathered there. They had brought pots and pans in their *aguayos* and invited us all to a not very appetizing meal of *quinua*, boiled into a kind of tasteless porridge.

Afterwards, business started in earnest. The first step was to elect officials, and a wiry little woman, with a thin, lively face, was unanimously elected President. She was not young, but you could tell from the aggressive tilt of her bowler that here was a person of considerable character and personality, who knew what she was about.

We did not have long to wait. The next item on the agenda was the choice of the club's name. The Bolivian head of the local rural development centre explained this concept carefully:

'It is usual,' he said, 'to select the name of some famous person—a national hero, someone famous in history. So you might like to think of, say, Bolívar, or Santa Cruz, or Sucre.'

For a moment or two there was silence and then the newly-elected president was on her feet, pointing in my direction and declaiming loudly:

'*El nombre de la señorita*'—'the name of the señorita.'

That too was carried unanimously and any embarrassment or surprise I felt at being thus apparently considered on a par with

79

the founders of Bolivian independence quickly became admiration for her astuteness: Bolívar and Santa Cruz and Sucre might be more famous, but they were also indisputably dead long since and the new organization could expect much more help from the living, even if they were less eminent!

Lastly, they discussed the kind of activities that the club should undertake. The Director of the Centre listed the possibilities: sewing, baby-care classes, cookery, social gatherings, etc. Up came the new President's hand again, flailing the air peremptorily.

'I,' she said, in a tone brooking no argument, 'want to learn to read and write.'

Nor was there any argument: literacy classes were given top priority.

Health improvements are the most difficult of all because you have not merely to fill a vacuum, as in education, but to substitute, or at least modify, deep-rooted traditional practices. Most illnesses, it is believed, are brought about by the machinations of witches or by evil spirits that haunt the *chullpas*, as the old Indian burial sites are called. Logically enough, the cures must also be supernatural. The *yatiri*, or witch doctor, diagnoses the malady usually by reading the coca leaves—*la suerte de la coca*—and then prescribes the appropriate treatment with herbs, weird potions and incantations. Some of the more lurid remedies involve hot fomentations of human or animal urine; sometimes the illness is sucked out of the patient and transferred to an animal or an evil spirit by slitting open a guinea-pig or a bird and laying it on the patient's body for several hours before placing the remains, together with other prescribed objects, in a place indicated by the way in which the coca leaves have fallen. Small wonder that the prosaic pills and sterilized instruments of modern medicine at first had little appeal. But here, where infant mortality rates are among the highest in the world, you can often do more to gain local confidence by saving the lives of one or two babies suffering from quite commonplace illnesses than by more spectacular cures. However, you have to be prepared to adopt empirical methods:

80

at first for instance, pregnant women greatly resisted pre-natal examinations. Then a doctor observed that the *yatiri* performed a magical ceremony at a certain stage of pregnancy and, by imitating some of its ritual, he persuaded the women to accept examination as part of the traditional rite.

Even when modern medicine has been accepted in a general way, there are still pitfalls, as the story of the Otavi donkey illustrates. Otavi was once a *hacienda* in the Quechua-speaking district of the same name, on land given by the King of Spain to the first Count of Otavi, early in the eighteenth century. It is three hours' journey from the mining town of Potosí in the southernmost part of the *altiplano*, which is neither so high nor so unrelievedly flat as the region round La Paz. Though the climate is more benign, it is still an umber landscape, deeply fissured by the ravages of erosion. After the redistribution of the lands, the old house crumbled in disuse round the cobbled patio that had seen so many comings and goings of horses and men. Then, in 1958, Otavi was made a rural development centre for the region, as part of the Andean-Indian programme. The old cobbles once again rang with activity, the ruins of the old buildings were restored and improved, and new ones were added. A small town grew up alongside with a market, and a school, a town hall and a library. And, nearby, on a crisp, sunny afternoon in March 1960, I laid the foundation stone of the first rural hospital in Bolivia.

The villagers themselves had decided to build it and bore the brunt of the effort. The equipment, and some building materials, were provided from outside contributions; but for three years or more, the local communities diligently dug rocks and made adobes and daily provided the voluntary labour of twelve men, who worked under skilled supervision. The hospital was a modest enough affair built of adobe; there was a public health clinic, three wards containing a total of fourteen beds—five for men, five for women and four for children—a simple operating theatre and a laboratory. The work grew slowly, not for lack of enthusiasm on the part of the local inhabitants, but because delays in obtaining sufficient outside funds often held up progress. Yet, despite the *campesino's* alleged lack of decision and willpower, local determination and support never wavered.

At last the hospital was finished. The local country-folk were bursting with pride, the government sent out a public health team to run the hospital and everything seemed highly satisfactory. Then a serious snag arose. Everyone was happy to be examined by the doctor, and to have pills prescribed, but it was quite another matter when it came to really serious medicine, especially if it meant using the spotlessly clean, tiled operating-theatre. No one could see any way out; for a few weeks it seemed as if all that money and effort had been expended in vain.

Then, one day, a meeting of co-operatives was held at Otavi. From far and near community leaders trudged over the hills in their homespuns and shapeless felt hats, exchanging news and chattering about the meeting. But one of them was silent and preoccupied. Behind him lagged an equally sad looking donkey: the donkey had been gelded, the operation had been badly performed and had caused a septic swelling. The road to the centre led past the long, whitewashed building inscribed with the words: 'Hospital Campesino'. This gave the community leader an idea. If this hospital was built to serve country-folk, why should it not help him by saving his donkey? So he entered, and a few moments later reappeared with the white-coated doctor. 'Yes,' the doctor agreed, vacillating only a moment, unorthodox as it was, he would operate on the donkey. Fortunately, he had been born in Potosí and was more familiar with the *campesino* mentality than with the finer points of medical etiquette. To have suggested that this was work for a veterinarian, would not only have been unhelpful, since there were only two or three in the whole country, but would have meant forfeiting local confidence for ever.

The donkey's legs were tied, he was anaesthetized with a pad of cotton wool over his nose and carried into the health centre. There, beneath the intent gaze of the whole group of community leaders, the wound was lanced and stitched together. Shortly afterwards, to the doctor's relief, the donkey shambled to his feet with an air of faint surprise at finding himself in these strange surroundings but once he had been led outside began to graze as if nothing whatever had happened. An unwitting guinea-pig, he had vindicated the doctor's skill before the eyes of the leaders from all the surrounding villages. From that day on people no longer hesitated to use the facilities of their new hospital. There was nearly an untimely sequel, however, because the donkey's owner, in his joy at finding the animal recovered, quite forgot to bring him back to have his stitches removed, and the hospital had to send messengers to his village to remind him of the need for this post-operative treatment.

The Andean-Indians are often described as dour, and lacking in gaiety or a sense of humour. The wonder to me is that they should have retained the power of laughter at all. Yet Cristina had as much sense of fun as any child brought up in a kinder environment, and was certainly more able to amuse herself. The grim, set lines of grown-up faces are transformed into smiles of quite dazzling brightness when they meet you—for their teeth are always white and perfectly formed—and women and young girls giggle infectiously.

Sometimes, they are downright mischievous: once, on a visit to an isolated hamlet, my mother was trying to persuade three young women, by sign language, to show her the baby that one of them was carrying, tightly swaddled in the *aguayo* on her back. The three girls understood perfectly what she wanted. They shook their heads mysteriously, smiled provocatively and half-promisingly, then changed their minds and wagged their fingers in negation. This tantalizing game went on for some time until at last they seemed to relent. With many ceremonious preliminaries, one of the girls began to unwrap the *aguayo* on her friend's back and uncovered—a bag full of *oca*, one of the root vegetables that grows on the *altiplano*. Shouts of delighted laughter all round celebrated the disconcerted expression of my mother's face and the success of their prank.

Dancing and festivities, it is true, have a largely ritual significance and are usually connected with marriages or

83

religious celebrations in which you can detect more than a hint of pagan observance in the dancers' dedicated concentration and the almost liturgical repetition of the rhythms beaten out by their feet. In every *altiplano* village at carnival time a long crocodile of indefatigable dancers follows the village band round the main *plaza* for days on end, twisting and weaving in the repetitive patterns of the mountain *huayño* as if their very lives depended on it. They are sustained for unbelievably long periods by the monotonous reiteration of the music blaring from the brass instruments and deep-sounding drums of the band, and by frequent intakes of alcohol, usually *chicha*, a potent, sour-flavoured brew made from fermented maize. During the feast of the Virgin at her shrine in Copacabana on the shores of Lake Titicaca fireworks fly with great abandon and little concern for the eyes and ears of the bystanders while the groups of dancers, each with its own banner, prance around for two or three days. The sole function of one of their number is to pass the bottle around to each member of the troupe in turn, a task requiring some skill and sobriety since, to save the performers' energy, and ensure non-stop music, he has to pour the liquid directly down their gasping throats.

Ritual solemnity does not preclude enjoyment. The Andean-Indians derive intense and lasting satisfaction from their feast days, which contrast brilliantly with the drabness of everyday life and have a cathartic effect. The magnificence of the clothes brought out on such occasions is the outward sign of a pleasure that penetrates to the very roots of the villagers' existence. Even the men come out in brilliant red and green jackets and bell-bottomed trousers, thickly embroidered with silks and sequins of every conceivable colour, and wear their brightest and newest *chullo* on their heads, with an incongruous gauze mask in brilliant pink with enormous, vacant blue eyes, hanging down from it. The women's dresses are still more flamboyant: their most sumptuous bell skirts in flaunting colours of silk or velvet billow out like spinnakers before a following wind over a myriad petticoats of different colours, sometimes as many as twenty or more; their blouses are richly embroidered, glittering with silver and sequins and on their heads, in the department of La Paz, they wear round hats, also thickly embroidered with sequins and pearls which dangle over the brim, dancing and tinkling in time with the rhythm. The whole outfit is so heavy that one wonders how they can manage to dance for so much as an hour, let alone for days; and yet, towards the end, you will see many of them, in addition, sustaining the weight of a husband at last flagging from enormous intakes of *chicha* and with a deft twist of a brawny arm twirling him remorselessly through the intricacies of the *huayño* like a rag doll.

On days like this, the sombre and subdued *altiplano* is transformed. Life becomes a comfortable and compact thing, its horizons no longer lost in the limitlessness of distance but safely encompassed in the four walls of the *plaza*, its essence no longer dissipated in the unremitting battle against an unresponsive nature but condensed in the warm colours and swirling skirts of the dancers and the reassuringly familiar strains of the music. If you see such a scene on the shores of Lake Titicaca, the dancers seem to trace an exotic frieze against the deep blue of its waters.

The Andean-Indian peasant also enjoys music for its own sake. Once, struggling to find our way in a jeep over a rapidly deteriorating trail, we came on a stony hollow between two hills. It was such a barren spot, high, cold and rocky, that even stout Aymara hearts had quailed at the prospect of cultivating it and there was no house for miles around. But there, trudging sturdily along, and playing at full blast, was a local band. In many villages, brass instruments are popular nowadays, but in more out of the way spots like this one the traditional, home-made instruments are still preferred. This group had *tarkas*, a square, wooden flute, *pinquillos*, a small double-reed flute sounding rather like the *quena*, and some massive *zampoñas* which are rather like the pipes of Pan and usually played alternatively in pairs by two players. There was also a huge *bombo*, or bass drum, carried by a wizened little man of evidently immense age who could barely see over the top of it or get his arms round the sides to beat it. They told us that they were on their way to a wedding—we had seen the marriage flags flying at a hut some five or six miles away—and were playing to keep themselves company and 'to make the miles seem short'. They seemed as delighted to entertain an unexpected audience as we were to hear *altiplano* music in surroundings that could hardly be more ideal.

The melancholy of this music has often been observed. It is true that the soft sonority of the *tarkas* and the *zampoñas* give a sombre effect, while the *bombo* beats out an underlying theme of sadness and the wild haunting cadence of the *pinquillo* and the *quena* echoes the solitude and mystery of the high Andes. Yet it is also resilient music, embodying in its buoyant rhythm the unquenchable spirit of man, still able to find beauty, even in these harsh highlands and translate it into song. They played for us enthusiastically and the aged drummer, eyes dancing in the crinkled folds of his face, thumped away at his drum with such verve that he nearly fell over backwards beneath it. When we looked back from the top of the next hill they were still playing with all their might and the tiny old man was scurrying along at the rear with little scampering steps to keep up with the rest, almost hidden behind the great hoop of his drum which he seemed to be bowling in front of him with the measured beat of his drumsticks.

Folk-music and dance are a living part of Bolivian life, not only in rural areas and villages, where they could be expected to survive, but also in the towns. Even in relatively sophisticated circles in La Paz you will find people making their own music in traditional style and the most formal state banquet in the Palacio Quemado is not complete if the dancing that follows does not include some stirring Bolivian rhythms in which the Head of State will join as readily as the humblest citizen. Many have been stylized and adapted into more sophisticated moulds, and owe much to Spanish music introduced by the colonists, but this very synthesis of indigenous and peninsular influences is typical of the quality which is the *leitmotiv* of Bolivian culture.

Drunkenness is inevitably quite common at feast days but the Indian is not an alcoholic. Drinking for him has a special significance, probably derived from the Inca concept that intoxication was a ritual necessity at certain ceremonies. The inebriated Indian does not usually become aggressive, but drinks until he can dance no more, even with the support of his partner. In the evening, after a *fiesta* in a nearby hamlet, the roads are full of wavering groups, trying to wend their way home, those only slightly fuddled trying ineffectually to support the really groggy ones between them. One roadside scene stays in my mind: a man whose legs had quite given out and whose two friends could no longer manage him, sat on the ground with his feet splayed in front of him while one of his unsteady companions held his lolling head and the other shakily poured the remains of a bottle of beer into the mouth he still held expectantly open. Compassion and abnegated concern were written large on the features of his helpers, who undoubtedly considered that the best service they could render in the name of friendship was to assist him in finding oblivion as speedily as possible.

Many would say that the chewing of the *coca* leaf is a greater vice, leading to addiction, lethargy and gradual degeneration. For the Indian, who has chewed *coca* since time immemorial, the leaf has magical and divine properties and is a source of physical strength, helping to overcome the effects of cold and high altitude and allaying the pangs of hunger. *Coca* is the 'green gold' of Yungas, grown in the warm, precipitous valleys on the eastern side of the *cordillera*, and the discovery of its properties has its own legend. In the dim past, it is said, Indians from the *altiplano* travelled over the *cordillera* to the Yungas in search of new land. The valleys, although fertile, were thickly forested and the settlers set fire to the undergrowth in order to make a clearing. But the fire became a conflagration and the smoke rose to the mountain crests, angering the Storm God who let loose a tempest which not only quenched the flames but destroyed all vegetation. The only plant unscathed was the *coca* bush, and the famished Indians who ate its leaves at once

87

experienced a return of strength which enabled them to find their way back to the *altiplano* and spread the news of their miraculous discovery. Nearly a century ago, the extraction of cocaine from this plant made a significant contribution to the development of anaesthesia in Europe.

It is believed that in Inca times the mastication of *coca* was restricted to the Incas themselves and the privileged classes, and also to those of whom great physical feats were expected, such as the *chasquis*. In the intervening centuries, however, the habit has become widespread and the cheek of nearly every Indian you meet on the *altiplano* is distended by a wad of *coca*, mixed with ash to intensify its effects. For him *coca* has also a ceremonial and magic significance; the *suerte de la coca*—the luck of the *coca*—is widely used in foretelling the future or diagnosing disease, and a well-chewed wad of *coca* is considered a fitting offering for the gods. If you wish, for instance, to ensure yourself a safe journey, you will not only add a stone to the cairn that marks the top of every mountain pass but leave your gob of *coca* there as well.

Though it is generally agreed that *coca* has an anaesthetic effect on the stomach muscles and renders one impervious to hunger, there is still controversy as to whether it actually increases physical endurance. Bolivian friends who first took up the habit during the Chaco War have told me that without it they would have been unable to withstand the terrible ardours of that campaign; and an infusion of *coca* is traditionally recommended to the new arrival in La Paz as an antidote to mountain sickness. What is certain is the Indian's conviction that it is essential to his survival. No simple government decree will sweep away this habit, contrary to the ingenuous belief of many of the most eloquent exponents on the subject, well-intentioned people, who I usually found smoked away incessantly at pipes or cigarettes as they held forth on the pernicious effect of *coca* addiction. It has, however, become clear from recent settlement projects in tropical areas of the country that the habit tends to die out naturally among the younger generation and the children of the colonists as they become used to a warmer climate and are better fed. Like so many of Bolivia's problems, the solution depends on development. You cannot expect the Indian to give up *coca*, his one luxury, until his life becomes more tolerable and he has enough to eat.

6 THE Japanese jeep inched its way up the mountainside along a narrow dirt-trail jutting like a shelf over the *altiplano*, now spread far below us. The thick tyres strained for a hold on the loose surface and the engine screeched in protest as the air became progressively thinner. We were on our way to visit one of the more promising drilling sites discovered by a mineral survey.

Lower down, the plain stretching southwards from Oruro had appeared the most barren part of the *altiplano* but here, where even the sparse fans of the *paja brava* had become more and more dispersed, the land took on the aspect of a tundra, incongruously transplanted to the tropics. Habitation in such an inhospitable wilderness seemed unthinkable and yet, on a sharp turn, we jerked to a stop to manoeuvre past a mobile tank which was gingerly edging its way down.

Higher still, where the track petered out after a last switch-back turn, a bustle of activity surrounded the twin triangles of two drilling rigs, clinging at a perilous angle to the steep slope below us. From this height of nearly 16,000 feet above sea-level their strictly functional arches framed in bizarre perspective a wild and beautiful panorama, embracing almost the whole of the *cordillera* and the southern *altiplano*. The ground on which we stood fell away into a deep valley walled in by hills pocked with old workings and criss-crossed with a network of gullies and ravines laying bare the very nerve-ends of this ravaged countryside. But there was a uniformity about its subdued blendings of sepias and dull yellows which drew the eye onwards almost hypnotically until one's gaze was held by the incandescent blue of Lake Poopó, lying nearly three thousand feet below, an enormous sapphire encrusted in a diamantine rim of dazzling white salt. Beyond, the faintly opalescent peaks of the Western Cordillera shimmered on the Chilean frontier, while to the north the horizon was girdled by the silver chain of the Royal Cordillera.

These glittering jewels of the landscape held little attraction, however, for the men working on the drilling site, spurred on by their determination to wrest more tangible prizes from the inmost recesses of the earth. Bolivia has never been prodigal of the mineral wealth hidden away in the tightly-sealed coffers of the *cordillera* and men have had to fight for her favours as they have also had to strive against overpowering odds in order to eke out a humdrum agricultural existence on the *altiplano*.

This site was no exception. Even with the advanced prospecting methods of today obstacles are many. Although the spot had been pin-pointed as a likely one for further investigations by an aerial geophysical survey and by geophysical and geological work on the ground, the most difficult task still lay ahead. First, it had been necessary to build a track strong enough to bear the weight of the vehicles transporting the drilling rigs. Even so one of the chosen spots had proved inaccessible and the second rig had to be levered into position on skids, a feat that seemed well-nigh impossible as we staggered towards it down an escarpment littered with loose rocks and shale. The air was so rarefied that even this effort left us gasping for breath and our lungs seemed to be seared by the crystalline coldness of the atmosphere. The faces of geologists and labourers alike were weatherbeaten and chapped, their lips parched by the relentless contrasts of a climate which burnt them with strong sunshine at midday and froze them with biting winds in the mornings and evenings.

Although it was after ten o'clock work had not yet started,

because water for the drills had to be pumped up nearly 3,000 feet from the Antequera river in the valley below and the sun was not yet hot enough to unfreeze it. Patches of ice still glistened on the hills around us and it was eleven o'clock before the welcome chugging of the motors reverberated across the valley. It was June, and since mid-winter coincides with the peak of the long dry season in the highlands, not only was running water scarce but sections of the 9,000 feet of piping which carried it up to the rigs frequently burst with the cold. But, with the usual contrariness of Bolivian seasons, drilling would be even more difficult during the heavy summer rains when the access trails became impassable for several months at a time. Field work had therefore to be concentrated during the winter, even though the frost set in again by four o'clock in the afternoon and brought the brief working day to a close. Then the men retired to their tents or to the dilapidated huts and offices of a small mine on the crest of the hill, a ramshackle hamlet of adobe and corrugated iron, well over the 16,000 feet mark, which contrasted grimly with the grandiose scenery.

It is easier to understand the excesses of the Bolivian miners when one has tasted, however briefly, the harshness of their existence. Life at our base camp in Callipampa, at a mere 12–13,000 feet, to which we retreated for the night, was uncomfortable enough, though we camped in what had once been the manager's house at a mine long since abandoned as uneconomic. In comparison with the accommodation on the site it was almost luxurious: the walls were still standing and there were unexpected traces of past splendour, such as the shell of a magnificent four-poster bed on which I was invited to array my sleeping bag. There was little other furniture, however, no running water, and for light only a hurricane lantern and candles. It was bitterly cold and a brief fire of *tola* twigs—one of the few stunted bushes which grows on the *altiplano*—soon spluttered itself into extinction.

No one who has not spent a winter night on the *altiplano*, when the temperature drops to between ten and twenty degrees below zero centigrade, can have any conception of how cold

above: A view across the *altiplano*.
right: Illimani as seen when flying into
La Paz from Cochabamba.
below: Huayna Potosí.

above: Aymara women going to market.
below: Aymara women working on the *altiplano*.

it can become in this altitude. Perhaps because of the very thinness of the air it seems to penetrate to the very depths of one's being. Even when you huddle almost fully dressed into a sleeping-bag the cold lies in ambush for you in the corners and seeps insidiously through all the protective layers, no matter how numerous, until every bone aches.

But it takes much more than cold and discomfort to quench the Bolivian spirit. As we crouched around the dying fire, washing down a rough meal with whisky to keep the circulation going, the Bolivian geologists brought out their guitars, which are as much a part of their field equipment as their hammers and compasses. Until well into the night they played and sang their folklore, now a poignant melody, full of the forlorn strangeness of the high Andes, now a spirited rhythm reaffirming the resurgence of life in the face of adversity, each mood merging into the other like the shadows that alternately flared and faded on the earthen walls around us.

Perhaps life would be intolerable all the same if one did not invariably wake the next morning to a sun-swept world beneath a lapis-lazuli sky. It is still cold, but there is already an incipient warmth about the air that encourages cramped limbs to stretch in anticipation. Even the frugal *altiplano* villages, where the people are beginning to creep out of their adobe houses, muffled up against the penetrating early morning air, take on something akin to beauty when limned in the clarity of this light. The absurd, wedding-cake church of Poopó becomes almost probable, and around the *plaza*, where the incongruous goal-posts at either end acknowledge its other use as a football pitch, wispy weeping-willows are putting forth tentative pink fronds towards a spring that is still distant but not yet despaired of.

Whatever the explanation, mining has always been a singular passion in Bolivian life, even though fraught with danger and disillusion because of the tortured conformations of the Andes. Most of the deposits mined today were known already to the Incas, although not all of them were exploited—tin, for example, only became of economic importance towards the end of the last century with the growth of the food preserving industry.

Yet the Incas' attitude to their mineral resources was quite alien to that which has prevailed since the Spanish conquest. Gold and silver played no central rôle in the economic structure of their tightly-knit communities. They were rather an adjunct, to be converted into ornaments valued not for their intrinsic worth but as adorning life with a new dimension of artistry and beauty, and because they bestowed on their wearers outward and visible signs of their inborn rank and prestige that were known and understood by all. Their function above all was ceremonial and aesthetic: the stone walls of the Inca palaces and temples were plated with gold, and sometimes even cemented with gold instead of mortar; the dress of the Inca, his family and his womenfolk was embellished with gold and silver ornaments and precious stones; and because all this wealth accrued to the coffers of the Inca, Cieza de León tells us, precious metals were used to make even kitchen utensils and musical instruments as well as the famous *osno*, or golden stool, upon which only the Inca or his blood relatives could sit. As the Inca had to leave the treasure of his predecessors untouched, much of it was buried with the dead; and it was decreed that anyone found removing gold or silver from Cuzco would be immediately put to death. Work in the mines was carried out under the Inca system of *mita*, or labour tribute, but conditions of work were not excessively onerous, because such spells of work lasted only two or three months each year, since mineral wealth was merely an embellishment of Inca culture and not its central pillar.

All this was overturned in the sixteenth century when the Spaniards burst into the secret, hermetic world of the Andes, impelled by their lust for gold, and overnight transformed this closed economy and closed society into the source of a stream of wealth which poured into the Spanish peninsula. Minerals ceased to be an accessory and became the *raison d'être* of the Spanish colonial empire. It was not only the economy of the high Andes and the life of its inhabitants which were transformed;

94

so too, were the fortunes of Europe and of Spain. By a strange streak of irony, the flow of bullion ferried across the Spanish main in fleets of lofty-prowed galleons helped to generate both the development of European capitalism, and the economic decline of Spain, which reached its nadir in the seventeenth century, and bequeathed a grim legacy down to the present day.

Perhaps no part of the ancient Andean empire was more affected than what is now Bolivia. The convolutions of the igneous rocks which form the *cordillera*, twisted into grotesque deformations by a series of violent geological upheavals, have ensnared in secret places far down inside the earth some of the greatest riches the world has known. Just as the *cordillera* has since time immemorial formed the physical spine of the country so the mineral resources concealed within its depths have, since Spanish times, come to form its economic backbone.

The term is perhaps misleading for it suggests a strengthening of the economic framework that is not wholly borne out by the facts. It is true that the present-day economic structure is entirely built around mining. But its metamorphosis from a marginal activity in Inca times into the mainspring of the economy led to a self-perpetuating distortion in the country's development which continued to bedevil Bolivia after independence and still does so today. In consequence, the country was turned relentlessly outwards, to the detriment of its internal integration and development. The concentration of the sparse network of roads and railways on the central mountain chain and the failure, until comparatively recently, to make any serious attempt to connect the eastern tropical lowlands with the ore-producing mountain area testify that the main preoccupation was not to join the country together, but to link the mines with the Pacific coast and provide an expeditious route to international markets.

Moreover, the strangulation of Bolivian development into one single and exceedingly narrow outlet could be achieved only at the expense of the complete collapse of the well-balanced agricultural system devised and perfected by the Incas. Agriculture is still suffering the consequences today and a small

95

population, with vast and potentially rich land resources at its disposal, is obliged to import a large proportion of foodstuffs in order to feed itself. The social consquences were also serious. The Inca system of *mita* was extended and applied with such abuses in the mines of the Spanish overlords that it became virtually a form of underground slavery and Indians who had been impressed to provide tribute in the form of labour in the mines for a few months were, by an iniquitous system of accounting for their clothes and food, soon reduced to such a degree of indebtedness that they and their children had to spend most of their lives in redeeming their supposed obligations.

This was the system by which the fabulous Cerro Rico of Potosí was exploited—mines which provided the vast bulk of the wealth of the Kings of Spain and which became so legendary in the sixteenth and seventeenth centuries that the name of this remote Andean fastness became almost a myth in the annals of the Spanish Empire and a household word in Europe: *'Vale un Potosí'* (it is worth a Potosí) was a common expression in Spain and the phrase 'as rich as Potosí' found its way into English literature.

It was a city that sprang up almost overnight in 1545 when an Indian, seeking a strayed llama, had stumbled upon the vein of silver which led to the discovery of one of the richest mines the world has ever known. But legend has it that a hundred years before the Spanish conquest the Inca Emperor Huayna Capac had started excavating the same mountainside, only to be halted by a terrible voice which said to him in Quechua:

'Take no silver from this hill. It is destined for other owners.'

Rich as the mountain was, the Inca's privileged successors had exhausted the best veins within thirty years and there was a marked decline in production, restored only by the discovery in 1572 of a refining process, through an amalgam with mercury, which made it possible to recover even low-grade ores. This technological advance, coinciding with the fortunate discovery of a mercury mine at Huancavélica in the Peruvian *sierra*, made it possible for the silver cycle to follow the gold in the Spanish colonies and assured the continued prosperity of Potosí. The census of 1611 enumerated 114,000 souls and these had increased to 160,000 by the middle of the seventeenth century. The city's first coat of arms, granted when the Emperor Charles V gave it the title of 'Imperial City' bore the legend: 'I am rich Potosí, the treasure of the world and the envy of kings', while the shield presented later by Philip II read 'For the powerful Emperor, for the wise King, this lofty mountain of silver could conquer the world.'

Everything in Potosí was more than life-size. Only eleven years after its foundation its citizens celebrated the accession of Philip II with a party lasting twenty-four days and costing eight million pesos. By the end of the sixteenth century there were fourteen dance halls, thirty-six gambling halls and one theatre. But although there were eighty churches when its fortunes were at the flood, the city hardly enjoyed a reputation for godliness. Duelling was one of the main pastimes and members of the town came to meetings armed with swords and pistols and protected with coats of mail. Sedition was also rife. The notorious 'Monja Alférez', Doña Catalina de Erauzo, the novice who escaped from a convent in San Sebastian in 1600 and spent twenty-two years in the Indies, as Spanish America was then called, disguised as a soldier, wielding her sword with the best, killing and carousing, curtly describes the uprising of don Alonso Ibañez which she helped to suppress:

'Thirty prisoners were taken, among them Ibañez. We had two dead and several wounded. Some prisoners confessed that their intention was to cause an uprising of the city. Fifteen days later they were hanged and the city became calm again. For deeds of valour I was made a sergeant.'

The city was alternately described as a sink of iniquity and the nerve centre of the realm. A Dominican disciple of Bartolomé de las Casas, appalled by the thousands of Indians who died there yearly called it 'a mouth of hell'. But still the silver ingots poured across the sea. It has been said that the ore extracted from this hill made almost of solid silver was sufficient to make a bridge of precious metal, one yard wide, from the Indies to

97

Spain, but it is also asserted that a parallel bridge could have been built with the bones of the Indians who died as *mitayos* extracting it. And then in the eighteenth century the fortunes of Potosí declined steadily with the discovery of other mines and the exhaustion of its dwindling treasure. When Bolívar entered in triumph after the Liberation it retained only a shadow of its former glory and was reduced to eight thousand inhabitants.

It is strange to visit Potosí today against the background of all that wealth and history. If it were not for the occasional noise of a combustion engine one might imagine oneself back in the seventeenth century, listening for the bells of the trains of llamas and mules carrying the precious burden of silver on the long journey across the frozen uplands of the *cordillera*, and so down to the coastal deserts of Peru and the Viceregal capital of Lima, where the Spanish galleons swung at anchor in the port of Callao, laden with the finest silks and laces, potteries and works of art that European ingenuity could send in return. Even nowadays the journey from La Paz is not easy. The road is unpaved and if you come by train it takes something like thirty hours and carries you over a pass which the Bolivians, ignoring the marginal claims of a rival in the Peruvian Andes, claim to carry the highest railway line in the world. You usually pass this point at one o'clock in the morning, or some other nocturnal hour when the vitality is lowest, but a solicitous engine-driver ensures that you do not miss the experience of a lifetime by noisily shunting backwards and forwards until you bounce awake in your hard wooden bunk to find your heart hammering away in your chest.

The llamas still tread delicately along the narrow cobbled streets; they carry a humbler cargo now but their proud mien seems a heritage of those more glorious times when they bore the treasure of the greatest Empire in the world and brought back satins and brocades to gown the haughtiest beauties of Potosí. It is a discreet city where Quechua women, looking like transplanted Welshwomen in their tall hats of black or brown, clutch dark shawls around them and murmur softly together at the corners of whitewashed alleys where no window breaks the thick walls tapering into the distance. Every street has its convent or church where life is turned inwards, rejecting even the unobtrusive eddies that stir these quiet backwaters. Now and again you come across an intricately carved doorway whose curlicued stone flowers and fruits seem almost an affront to the straight symmetry of the surrounding walls.

But the roofscape of Potosí is its most changeless prospect: a pattern of mellowed tiles and overhanging eaves, intersected by countless towers and turrets, domes and spires, whose melancholy bells have chimed the passage of the centuries and still stir the weary traveller at dawn with echoes of the bullion trains of old. Yet, though the churches predominate, it is the worship of another deity that permeates this city. The russet roofs ascend the hillside, like sacrificial steps before an altar, towards the gutted cone of the Cerro Rico which overhangs the town like the gaunt, decrepit deity of some forgotten cult.

At a respectful distance the new and rival rites to the 'Devil's metal', as tin is called, display their pyramids of tailings, their endless temples of corrugated iron from which a constant hymn of whirring machinery rises skywards. But the old town resolutely turns its back on such new-fangled notions and seems immersed in its memories of the two splendid centuries when Potosí was the largest and most famous city in the New World; when its cobbled streets rang with horses' hooves drawing luxurious carriages, in which rode dandies and fine ladies decked out in the latest fashions that had survived the long and arduous journey from Europe; when culture flourished and a host of indigenous artists, some anonymous, some who, like Pérez de Holguín, have handed their name down to posterity, combined their talents to make the Potosí School of painters famous in Hispano-America; when silversmiths beat out painstakingly by hand the goblets and altarpieces, the chalices and salvers, plates and candlesticks that one can still find in dusty backstreet shops or buy from antiquaries in La Paz.

It is a city that has died by inches as the marvellous mountain, now honeycombed by a thousand passages and galleries, shafts

99

and adits, gradually exhausted its treasure. Yet it has not decayed but has shrunk in a genteel way, still trailing a few tattered fineries of past glory and wearing with dignity those ornaments that time has not tarnished. Not the least of these is La Casa de la Moneda, the old Mint that served the Spanish Empire and the early years of the Republic. Now a museum, it has been carefully preserved and restored. You step into its quiet cobbled patio, overhung by broad wooden balconies running round all sides of the massive stone building, as you might step back into the seventeenth century. There is no sound save that of the water plashing in the central fountain. Inside, the heavy oak beams and crude mechanism of the massive press, brought from Spain and lugged piece by piece over the mountains to stamp out the silver coins with the Emperor's head, are still. Yet it is as if they ceased only yesterday and as you peer down between the crevices to the dark dungeon below you can almost see and hear the Indian slaves toiling round and round to push the cumbersome, creaking machinery into operation.

In the old part of the town only the *plaza*, with its strait-laced iron railings, its stunted trees blown asymmetrical by the wind, and its emaciated flowers and grass—for here we are higher than La Paz and well over 13,000 feet above sea-level—seems to defer grudgingly to the demands of latter-day bourgeois respectability. Yet here, too, in the early evening, and at noon on Sundays, sedate families, well-chaperoned young girls, and scrubbed young men solemnly parade as, four centuries ago, their ancestors, nostalgic for the old customs of Spain, must also have done, defying the rigours of a less clement clime.

The final blow to Potosí's prosperity came with the decline of silver on the world market and its substitution by tin in the latter half of the nineteenth century. Although there was tin around Potosí—for the two metals are often found together and the tailings of the old colonial silver mines frequently contain much tin that was discarded as a waste product in those days—and it is still mined there today, the centre of the mining industry moved farther north to Oruro and Uncía. The fame of the Cerro Rico was usurped by that of another mountain of almost solid metal but this time of baser ore—Catavi, thickly veined with tin, which was discovered by Simón Patiño at the turn of the century and made him one of the richest men in the world.

Although methods of extraction had improved by then, tin-mining proved no easier, and no less prodigal of human life and welfare than the silver mines in olden times. Once again nature has been guided by a perverse sense of humour; although there are many vast tin deposits, they are not easily accessible as in the other main producing areas of the world but deep in the earth, which has to be practically disembowelled in order to extract the metal. Most of the mines too, are at extremely high altitudes and it is not surprising therefore that Bolivia is a high-cost producer.

The price is also paid with the lives of men. Often the entrance to a mine is anywhere between eleven and fifteen thousand feet, while the workings may be several thousand feet lower, so that the miner is subjected to extreme differences of temperature and pressure. At Pulacayo, one of the worst mines in Bolivia, the galleries are at such a depth that the miners have to work stripped naked and water is constantly sprinkled on their bodies to enable them to resist the heat; yet they enter and leave the mine high up on the *altiplano* where winter temperatures fall well below zero. In all the mines disease is rife, particularly tuberculosis and silicosis, and accidents are frequent because of defective machinery and inadequate safety requirements. The average Bolivian's expected span of life is not very long by the standards of the developed world at forty-six years, but the miner's is even shorter, being only around thirty-three.

It is difficult to see what advantages the riches of their sub-soil have brought to the Bolivian people. Although minerals have for long provided nine-tenths of their exports and have brought unimaginable wealth to a few Bolivian citizens, only just over three per cent of the working population, or two per cent of the total population, is employed in the mining industry and they work and live in Dickensian conditions of poverty and squalor, with danger and disease as their constant companions and the prospect of an early death as their only expectation.

For many years most of the mines were in the hands of three companies, Patiño, Aramayo and Hothschild, the Big Three of Bolivian mining. Their monopoly position predictably gave them great wealth, most of which was squandered in the fashionable centres of North America and Europe, while little was ploughed back into the country or even into the mines themselves. More important still, however, it also gave them overwhelming power in affairs of state. If the years of the hegemony of the mining interests in the first quarter or so of this century were years of comparative tranquillity and stability politically speaking, they also established a tradition of corruption that has proved difficult to break, even though circumstances have greatly changed. The three mining companies were known as a superstate within a state, and many attempts to break their dominion were doomed to failure because of the very strength of their influence. Busch, the first Bolivian President who tried to regulate the financial activities of the mines, committed suicide in 1936 in strange circumstances when he was about to sign a decree introducing state control of mineral exports. Villaroel, who tried to continue similar policies in the next decade, met a dreadful end hanging from a lamp-post of the Plaza Murillo in La Paz, after having been lynched during the revolution of 1946.

When the MNR came to power after the 1952 revolution, the three giants were finally brought to heel. Their mines were nationalized and handed over to a vast state company known as the Corporación Minera de Bolivia, better known as COMIBOL, and one of the largest mining operations in the world. But whereas the political necessity for such a move was beyond dispute, its economic rationale was less convincing. A new and inexperienced government undertook the management of this vast enterprise at a time when the price of metals on the world market was falling after the artificial boom caused by the Korean war; when the richest veins in the known Bolivian mines were nearing exhaustion; and when the mines themselves were decapitalized, and little had been spent on their equipment or on new exploration for a number of years. These difficulties were aggravated by the award of retroactive wages and the concession to the miners of a number of social benefits, as well as a good deal of say in the operation of the mines.

No one who has seen the conditions in which the miners work, or has read the graphic description of their exploitation in Augusto Céspedes's novel, *Metal del Diablo*, which is based on the life of Simón Patiño in the guise of the protagonist, Zenón Omonte, can doubt the crying need for drastic reform. But the changes were so sweeping that, combined with mismanagement and the increase of state bureaucracy at the top, they brought disaster in their wake. If the three giant companies were the ugly sisters on the Bolivian political and economic scene until 1952, COMIBOL, however inadvertently, has been the wicked uncle since then, always hovering somewhere nearby in the wings, whenever some particularly violent drama was being played on the stage, on the few occasions when it was not itself occupying the centre of it. An industry naturally doomed to produce ore of diminishing grades at ever-rising cost in comparison with its main competitors in other parts of the world was further burdened by increased labour costs and decreased productivity.

One of the answers must be complete reorganization of the state mining industry, and another the discovery of new deposits of high-grade ore to eke out the rapidly disappearing reserves of diminishing quality in the existing mines. Some new possibilities have been opened up over the last seven or eight years, by a number of mineral surveys. The problem of reorganizing the mines on a more rational and economic basis is more intractable, however, because it involves the human difficulty of redisciplining a body of workers, who have tasted political and syndical power, and easier working conditions, after generations of near-slavery of which the tradition has been handed down to them by their fathers and grandfathers. Moreover, in order to increase productivity, the labour force has to be considerably reduced in circumstances where re-employment is doubly difficult because of the country's general economic situation and the inadaptability of the miner. The military régime, which overthrew the MNR in November 1964 and its successor government elected to office in August 1966, have managed to transform the deficit, which has dogged COMIBOL ever since it started operations, into a surplus. But rationalization could only be achieved by drastic measures causing more hardship and even loss of life in what is historically perhaps the most long-suffering sector of a much misused people.

Examined dispassionately against the backcloth of history, mining seems to have been the scourge, rather than the saviour, of the Bolivian nation, a wrong turning in the country's destiny. The pursuit of mining to the exclusion of most other things has left its impress on the landscape and on the nation and has changed the course of history. The slagheaps at the big mines of Catavi, Llallagua and Siglo Veinte have created a new orography to rival the mountains of the *cordillera* and added new dimensions of desolation to the forbidding prospect of the *altiplano*. It is a harsh, abrasive land that grates on the soul. The very entrails of Bolivia's soil lie exposed as if in vital testimony of the extraordinary telluric force of these highlands and of the indissoluble link between the land and the people who not only eke subsistence from its surface, but delve into the bowels of the earth, often giving up their lives in return for the so-called living of which they have gone in search. The dream of stumbling on some undiscovered treasure of immense wealth illumines every Indian heart, and each slope in the known mining areas is pocked with the scars of primitive workings, ugly quarries torn in the side of the mountain and abandoned when the ore has given out or the hoped-for lode has proved as elusive as fortune.

At every turn in Bolivian history the influence of mining can be detected, guiding the course of events. The existence of precious metals determined the Spanish conquest of the Andes and the way in which their subsequent exploitation developed. After independence, the discovery of nitrate deposits in the

Atacama desert in 1866, at first exploited under a concession by Chilean and British capital, caused the conflict of interests which led to the disastrous Pacific War, and the loss of Bolivia's outlet to the sea. Later, during the first part of the present century, the political destinies of the country were governed by the dictates of the mining magnates—the Tin Barons, as they came to be called. By this time the deformation of several centuries had irrevocably cast the country's economic structure in the mining mould.

Yet, in certain curious ways, the mistaken predominance of mining was not wholly negative. It was the control of this key industry and the controversy over the need to re-channel its profits to the benefit of the country rather than to interests abroad which formed the crux of the struggle for power between the entrenched mining establishment and the new nationalist school of thought represented by the MNR. That the latter were at last victorious, after a contest that had lasted over fifteen years, and had been characterized by violence of the most bloody kind, massacres of miners, lynchings of public figures, riots and revolutions, was largely due to the miners. They were the only group among the mass of the people that was in any way organized or politically conscious and it was their intervention on the side of the revolutionary forces, and their victory over the regular militia, that turned the tide of the fighting in April 1952 and so brought the MNR into power. Thereafter, the mine-workers' unions became the most important political force in the country and their power was based on armed strength.

It is a curious paradox that the workers in the sector that has been the root cause of the stagnation of Bolivian economic life have become the agents of the profound transformations that have taken place in the country over the last fifteen years. Many of these changes have been Marx-inspired and within the context of his teachings the miners, though forming such a small proportion of the total population, would seem to have acted the rôle which he ascribed to the proletariat. Only since the 1952 Revolution have the peasants come to develop into

105

politically conscious groupings, whereas the miners were prime movers in bringing that revolution about.

At every crucial moment in Bolivian politics since 1952, whenever the gains achieved by the revolution seemed to be in jeopardy, lorry-loads of miners have rumbled into La Paz, firing their rifles into the air, their pit-helmets with their inset lamps worn, not as if they were the symbols of their trade, but rather like the helmets of some crack regiment. One wonders whether this predominance of the miner as the active element for change in Bolivian society does not at least partly explain the prevalence of violence in the country's political life. It is true that violence is already endemic in the tortured rocks of the *cordillera* and in the jagged horizons of the *altiplano*. One senses a latent, pulsing force behind this landscape whose menacing contours, twisted into the shapes of ferocious animals, spring out and pounce upon the unwary traveller. In the miner, however, this innate tendency towards violence has been magnified by the savage realities of his everyday existence, in which the value of life is constantly disavowed by the prevalence of disease and by the daily flirtation with death as he descends to dizzy depths by rickety ladders, or crawls along the narrow tunnels in constant danger of being buried by a fall of rock, or asphyxiated through lack of oxygen. Then, too, dynamite is the staple tool of his trade, though in this context it is treated with healthy respect. In *Metal del Diablo* August Céspedes tells how Omonte, on his way to excavate the concession which was to make him one of the richest men in the world, instructed the Indian *peones* to carry the dynamite strapped to their stomachs; but that the Indians already knew that the only way to prevent it from exploding at the slightest blow was to keep it at body heat underneath their shirts.

But dynamite is more than an instrument of the miner's craft and has become part and parcel of everyday Bolivian life. As you pass through an *altiplano* village, you will often see a notice scrawled in chalk on a blackboard hung lopsidedly at the door of the dingy general stores which seem to be housed in every other cottage, announcing: '¡Llegó dinamita!'—'Dynamite

106

has arrived!', as if proclaiming the advent of some particularly succulent comestible or a much-vaunted article of latest fashion.

Dynamite is much in demand for *fiestas*: crude fireworks are made from it and whole salvoes of explosions reverberate against the hills to herald the dawn of some special saint's day or other festivity. There is a certain bravado about how long the person who lights the fuse hangs on to the charge and there is hardly a village in the Bolivian highlands where one may not meet two or three men who have lost a hand or an arm or a foot, or whose blind eyes stare out at you from faces distorted out of all resemblance to human physiognomy. '*Dinamita*' is invariably the laconic reply to any enquiry about how the accident came about, as if this were explanation enough of an accepted hazard of daily life. It is hardly surprising therefore that such a handy and easily acquired armament should be the concomitant of every revolution or riot. The hardened dweller in La Paz, shaken into wakefulness by a shattering explosion in the middle of the night, mutters equally laconically to himself '*Dinamita*' and rolls over to sleep once more. Things have not really become serious until more sophisticated arms are used and the artillery has been brought into the fray.

The spectre of violence stalks in every mining town. It is presaged in the rusty shanties that cling tipsily to the eviscerated hillside and lurks behind the eyes of those who dwell in them. Early on in my years in Bolivia I was told of a parti- cularly gruesome episode when visiting a UN-assisted centre for rural development. The accounts, they explained apologeti- cally, were not in order because the book-keeper had not returned after the weekend from the nearby mining town of Huanuni where his family lived. Later they learned that he had discovered his wife with the miner who had usurped his bed and home during the weekdays when he was away. There had been a fight, but this had been patched up and developed into a drinking bout from which the wronged husband had emerged greatly the worse for wear. The lovers then filled his pockets with dynamite as he lay slumped under the window, trailed the fuse outside, and lit the end from the street. He was a long time

107

dying, but when his moribund groans were at last heard by a passer-by and the forces of law and order were called to investigate, the guilty pair were found sleeping peacefully in bed, not a yard from their victim. As a tale of love and death inextricably intertwined this surpasses even the most ghoulish examples of traditional Spanish drama.

As elsewhere the strike is the classic weapon of the mining syndicates but it is usually reinforced by less conventional measures, designed with almost devilish ingenuity to bring a recalcitrant government to heel. Thus the miners will think nothing of threatening to string up the President there and then if he does not meet their demands. When they did attempt this tactic against Dr Hernán Siles Suazo in the same mining town of Huanuni in January 1960, a tragic outcome was averted largely through the courage of their potential victim; this was the incident which added yet another difficulty to my ill-timed journey overland to La Paz from Montevideo.

A more usual ploy is the taking of hostages. At the first sign of trouble any handy foreigner, be he mining engineer or geologist or whatever, is promptly clapped into detention and held there while in La Paz the various Ambassadors concerned queue up at the Ministry of Foreign Affairs to demand guarantees for their subjects from a harassed government torn between the need to resist the miners' pretensions, humanitarian considerations and the requirements of diplomatic practice. On one occasion the dilemma acquired a new and diabolical dimension when the miners lodged their hostages in a dwelling whose lower storeys were well-stocked with dynamite and kept the government on tenterhooks by metaphorically waving a match near the end of the fuse. What the psychological effect on their unfortunate prisoners must have been one can only too readily imagine, although in the end they escaped unscathed.

Sometimes, however, there is a refreshing note of comic relief. Once when La Paz was parched by prolonged winter drought someone hit on the bright idea of sending a contingent of soldiers to dynamite a few glaciers in the nearby Cordillera and so increase the flow of water into the Zongo Lake which

Aymara child with kid.

above: Market day in Otavi.
below: Author visiting an improved house on the *altiplano.*

supplies the city. Apparently no one remembered that the only approach to the narrow *col* in the Cordillera—a marvellously beautiful place, where the jade waters of the lake mirror the snows of the Huayna Potosí, and seem almost to lap the sky—led through the Milluni mine which straddles the single trail just below the skyline. At any rate, no one thought to acquaint the miners with what was afoot. The miners drew their own conclusions. Dynamite and soldiers together meant business to them, and business of an unmistakable kind that must be thwarted. Without more ado, they surrounded the unsuspecting soldiers and took them prisoner. Passing through equally unsuspectingly some time later, I was severely interrogated by the miner guarding the road barrier at the mine entrance, who proved singularly hard to convince of the attractions of Lake Zongo for an innocent Saturday afternoon's outing. Eventually allowed grudging passage I was even more surprised to see soldiers and miners—the most incongruous mixture one can imagine in Bolivia—crowded together in a lorry being driven off at great speed, while another group of soldiers, unarmed and under guard, sat sheepishly on the mountainside. Not until the next morning did I discover the explanation on opening my newspaper. Some days passed before the military hostages were released and the government had great difficulty in extricating itself with dignity from a ludicrous situation which appealed greatly to the irreverent spirit and merciless wit that typify the *paceños*.

Despite his wilder excesses, sometimes verging on anarchy, one cannot suppress a lingering sympathy for the miner, so often misled by the false promises and exhortations of his leaders. It is more than the compassion aroused by the unutterably cruel circumstances in which he lives and works, though that counts for much. One also admires the resilience with which he does not merely survive these hardships but retains a sufficient margin of energy and purpose to try to alter his situation. That these efforts are often misguided is more a token of bad leadership and of the accumulated grievances of centuries of oppression rather than an expression of innate evil. Nor do the miners flinch before the sacrifices that are in turn exacted of them. Their blood too has flowed in the massacre at Catavi in 1941, in the April revolution in 1952, and in the pitched battle of Sora-Sora in 1964 when they confronted regular troops who barred their entry into Oruro. Soon after, the two adversaries combined to oust the government of Dr Paz Estenssoro from office but the alliance was short-lived: in May 1965 the main road coiling up to the airport from La Paz was criss-crossed with automatic fire between troops and workers from the Milluni mine—the same who, earlier, had so lightheartedly kidnapped a regiment—and the miners only surrendered when many of their number had been killed by bombing and strafing raids carried out by air-force planes.

For all the vicissitudes of the past years, the miner represents a reserve of courage and determination which, if properly directed, could constructively assist in the task of nation-building. Their rôle in the revolutionary transformation of the country from near-feudalism was decisive; there is no reason why they should not play an equally constructive part in the much more complex period of consolidation that must follow every political and social upheaval if its effects are to last. The miner has the same dour and obdurate cast of face as the *campesino*, but whereas the latter's expression is inured to passive resignation and suffering, every line etched deep in the miner's countenance is stamped with determination and a thrusting resolve to fight for his rights. With the rapid social transformations of the last sixteen years the *campesino's* status has changed and he himself has evolved. Why should not the miner evolve simultaneously in such a way as to diminish the differences between the two? The attainment of such an ideal will take a long time but is surely not impossible.

It is all the more sad that recent years have seen an increasing tendency to make each group—and sometimes even subdivisions of them—into the toy of rival political factions and leaders. These attitudes must change if the process of developing a unified nation is to continue unimpeded. A more hopeful sign is the gradual change of attitude towards the rôle of mining.

It is still of paramount importance and must remain so for a very long time, but there is a growing and healthy realization that a panorama of the future framed solely in the narrow angles of a drilling rig can only produce a distorted perspective.

7 PERHAPS there is nowhere more symbolic of the miner's life than Oruro: the illusion of fabulous wealth followed all too often by the reality of poverty and squalor. From whichever side you approach, Oruro coquettishly hides behind a shimmering haze which entices the traveller on like a will o' the wisp. To the north dust-devils ring the horizon with their probing question marks, querying the town's very existence; to the south, the pink flamingoes wading and preening in Lake Urus, and rosily reflected in its waters, lend an incongruously exotic touch to the sere distances of the *altiplano*. And after all, you remind yourself, Oruro is the centre of the whole of Bolivia's vast tin mining area, just as Potosí was the hub around which the silver trade revolved. You do not, obviously, expect the same traces of colonial elegance or the aura of spent glory that pervades the cobbled streets of Potosí, but perhaps some solid middle-class comfort, unpretentious but respectable, an Andean Manchester, in keeping with the more mundane mineral to which it owes its origin.

Oruro does not meet even these modest standards. It is a mean, forbidding town, hugging the bare hillside, its streets drawn out in a strict chequered pattern and bordered by ill-favoured houses mostly one storey high. Individuality has no place here: all is grey monotony even in the noon sunlight of a bright winter day. One street is much like the next, foiling the traveller in his search for the centre of the town which, indeed, is distinguished from the rest only by its taller buildings. Here a few scrawny trees, twisted into tortuous shapes by the unending conflict with the elements, try vainly to invest the *plaza* with a suitable degree of civil dignity and on Sundays and holidays a melancholy brass band lugubriously summons up breath to play sedate airs from the rickety bandstand.

Plaster peels off the walls of the houses; inside, the uniform pattern of grey lace curtains, antimacassars and a plethora of ugly china ornaments and faded photographs speak of lives consumed in boredom.

'It was different,' the old, conservative Orureños will tell you a little wistfully, 'in the old days when all the *gringos* were here.'

But it is difficult to imagine that it was ever any different, for the essence of Oruro is the unrelenting sameness of everything. The *gringos* are drifting back now, no longer the lone adventurers or representatives of private companies of former times, but the employees of bilateral and international aid programmes sent out to help save the tin industry from bankruptcy. Oruro unrepentantly clings to its air of a gold-rush town that did not quite make the grade.

Even its occasional claims to glory seem to misfire. Melgarejo, the colourful dictator whose extravaganzas have become legendary, and have certainly lost nothing in the telling, is said to have been in the midst of a sumptuous and well-liquored banquet here in 1870 when the news of the Franco-Prussian war reached him. An ardent admirer of Napoleon III, he at once declared that Bolivia would speed to the aid of France. When a few faint-hearts enquired how the army would cross the ocean he brushed their doubts aside:

'If necessary, we shall swim there,' he cried, and marched his soldiers out of Oruro and across the windswept *altiplano* in the middle of the night.

Dawn found them in a more sober frame of mind, shivering on the banks of a torrential river which they could not cross. But Melgarejo had no compunction in ordering the return to Oruro.

113

'After all,' he said philosophically, 'the Emperor will know that we have done our best.'

A pioneer spirit still pervades the hotels in Oruro and throughout the main mining area, including Potosí, for they hardly seem to have changed since the first great tin boom at the turn of the century. They operate on the principle of packing in as many clients as possible and rates are quoted per bed and not per room. If you crave privacy then you must pay for all the beds in the room allotted to you; the charge is not high but the creature comforts are proportionately exiguous. Some cunning architectural hand, guided no doubt by Andalusian memories that momentarily obliterated the realities of the *altiplano* climate, has designed most of them round a central patio, and taken infinite pains to ensure that each room has at least two, if not three, outside walls. Sanitary arrangements are primitive and invariably equipped with a defective lock which becomes a constant *casus belli* between whoever happens to be in occupation at the time and the next aspirant. Washing is a perfunctory operation often carried out in a corner of the patio with icy cold water in a chipped enamel bowl, but even with more sophisticated facilities there are still compelling deterrents against removing more than a minimum of clothing. Nights here are cold the whole year round and in winter, when most people prefer to travel because there is less danger of becoming marooned in the mud or in a swollen river, the thermometer goes down well below zero centrigade. There is no heating but in the towns there will be electric light in the bedrooms, usually dispensed by one fly-specked naked bulb, of the lowest wattage available, which flickers wildly with the fluctuations of an uncertain current, to expire utterly by eleven o'clock. And once I had the disconcerting experience of leaning against a wall to find that it was only made of wallpaper stretched between wooden slats, so that I nearly fell into the next room and was kept awake for hours by the booming River Plate accents of its Argentine occupants.

The human element restores the balance, for the concern of

the innkeeper for the comfort of his guests seems always to operate in inverse proportion to the possibilities of translating his desires into action. Waiters may be grubby and unkempt, and probably not very bright, but they serve you spiced *altiplano* soup and a steak that successfully defeats all efforts at dissection, with a solicitous zeal born of an evident determination to please, however great the odds may be. This imperviousness to the harsh facts of life around them is one of their most delightful qualities and breeds a fatalistic insouciance in the face of all disasters. When once, during the rainy season, we called the landlady to our hotel room in Oruro to show her a pool of water that had dripped through the roof into the accommodating depression of one sagging bed her capacious bosom shook with mirth as she exclaimed, in a rising crescendo:

'*¡Aa y-y-y, Dios!* The rain does this *every* year.'

There were overtones of indignation to her hilarity, all the same, as if she were also enquiring of the Almighty how much longer she would be the victim of an unco-operative and freakish nature.

One's companions are usually mining folk, engineers or geologists or prospectors, for tourists are not frequent, even in Potosí, and haunt Oruro only at Carnival time. The wayside inn does not merely provide food and a roof for weary travellers but also the setting for warm sociable gatherings. On one occasion, when I was returning with two or three United Nations experts from a visit to the rural development centre in Otavi, we were unable to sleep in Potosí because the previous occupants of the rooms we had booked had decided not to move on after all, an explanation that everyone beside ourselves seemed to find perfectly reasonable. Everything else being full because of the unlikely coincidence in the Imperial City of an assembly of dentists, a conference of accountants and the imminent arrival of the President of the Republic, we drove on dispiritedly northwards and after about two hours the headlamps of the Land-Rover picked up a welcome sign announcing '*Alojamiento*' in a narrow village street.

The lodgings offered turned out to be one long narrow room

115

reached by a steep staircase over a patio. It held about ten iron bedsteads lined up against the wall, and covered with rough Indian blankets woven in a gaudy combination of colours. On the other side of the road the owner kept a small mud-walled bar where we sat on benches at a rough wooden table and ate a meal, well seasoned with *llajhua* (or *jallpja-huaica* as they call it in Aymara), a fiery sauce of hot peppers, tomato and the herb *quilquiña* used to pep up most *altiplano* food and which helped down the unpalatable, blackened *chuño*, an acquired taste that I never seemed to acquire.

Our host was delighted to have some *gringos* as his guests and produced some raw-tasting *pisco*—a sort of eau de vie made from fermented grapes—that burnt the back of one's throat comfortingly after a tiring day and the cold night drive. It was a convivial evening, the conversation as highly spiced as the food, and it must have been midnight when we climbed back up to our room and rolled ourselves in the garish blankets. Hardly had I got to sleep, however, when I was jerked into wakefulness by the sound of boots clumping on the staircase outside and then of the door opening stealthily. I felt very glad to be flanked by two stalwart male protectors at that moment. But there was nothing to be afraid of:

'*Buenas noches*,' said the dim shape by the door courteously and shuffled to one of the empty beds at the far end.

Wayfarers continued to arrive at intervals during the night until our communal dormitory was full and loud with snoring. In the dawn we cemented the anonymous companionship of the night by gulping down hot coffee of rasping strength together before travelling on our separate ways.

Yet, despite the Spartan conditions, there is one season when Oruro's modest hotels are packed out; and not only the hotels, for the antimacassars are snatched off the high-backed old-fashioned sofas in threadbare parlours and every conceivable article of furniture is pressed into service to accommodate the hordes of visitors who flock into the town at Carnival time. The Oruro Carnival is the most famous in all Bolivia, and, to the discerning, in all Latin America, for in its own special way it can hold its own even with the sophisticated festivities in Rio de Janeiro. The town is transformed and for a few days its habitual drabness acts as a foil for the kaleidoscopic colours and hypnotic music of the Devil Dancers, the Morenada and all the other groups that traditionally perform at this time.

The most celebrated of all are the Devil Dancers. This curiously hybrid dance, still a remarkably alive and developing popular manifestation, is a creation of the miners, although it has been enthusiastically taken up by the rest of the town's inhabitants. Rooted in a combination of pagan and Christian myth, it is an interesting example of the duality that still runs through everyday life in Bolivia. At this time the miners renew their allegiance to La Vírgen del Socavón—the Virgin of the Mine—and ask for her protection.

There are various versions of how this cult originated but common to them all is the legend that on the Saturday of Carnival, some time in the late eighteenth century, a certain Anselmo Belarmino, who was also a celebrated bandit, known variously as 'Nina-Nina' or 'Chiru-Chiru' was mortally wounded in a street fight and then succoured by the Vírgen de la Candelaria to whose image, painted on the decaying wall of a deserted house, he had dedicated a candle every Saturday. According to the most romantic legend, told in very flowery language by Padre Emeterio Villaroel in 1908, Nina-Nina, whose 'name alone made our grandfathers' hair stand on end and forced them to retire to their homes when the soft crepuscular light had barely dissolved in night', was also the ardent suitor of a young belle named Lorenza, whose father, though ignorant of his true identity, did not encourage his attentions. The story is not without a touch of melodrama. Bursting into the shop where Lorenza was serving on that same day of Carnival in 1789, the young gallant demanded a glass of eau-de-vie, and then, tearing off his false beard, eloped with her. An encounter with her father in the street led, however, to the fight in which the bandit was stabbed and left for dying, only to be rescued by the Virgin he had served who, disguised as a 'beautiful young

117

girl dressed in black', bore him off to the hospital so that he could receive absolution before expiring.

Chiru-Chiru's amorous exploits do not enter into the legends about him. He seems to have been a Robin Hood type of character who robbed the rich to help the poor but who was eventually caught when stealing and stabbed; somehow he was carried, or made his way, back to the cave or cottage in which he lived on the hillside above Oruro and there, on his death, a life-size image of the Vírgen de la Candelaria appeared painted and sculpted on the wall. This is supposed to be the site of the present-day temple of the Vírgen del Socavón.

There is nothing remarkable about such a story; many other regions of Bolivia and Latin America have their own local tradition of miracles performed by the Virgin. The interesting feature here is that the Virgin's devotees pay homage to her by dancing for days on end in the guise of devils. This seeming anachronism has several explanations. The most plausible is the miners' own superstition relating to rites practised in these hills long before the Catholic religion spread the cult of the Virgin. In pre-Spanish Andean mythology, a spirit known as *Supay* lived in the centre of the earth; it was a spirit of evil, but could also bestow blessings and protection on people if suitably appeased. This ambivalent image of the *supay* became further confused, according to some writers, when the Spanish missionaries arrived and decried all the old Inca idols—whether representing good or evil spirits—as *supayas*, and their priests as the intermediaries of all evil spirits. Since the Indians received only suffering at the hands of the earthly followers of the new Christian God whom they were asked to serve, and since the exponents of this new religion insisted that their former cult had been devil-worship, the *supay* or devil came to seem a kindly spirit in contrast to what had come after.

The miner, who is very superstitious, has developed this concept into the cult of the *tío*, a spirit who lives in the centre of the mine and who is the owner and donor of all the rich veins of ore. His goodwill has to be assured if the miner is to be successful and is to escape harm from the myriad hazards which lie in wait for him inside the mine. The vitality of this belief is well illustrated in Augusto Céspedes's book *Metal del Diablo*, when one miner, with his faint light, suddenly sees an enormous black and hairy face, adorned with huge ears, like horns, rise up before him, and rushes out screaming '*¡El tío! ¡el-tío!*' The panic spreads among the rest of the miners until it is discovered that the apparition was merely one of the blind pit mules which had wandered into a disused gallery.

At the entrance to most mines you will find a small clay or stone figure, with horns, standing sentinel over the adit. This represents the *tío*, and every miner, each time he goes underground, presents the image with his well-chewed wad of *coca* leaves as a votive offering. The *tío* is a very jealous god, and the name of Jesus must never be pronounced in any mine lest the *tío* cause the ore to disappear. Priests are not welcome in most mines either, though it is not clear whether this is an extension of the superstition that there will be a death if a woman enters the mine (and indeed, women are not allowed in most mines), by virtue of the priest's long skirts, or whether it arises from fear of displeasing the *tío*.

Thus, although there is also an altar to the Vírgen del Socavón at the entrance to the Oruro mine, throughout the year the miner's daily devotion is directed mainly towards the *tío*, who is supposed to watch over him while underground. The duality is given a new twist when, at Carnival time, the miner reaffirms his devotion to the Virgin by identifying himself with the diabolical personage whom he reveres throughout the year. This ambivalence is not exceptional but a particularly striking expression of the Andean-Indian's syncretic approach to religion. The new faith does not supersede the old one. Nothing is discarded, but the new dogmas are absorbed into the existing framework of beliefs, and the two become so closely intertwined that it is no longer possible to unravel them. No one finds it in the least strange that after three days of fervent veneration of the Virgin, Carnival Tuesday is traditionally— as elsewhere in Bolivia—the *Día de la ch'allá*, the day when oblations are poured to the Pachamama, the Earth Goddess,

119

who, in some scarcely defined way, also represents the Virgin. Everything which is *ch'allá'd* on that particular day will be blessed with the protection of the Pachamama and of the Achachilas, the spirits that inhabit the mountains, the rivers and the lakes.

The *diablada*, as the devil dance is called, is not a celebration lasting only a few days. It is a highly-organized affair, and preparations for it occupy almost the whole year. Although tourists, foreign and Bolivian, pour into Oruro every year to watch this spectacle, it is in no sense organized for them but is the intensely popular expression of a closely-knit and normally rather isolated society. Spectators are, as it were, extraneous; the celebration will be unaffected, whether they come or not. This is strange when one considers that, so far as can be gathered from the scant records, the *diablada* in Oruro had fallen into complete decadence in the early part of the last century and was only revived comparatively recently. That it is an exceedingly vigorous popular tradition is beyond doubt: nearly every family in Oruro is represented, irrespective of professional or social standing, and over the years new features have gradually developed. By no stretch of the imagination can it be called a static or moribund phenomenon of a fast disappearing folklore.

At the same time there is something curiously mediaeval about it. The different *comparsas*, or dancing groups, are often composed of guilds of *gremios* representing a certain occupation. The two most famous are those of the miners and the railway men. The full version of the dance—the *relato* as it is called—is obviously a close cousin of the mystery and morality plays of the Middle Ages. Similarities have been traced with Catalan *entremeses* of the twelfth century and with an ancient Catalan dance called 'The Seven Capital Sins' in which the Vices argue with a lady who represents Virtue, apparently a forerunner of the present-day *Ball des Diables* of Tarragona. It has much in common, too, with the *autos sacramentales* that so enriched Spanish religious drama in the sixteenth and seventeenth centuries, and were preoccupied with the temptations of the

120

flesh, except that it is simpler in conception and does not have the eucharistic significance of the *auto sacramental*, which was customarily performed at Corpus Christi. Again, there is something of the Quixotic concept of chivalry in the vigil that is observed on the first night and this, combined with the cruder aspects such as the buffoonery of the bears and condors, produces an almost Cervantine polarity of the romantic and the picaresque.

Though much of the *diablada* is Creole-inspired—from ideas and forms transplanted from Spain's Golden Age by the eager conquerors of the New World and preserved through the centuries—there are also indigenous aspects going back to pre-Colombian times. As they execute their flying leaps and curvets at the apogee of the dance the masked performers with their short flaring skirts and flowing capes might be the personification of the winged figures decorating the frieze on the Gate of the Sun at Tihuanacu, or of the dancers depicted on ceramic plates found at Nazca and Mochica in the coastal areas of Peru.

The *diablada* is a religious dance, and all the roles are performed by men, including that of the *China Supay*, the wife of the devil, who is pictured as a lascivious woman. It demands rigorous training and exceptional physical stamina, for it is a wild leaping affair and the performers dance practically without ceasing for four days at an altitude of 13,000 feet, borne up only by their religious fervour and, be it said, by large quantities of the beer and *chicha* that accompany all festivals on the *altiplano*. It is a mimed representation of the submission of the Devil to the Queen of Heaven, an atonement, as it were, for the superstitious cult of the *tío* which the miner observes for the rest of the year. The dancers are in the service of the devil until the Monday afternoon when they remove their masks and transfer their allegiance to the angels.

The public part of the ceremony begins on the Saturday afternoon with the *Entrada del Sábado*. The *comparsas* dance in procession through the main streets of Oruro and so up the hill to the church of the Vírgen del Socavón which dominates the whole town. Each group is accompanied by its *pasantes*, or

121

sponsors, usually two or three devout, portly ladies, who carry the group's standard, ornately embroidered with their name and an image of the Virgin. At the head goes the *cargamento*, a fabulous display of silver, hand-beaten salvers, plates, spoons and ornaments of all kinds, of great antiquity and value, arrayed on *aguayos*, the brightly-hued Indian shawls, which are draped over the roofs and bonnets of a whole line of cars. Sometimes, as a relic of an older and more picturesque tradition, the *cargamento* is carried on the backs of donkeys or oxen, and occasionally even of a llama, or a small calf or lamb. Some of the guilds are immensely rich and on the Saturday of Carnival a breathtaking amount of wealth is solemnly paraded through this town, which normally wears such a down-at-heel air.

Behind, to the traditional strains of the *diablada*, come the dancers, headed by the diabolical and richly dressed trio of Lucifer, Satan, and the *China Supay*. The costumes of all the devils are ornate and extravagant in the extreme. They consist of a breastplate thickly embroidered with silver thread and stones, and fringed with silver, a short skirt divided into five leaves and worn over white tights, white boots laced in red and a small shoulder cape, usually also embroidered. The boots are spurred and each devil carries in his right hand a viper, or, more often nowadays, a brightly-coloured kerchief. The costume is rich in colour, bright blues and reds and greens overworked with silver and glittering stones, but it is quite outshone by the monstrous, baroque magnificence of the mask that each devil carries on his head. Bulging, billiard-ball eyes studded with bright artificial stones and huge grinning silver teeth, hideously pointed, leer grotesquely out of an exuberant tangle of horns and ears and tusks, painted in a wild cacophony of colours, and crowned by a three-headed viper or other misshapen reptile. The whole contraption is fashioned from plaster of Paris and weighs several pounds, so that it is no mean feat to dance for hours on end encased within it.

Lucifer and Satan are distinguished by their even more luxurious dress, long embroidered capes reaching down to their knees, flowing manes of blonde hair and even larger and more magnificent masks. Lucifer wears a crown on top of his mask and carries a gilded sceptre. Between them pirouettes the *China Supay*, decked out in the typical *chola* dress of about 1930—a richly embroidered blouse with a peplum, over a brightly-coloured velvet skirt puffed out by layers of other skirts and starched white petticoats, white stockings and high-heeled white boots laced up over the ankle. Her mask is pink and white with the same bulbous eyes, conveying an impression of pop-eyed innocence rather than the lust and temptation of the flesh which she is supposed to represent, and is topped by a pair of horns, a crown, and a female wig with long braids hanging down her back.

The Archangel Michael follows the main contingent of devils, a celestial figure in pale blue and white, glittering with sequins and silver embroidery, with long feminine locks cascading down his back to tangle with his gold and silver wings, and bearing in his right hand a curving silver sword and, in his left, a shield aflash with mirrors. His mask, too, is pink and white, and dominated by the same protuberant eyes, this time in a seraphic blue. The overall effect is somehow pallid and emasculated compared with the lusty vigour of all these Mephistophelian figures prancing ahead. A brass band brings up the rear, blowing away at the traditional, diabolically martial music. In the larger troupes there may be as many as a hundred devils, besides two or three clowns, traditionally disguised as bears or condors and sometimes accompanied by children, who provide comic relief and perform the useful function of clearing enough space for the dancers.

When the more celebrated *comparsas* are about to arrive an almost religious expectancy enthrals the crowd that throngs the streets, leans over grossly overloaded balconies or perches insecurely in the rickety trees round the *plaza*. Suddenly around the corner they come, caracoling and curvetting, a hundred pairs of feet or more dancing as one with marvellously formal precision, and the workaday street explodes in a blinding galaxy of light and colour, like some immense pyrotechnic display. One is caught up as if mesmerized by the movement,

123

the pattern of interweaving colours, the compulsive rhythm of the music. The onlooker loses his identity and is at one with the dancers, tapping out the irresistible beat with his feet, turning now at the head of the column to weave his way back unerringly through the forest of flaming cloaks and kerchiefs in a series of gyrating caprioles executed as to a metronome. Not a murmur is to be heard from the crowd which watches utterly absorbed, in pent-up exhilaration that finds relief in applause only when the dancers have completed their intricate movement and the cavalcade has moved on. It is a cathartic experience shared by performers and audience.

Not all of the procession attains this high point of emotion. Some *comparsas* are acknowledged veterans who can evoke such a response from their audience; others are more ragged in performance. Other types of representation also traditionally take part in the Oruro Carnival: the Morenada, a grotesquely-dressed group with black masks and enormous skirts laden with sequins and tinselly decorations, who personify the Negro slaves brought to the Indies by the Spaniards and shuffle round sedately—for their cumbersome skirts preclude anything more boisterous—whirling *quirquinchos*, rattles made of the carapace of the armadillo; the Incas, who represent their pre-Colombian ancestors, and hilariously burlesque their Spanish conquerors with a buffoon-like Conquistador staggering about in helmet and chainmail; and the Tobas, equipped with enormous feather headdresses and spears, who perform the acrobatic war dance of a tribe once numerous in the lowlands which, in the words of Alcide d'Orbigny, 'made the Spaniards and the neighbouring nations tremble'.

At the church the mood changes. The contained passion and virility of the dance humbles into devotion. As they enter the temple, the devils remove their masks and spurs, and, preceded by the *pasantes* with their banners, advance to the High Altar. The dehumanizing effect of the masked headgear and bizarre dress has been so complete that it is disconcerting to see the faintly mongoloid features and coffee-coloured skin of an Oruro miner or railwayman emerge from his gaudy finery. Each

124

comparsa sings its own special *copla de llegada* to the Virgin, a ballad of arrival. They are simple songs, unpretentious in both music and words, usually sung by the man playing the Archangel Michael, while the chorus of devils joins in the refrain. Once the priest had blessed them, the groups retire, without turning their backs on the altar.

That night there are visits to the houses of the *pasantes* and the people who have provided the *cargamento*. There is little sleep for the devils and for them the night hours take on the character of a vigil. For the town's dignitaries and the important visitors, a masked dance goes on until dawn, but if you climb back up the hill to the church you will find a more plebeian *fiesta* in full swing. *Cholas* and *cholos* and *campesinos* who have come in from the outlying villages for the occasion will be stamping out the rhythms of *cueca* and *huayño* to the music of *charango* and guitar, skirts and petticoats belling out shadowily in the uncertain light of a few flares. There do not seem to be many people, but when you pick your way along the steep stone-strewn paths that lead to the entrance of the mine you discover that the place is alive: faint candle flames suddenly flicker out under the lee of the boulders, glimmering on dark faces; people are sleeping here, or quietly murmuring about the events of the day; here and there makeshift stalls have been put up, food and beer are being sold, there is the subdued glow of a charcoal fire and the titillating peppery smell of *empanadas* or *sajta de pollo* or some other *altiplano* delicacy. Below, Oruro is spangled with light, for all the world like the great metropolis it undoubtedly seems to the people passing the night hours on the hillside.

Even if you do get to bed, there is not much sleep to be had. Music jangles out interminably from every bar and private house. Bands roam the streets. Long before dawn, bells all over the town begin peremptorily banging in the new day. There is the crunch of many footsteps as the *comparsas* and their hangers-on dance up to the church to salute the Virgin at dawn. Soon after breakfast they are on the march again. The little town throbs with the music of a hundred bands. Lucifer's bright hosts advance in every direction like some diabolical occupation force. Small, over-excited children, dressed in their Sunday best, dash in and out of the white-stockinged legs of the devils while parents try vainly to keep them under control.

The open space before the Virgin's chapel is now completely encircled by triumphal arches of wooden poles bound and draped with *aguayos* of many colours, and decorated with the antique silver objects and ornaments carried yesterday in the *cargamentos*. Once mass is over each troupe of devils, headed by the priest and his acolytes, dances down through the arches to a broad esplanade where the full version of the *diablada* is played out before a colourful audience seated in tiers up the hillside and plied by vendors with sweets and fruit and pork crackling. The basis of the dance is the same as the previous day, but the figures are more complex, words are added and the full allegorical meaning is revealed. With blood-curdling Satanic cries the dancers represent first, the rebellion of the angels, who fell from heaven to become devils, and then their subjection by the Archangel Michael, who dominates one by one the seven cardinal sins, each represented by one of the devils. The drama itself is rather crude but is not lacking in a homespun humour: Sloth has to be pushed into going to receive his punishment and when it comes to the turn of the *China Supay* she is unrepentant enough to try her seductive charms on the angel. In the end, the Archangel Michael leads them all in a final dance under the tutelage of his curving silver sword.

On the Sunday afternoon there is another *entrada,* but this time it is a carnival cortège without the *cargamentos* and by one of the strange paradoxes so characteristic of Bolivia—or perhaps it is merely that by this time the enormous quantities of beer and *chicha* consumed in an effort to keep the dancers on their feet have begun to have a counter-productive effect—it is a much more uninhibited display than the semi-religious procession of the previous day. Coloured bunting—*serpentinas* they call them locally—streams from the baroque configurations of devils' masks and the geometric precision of yesterday's marshalled ranks softens into a more flowing movement, reflected in the abandoned joy of the dancers. On Monday they are still capering, admittedly more raggedly, but enough to justify the *Orureño's* boast that he can withstand both altitude and fatigue, until, at dusk, the plaintive, Inchaic strains of the *kacharpaya*, the farewell, bring the revelries to an end.

Usually, though, the casual visitor has departed long since, and already by Sunday afternoon is retracing his steps to La Paz, through villages thronged with Indian dancers, decked out in their carnival best, tirelessly weaving an unsteady trot between the bystanders and the impassive vendors of food and drink squatting on the ground, like some outsize and animated *serpentina*. Above the *plaza* crouches a stumpy church, a benevolent dwarf who has also entered the spirit of carnival.

But the jealous spirit of the mountains is not so easily appeased and the spectre of death is never far away. Even with the miracles of modern technology men may not be immune to the dangers but simply become vulnerable in new ways. In August 1963 one of the planes carrying out the aerial geophysical survey for the United Nations crashed in the mountains to the south of Uncía. There were two planes, flying in accordance with technical requirements at 400 feet above the ground and with 600 feet between them, as they had done for many months despite the high altitudes—sometimes over 16,000 feet above sea-level—and the jagged terrain. That bright morning they flew up a deceptive defile. The crest of the hill at the end was hidden and suddenly reared up as an insurmountable wall beyond what had at first seemed to be the end of the valley. The first plane was too near to be able to escape, stalled, and crashed to the ground. The second banked only just in time and flew to Uncía to give the alarm and organize search-parties which set off immediately on foot.

Yet it was two days before we could retrieve the bodies and take them back to La Paz. The site of the accident was almost inaccessible: even the nearest track, already several miles away, was eight or nine hard hours' driving from La Paz. The mines were going through one of their periodic states of unrest and although the accident was reported to me by radio in the morning and confirmed in the afternoon, we could not leave the capital until eleven o'clock at night, so as to arrive in Catavi, the centre of the mining troubles, at first light. A sentry shot at us as we sped past the *Alto de la Paz* but after that we drove without incident to Oruro where we had to change to a Land-Rover. The *plaza* there at two a.m. was bare and windswept. It was impossible to imagine the shining hosts of devils that danced there at happier moments, and the whisky we sipped to keep warm in the bitter cold did nothing to lighten our spirits.

At six a.m., as dawn was breaking, we arrived at the first checkpoint at Catavi. A rifle butt was thrust through the window at me and a stern-faced miner's picket, swathed in scarves, glared mistrustfully at this car-load of *gringos* and asked our business. We had agreed beforehand that it would be less suspicious if I, as a woman, spoke to them. I explained about the accident and of our search for the three Swedes in the plane, who were all too probably dead, though we still harboured some hope that they might be alive but injured. At once the attitude of the guards changed. This was something they could understand. The rifle butt was removed from my ribs and we were waved on with gestures of sympathy.

Some hours passed before we found the right track and arrived at the point where the search-party had struck off into the hills on foot. Even in the brassy sunshine of midday it was a desolate spot with no sign of habitation. We had not climbed far through the stubbly *ichú* grass, tired as we were from lack of sleep, when we saw a group of people moving towards us over the farthest spur of the hill. As they came near the last of any faint hopes remaining disappeared. There were thirty or forty Indians of the region descending the hill at a fast jogtrot, carrying between them three improvised stretchers on each of which lay a bundle shrouded in blankets. The Indians managed to keep up this punishing pace by running in relays, like the *chasquis* of Inca times. Every few yards, without a word being said, new carriers sprang forward and grasped the sides and the ends of the stretchers. There was no pause in the headlong descent during the changeover, nor did the bare feet stumble once on the rocky ground. The Indians were Quechuas, poor people scratching a living somewhere back in these lonely hills and not much touched by civilization. Their dress had not greatly changed for centuries: they wore feathers in their round fawn felt hats, shapeless and stained with age, homespun jackets of brown llama or alpaca wool and trousers of the same material reaching barely below the knee. Round their waists broad, bright red cummerbunds contrasted with the tragedy of the occasion. They had found the wreck before the pilot and crew members of the other plane, who now followed, had reached the spot from Uncía. Not a thing had been stolen.

The sad cortège passed us down towards the trail below. The scene is still impressed on my mind as I write. On the last stretcher the long dark hair of one of the Swedes—a young man I had often seen at work and at parties in La Paz—had escaped from the confining blankets and was tossing up and down with the motion of the runners in a macabre lifelike imitation.

There was silence in Uncía when we passed through, but no surprise. They were used to seeing trucks carrying other mangled remains, those of the victims of the existing mines. It did not seem strange to them that the would-be plunderers of wealth as yet undiscovered should suffer a similar fate.

The ordeal was not over at Uncía, even when the gruesome autopsy had been carried out and coffins had been found. The bodies still had to be transported back to La Paz, and the plane we had hoped for had not materialized. Finally, the mine lent us a small lorry. It was too small for the purpose and, in the manner of such vehicles on the *altiplano*, was worn out long before its time by rough roads and poor maintenance. It was again nearly midnight before it was ready to start out and it must have been around two or three o'clock in the morning, when, somewhere on the long, stony road between Oruro and La Paz a tyre burst. Because space was restricted the tool box was under the three coffins which had to be lifted one by one into the road before the wheel could be changed. The moon was high that night and cast a leprous light over the long mournful plain; one might have imagined that this ghoulish operation was taking place on the moon had the moon not been plain to see above.

Later—years later it seemed after the horror of those scenes and the exhaustion induced by lack of sleep for nearly seventy-two hours—the coffins lay under the blue and white United Nations flag in a government building in La Paz. A minister who had come to pay his last respects, a cultivated man deeply interested in the development of his country, who had lived long abroad in exile and been much exposed to foreign scepticism, said to me quite seriously:

'You see? The mountains were angry at the intrusion: they have claimed their own.'

The *Supay* had had the last word.

8 A GENTLER world lies beyond the mountains, in the long valleys tumbling helter-skelter down the torrid eastern plains. There is green here, the 'green-gold' of the plantations of *coca* bushes in the Yungas, as these valleys are called locally, the glaucous bloom of rain forests and of lush vegetation nurtured by the heavy precipitation that falls on the eastern side of the Cordillera.

Yet the approach to the Yungas is anything but gentle. The roads, where they exist, cast themselves headlong over the precipice and a cool head and a strong stomach are required of driver and passenger alike. But the mountaineer has the best view. You start from La Paz at four or four-thirty in the morning, wake the startled guard at the control post on the Corioco road and by first light are easing your car along a narrow track through frosted grass just below the Cumbre de Yungas—the Yungas pass, where the main road itself reaches a height of 15,250 feet—to the foot of a group of gently-rounded snowcaps. The ascent, with crampons, is not difficult over hard, crisp snow that sprays up like silvered spindrift in your tracks, provided your lungs are stout enough to withstand the climb to 17,000 feet or more. The cold is glacial, almost a tangible enemy against whom you struggle for survival and the scant air rasps into your lungs with all the sharp pain of a probing icicle. But at eight o'clock, if you are lucky, you stand on a

crest unsullied by any other footmarks, and eat a sparse breakfast in one of the loneliest and most beautiful places in the world.

That world seems to drop away at your feet. Immediately
below a sheer black cliff plummets down. If the warm air has
not yet risen from the valley below and condensed into the
thick mantle of cloud that perennially muffles these peaks—and
this is the point of starting in the middle of the night—snow-
capped pinnacles surround you on every side like airy stalag-
mites, refulgent in early sunlight against the mazarine vault
of the sky. The rivers that run eastward to the Atlantic, here
no more than mountain torrents or cascades of water that hurtle
down the rock face, seem to gash a channel out of the escarpment, carving out deep ravines and eroded gullies. In between
them the road threads its way down like some minute capillary
vein.

One can see for miles in a vertical as well as a horizontal
direction. Beyond the blue glimmer of the forests—a hundred
miles or more away in the distance and two or three miles
below—the broad plains and lazy rivers of eastern Bolivia, the
Oriente, shine mistily under a flaccid tropical sun, seemingly
a different planet from that dispensing the hard mountain sunlight which outlines every smallest pebble with crystalline
clarity, and impresses every image indelibly and discretely on
the retina. Here on this mountain top where the air is diamond
sharp, where decisions are clear-cut and identities well-defined,
the blurred edges and somnolent afternoons, the humid haze and
happy-go-lucky charm of the *Oriente* belong to an alien world.

The approach to the Yungas by road is almost as dramatic
and certainly more hair-raising. At its highest point, the road
runs just below the snow-line across a tundra-like waste inhabited only by apparently untended herds of llamas and alpacas
that galumph off at the car's approach and, strangely, by dogs who
lie by the roadside and wait for titbits to be thrown to them.
Sometimes, in the rainy and, paradoxically, the warmer season,
snow may cover the road itself for a number of miles at its
highest point and then the going is really dangerous, for once
over the top the road drops dizzily down in a series of tight

corkscrews. All the valleys are deep and narrow, and strewn with boulders. Houses and the walls encircling the tiny fields are made of stones that are neither cemented nor hewn in any way but cling together by some weird necromancy of their own. In the higher places, where the numbers of ruined dwellings are many, they have followed their former owners' example and have ceased to fight for survival against such overwhelming odds.

The vegetation changes quickly, with the effect of frequent rainfall and the rapidly decreasing altitude. It is already exuberant just beyond Unduavi, a sad village of petrol pumps, roadmenders and sleazy cafés—a last echo of the *altiplano*— where the road divides to Chulumani on the right and Coroico on the left. Neither road is prescribed for the squeamish but that to Coroico is decidedly the more alarming. It is a relief to most travellers to grope their way down it through thick cottonwool cloud, which mercifully obscures the abysses that constantly yawn on one side or the other, and, over some uncomfortable stretches, on both at once. The road is only wide enough for one vehicle in most places and its earth surface is almost always wet and slippery. There is barely more than a hundred yards continuous straight along the top of the rock face and the bends are so tight that even the term hairpin fails to describe them adequately.

It is at such corners that one slithers to a precarious stop in the path of one of the many heavy lorries that lumber up from the Yungas, laden with fruits and vegetables which not only have to withstand the rigours of the journey but also the weight of the crowd of Indians who, with admirable sangfroid, lounge on top of them. Advice is never lacking on such occasions. The lorry driver's mate and half the passengers leap down with alacrity and start to shout directions, cajolements and curses in the most confusing way, especially unnerving if you have never been at your best when reversing a car. It is surprising how greatly you improve when a false move would pitch you over a thousand foot precipice. When one vehicle has at last manoeuvred itself back to a slightly wider place, the climax of the operation arrives when the two vehicles have to edge past one another. Then the chant of counselling—and contradictory —voices rises to an absolute crescendo and someone always tests the edge to show how easily it will crumble away into the void at the slightest pressure. One wishes they wouldn't. And then somehow, the operation is successfully accomplished, the occupants of the lorry scramble back into their niches and you are both on your way again.

Not that accidents are unknown. Sometimes lorries or cars fail to stop in time or take one of those treacherous corners too fast. Whether the Bolivians are less addicted to the lugubrious Latin American custom of erecting a rickety cross wherever someone has gone over the edge or whether there are in fact less accidents than, say, in Colombia—where the road from Bogotá to Mesitas del Colegio is almost literally fenced with crosses and every Sunday one may come across a group gazing forlornly down into the gulf where a car or a bus and its hapless occupants have disappeared—such insignia are rare on the Coroico road. The group of large crosses that marks the headland of Chuspipata is therefore the more striking. They stand at a spot where the drop is said to be highest, though the eye cannot measure it because of the inferno of swirling mists below. It was here, at one of the more sombre moments of Bolivian history, that a group of political prisoners was shot in 1944 and their bodies sent crashing down into nothingness.

Landslides are the most common hazard. At times the whole mountain top seems to have moved and pitched forward over the road, dislodged by the water continually running down their sides as rain or mist, or even in the form of cataracts that come hurtling down with such impetus that they overshoot the narrow road altogether and enclose the traveller behind an iridescent curtain. Long lines of standing vehicles glimpsed ahead through the brume warn of the landslip. Sometimes they have been there all night and if you are really unlucky you may turn back from an outsize fall, which will take many hours to clear, only to find that your retreat has meanwhile been cut off by another subsidence farther up. All this adds to the general camaraderie

134

of travel and provides plenty of scope for the Bolivian's natural gregariousness. Food and drink are exchanged between groups previously unacquainted with one another, the more able-bodied assist in shovelling away some of the débris (though nowadays there is a well-equipped and highly efficient road service which performs marvels in keeping this particular track open at most times of the year) and advice is generously proferred. The Bolivians are great ones for giving advice to other people on how to manage things, a curiously Spanish trait.

When finally you reach Coroico, it is with the feeling of having survived some lengthy and perilous voyage. By contrast Coroico is a warm, enclosing haven; you might be in another country. Here there are no vast open spaces as on the *altiplano*; each valley is sealed off from the next and forms a circumscribed world of its own. The pattern is repeated in the tiny town of Coroico where the miniature whitewashed houses lean companionably over narrow streets, as if to embrace each other, their rickety balconies almost touching. Cobbled lanes lead to an equally neat and circumscribed square and through the doorways of the houses the passer-by glimpses shady patios where green leaves spill over the walls and begonias and bougainvillea run riot. It is a world turned inwards upon itself, as if, once the traveller has successfully completed the perilous journey, he has wished to look no further.

But access to this world, difficult as it is, has not been restricted to recent times. The Incas came here in search of gold, and found it, as evidenced by the frequent repetition of place-names prefixed by *Coro*—the Quechua word for gold—Coroico, Coripata and so on. The Spaniards followed them on the same quest, but, unlike the Incas, who returned always to their highland empire, some of them made their homes in this more congenial climate and there is a faintly Andalusian air about the small townships which shelter in the lee of the tall hills.

Not so Tipuani, however, which lies a little farther to the north and has all the transient characteristics of a gold-rush town. Gold is still mined there in large quantities and supplies a large part of the country's production. Where the wild cascade of the eastern *cordillera* towards the Atlantic is at last checked and the rivers become broader and gentler, placer deposits are exploited by large-scale foreign concerns. Higher up, where the Tipuani river is still narrowly caged in rock, individual miners and small co-operatives use more primitive methods to extract the gold, which is often deeply embedded in the mountainside or even under the river-bed itself.

Tipuani seems to be locked in by mountains. When I went there the journey by land was on foot or muleback and took anything up to five days. By air it lasts exactly thirty-three minutes but the emotion concentrated into that brief span, as well as the discomfort of passing abruptly from 13,000 feet to 19,500 and then just as swiftly to 1,500 feet above sea-level, make it seem more like a lifetime. You are surprised as well as glad to find that you are still alive at the end of it.

You fly in a battered DC–3, that relic of the Second World War about which people are apt to make the comforting remark that it can land anywhere. The one in which I made the trip in early 1964, when I went to investigate the possibility of assisting the gold mining co-operatives, looked as if it had done just that almost once too often. It was the C–47 version, with the cargo lashed down the middle of the fuselage, and a hard metal bench along the sides for the passengers. There were no seat belts and during take-off and landing one clung like grim death to the ropes binding the cargo. The trade between Tipuani and the outside world is simple enough: gold comes out, and beer goes in, in incredibly large quantities.

The rains lingered late that year and although we were waiting by the dismal corrugated iron sheds in an out of the way corner of the airfield from very early, the *cordillera* remained obstinately huddled in cloud. At last, in the middle of the morning, the peak of the Huayna Potosí appeared briefly and the pilots decided that we could leave. To the uninitiated visibility in the high mountains still looked dangerously poor, but all doubts were airily waved aside.

'So long as we can see the football pitch at the Milluni mine,

immediately before crossing the *cordillera*, then all is well,' said
our pilots.

So we bowed to their superior lore and clambered aboard the
ramshackle aircraft. We made one circle, climbing steeply,
for within a few moments of take-off the plane had to rise from
the 13,000 feet of the airport to nearly 20,000 feet in order to
cross the high narrow pass between the Huayna Potosí and
Chacaltaya. Sure enough, the football pitch at Milluni was
clearly visible just under the brow of the pass, and only a few
feet below us. When you are on the ground on the track that
runs over these mountains and down into the Zongo valley,
planes on their way to the *Oriente* roar so low overhead and hug
the contours of the land so closely that you hold your breath
until they have safely hedge-hopped the top, almost at the
limit of their altitude range.

There is a friendly atmosphere about travel in small planes
in sharp contrast to the technological mystique that shrouds the
mammoth jets. The pilots called me up into the cockpit so that
I could have a closer view of the snowbound defile as we passed
through it, but my enjoyment was abruptly curtailed by the
sight of an impenetrable featherbed of cloud billowing ahead of
us.

Seeing my expression the pilots hastened to reassure me as
we dived into it: 'Do not preoccupy yourself! From now on we
shall be flying on instruments.'

To my untutored and timorous mind the instruments seemed
to consist merely of a stop-watch, a compass and an altimeter.
The co-pilot called out the minutes from the stop-watch while
the pilot steered the aircraft on a certain course and dropped
height at a vertiginous rate of something very near a thousand
feet a minute. The physical discomfort of gasping for air in the
rarefied atmosphere—for there was no oxygen available, except,
one was glad to see, for the pilots—and of ears reacting to the
rapid changes of altitude, was not made any better by the unnerving sight of the green tummocks of hilltops popping up
through the clouds on every side like floating ant-hills.

The pilot said encouragingly: 'We continue on this course and at this rate of descent for another five minutes to see if the visibility improves.'

'And if it doesn't?'

'We turn round, gain altitude as quickly as possible, and head back for La Paz as fast as we can.'

Somehow it was preferable to creep back to the hard metal bench in the rear of the plane where the tiny windows discreetly admitted the sight of only one of those waiting hillcrests at a time. But when the air suddenly cleared and we were approaching Tipuani, there was no way of refusing the pressing invitations to return for a cockpit view of the approach and landing, famed as one of the most dangerous in a country where air hazards are commonplace. The entrance to the air-strip was guarded by a pair of green hills, so close together that it seemed as if even the narrow wing-span of a C–47 would be hard put to it to ease its way through. As the pilot steered his way towards the narrow gap with infinite precision, the co-pilot continued to drone away the passing seconds. One soon saw why. At the mid-point of the passage through the gap the aircraft had to swerve full tilt to the left to avoid another spur of the hillside jutting out beyond the first. At this point I shut my eyes tight and they were still shut—I believe I was subconsciously steeling myself for the crash of impact—when, brief seconds later, we were bucketing madly over the grassy airstrip. By a final quirk of nature this was scimitar-shaped and curved back in the opposite direction, rightwards, following the course of the river-bank. Passing through the gap, turning to the left, landing and then swinging back to the right were motions that followed so swiftly upon one another as to be almost simultaneous. Split-second timing and consummate skill were necessary to avoid disaster. Yet, as I learned later, there had been only one accident in twenty years or so in this place, though the local inhabitants were still shaking with mirth—hard to share at the moment of arrival, with the prospect of the return trip still hanging over one— at the memory of one plane which had failed to stop in time a week before and had very nearly crashed into the fast-flowing river which curls back across the end of the runway.

That day and the day of our return to La Paz later that week the two pilots made this hazardous flight four or five times. Apart from the intense mental concentration required, the men's physical resources were taxed to the utmost by the extremes of temperature, climate and barometric pressure to which they were exposed in the brief space of thirty-three minutes. Even though they took oxygen over the highest part of the *cordillera*, you could not help wondering whether the continued strain of performing this minor miracle several times daily would not, in the end, sap their strength and mar their judgement.

Those thoughts echoed again through my mind when, five or six months later, I read in the newspaper that the plane in which I had travelled was missing. It was later discovered to have crashed, not at the needle-eye entrance to Tipuani, but high on the snowy slopes of the Huayna Potosí. The same two pilots who had been so proud of their skill and their infallibility were both killed, together with two or three of the casual passengers who always travelled with the cargo. Visibility had been especially poor that day, the authorities said, and the pilots had been warned not to take the risk. Yet they had gone, perhaps because they could, after all, descry the football pitch at Milluni or because they placed too much faith in the magic of their 'instrumental' approach. Most probably they went because long association with the mountains had bred familiarity, a liberty that the *Achachilas*, exacting their tribute of worship and fear, could not condone.

Flying is a nonchalant business in Bolivia at the best of times. And even when tragedy has struck, the same insouciance, or perhaps fatalism might be a better term, continues unabated. For years the national airline, Lloyd Aéreo Boliviano, (LAB), had an excellent record. In March 1963, however, one of its largest aircraft, a DC–6 disappeared on the short flight up from Arica, the Chilean port on the Pacific coast, and after a long search, was found crashed at 15,000 or 16,000 feet up on the slopes of Mount Tacora in the western limb of the Andean Cordillera, near the point where the frontiers of Peru, Chile and

Bolivia meet. One of the forty-odd passengers who perished was a United Nations expert and I therefore had the grim task of identifying his body and bringing it back for burial. Access to the site of the crash was extremely difficult and American helicopters were specially flown in from the United States to assist in the salvaging operation.

On the Bolivian side the nearest point of habitation was a desolate village called Charaña, which existed more by virtue of being the last station on the Bolivian side of the La Paz-Arica railway line than on account of any natural advantage, since scarcely a blade of grass managed to push its way through the arid soil for miles around. We were flown there in the inevitable C–47, although this one had three or four single seats down each side. There was even some pretence that this was a normal flight, vouchsafed by the command 'Fasten seatbelts' but this soon faded before the abrupt discovery that some of the seats had not been screwed to the floor, and inexorably began to slide towards the back of the aircraft as its nose tilted upwards, while their captive occupants struggled to extricate themselves from their seatbelts or hung on to the sides of the plane. Even more disconcerting was an icy blast of air bringing with it the realization that at the moment of take-off the door of the plane had blown open. We were swiftly and soothingly reassured:

'Don't worry. This always happens with this plane; there's something wrong with the catch and we can't get the spare part to fix it.'

So a man was sent down to the back of the plane, with another man to hang on to *him*, while he leaned out over the widening gulf which stretched between us and the *altiplano*, dotted with brown homesteads like fairy rings of toadstools, far below, seized hold of the door and dragged it shut, securing it with a rope.

During the next couple of days we practically lived in that plane. At Charaña there was no news of the American helicopters and so we flew on to Tacna, in Peru, where they were being prepared for the rescue work, and next day ferried back the

140

reserve petrol for them to Charaña. The take-off procedures became a familiar routine. No sooner had we fastened the useless seatbelts round ourselves than a hapless man would be sent scurrying back, with a companion to hang on to his middle in order to make a grab for the door which blew open with monotonous regularity. Finally I could stand it no longer.

'Don't you think,' I asked the pilot tentatively, 'that since the door keeps flying open it might be better to tie it up with the rope *before* take-off, rather than after?'

He looked momentarily startled, but then gave the necessary orders, though with a reluctance that made me feel something of a spoil-sport.

We were about to take off from Tacna at the time with our volatile cargo of petrol barrels lashed down the centre of the plane. On board there were a couple of consuls on the same quest as myself and a man from the International Civil Aviation Organization investigating the scene of the crash. At the pilot's pressing invitation I was once again sitting in the little bucket seat behind him, an honour I could well have foregone, had it not been impossible to refuse without appearing ungracious.

Beyond us on the tarmac stood the huge Globemaster which had disgorged the helicopters a day or so before. These were now scattered around it in various stages of dismantlement while men worked furiously to adapt them to extremes of altitude far beyond their normal limits. The plan was for us to go ahead, survey the crash scene, and set up a fuelling depot in Charaña. The recalcitrant door was secured, the pilot exchanged the usual cabbalistic signs with the men on the ground, checked his instruments, and pressed a variety of buttons and switches with his right hand, while his left still sketched gestures of farewell through the window. Nothing happened. The engine did not make so much as a murmur. With an air of disbelief the pilot went through the whole manoeuvre again with no greater success. During the night the battery had died. There was a general feeling of anticlimax and ignominy when the Chileans had to push a huge generator over to us in order to resuscitate it.

It was hardly an auspicious start for our second flight over the scene of the crash but at least the weather was sunny and relatively cloudless, in contrast to the previous day when scudding rain had mistily obscured the mountain-tops. After one turn out over the Pacific we climbed to the *cordillera* and located the bare hillcrest where the remains of the wrecked aircraft lay broadcast over a wide area. They looked no bigger than the fragments of a broken toy that a child has thrown petulantly to the ground and we should hardly have made them out but for the waving figures of the rescue workers who had at last managed to climb to the spot from a narrow track several hundred feet below. The fresh mountain sunlight of early morning seemed to delineate that scene of death and destruction with a cruel intensity.

The plane swooped low over the wreckage, then banked steeply to avoid the crown of another hill that loomed crazily up at us. Peaks bristled on every side, yet the pilot seemed to keep only one absent-minded hand on the controls, while he speculated aloud about the cause of the accident.

'I cannot understand it,' he concluded 'he was our very best pilot and had very long experience.'

'Perhaps for that very reason he was over-confident,' I ventured, as we seemed to shave the short-cropped grass of another crest with one dipped wingtip.

The American Consul, who had been a helicopter pilot in the Navy, came forward to say that the ropes holding barrels of petrol in the back were loosening and that the barrels had begun to roll a bit. But he turned as grey as the next hilltop which shot at us with all the stomach-tilting speed of some mammoth switchback and retreated hastily. Round we went over the crash site again, at an even lower angle.

I tried another gambit. 'Doesn't it ever worry you that the same thing might happen to you?' I asked.

'Oh no,' came the confident reply 'I am quite sure that I shall not die in the air.'

I found it hard to concentrate on the explanation that followed for it engrossed so much of his attention that his head was half-turned towards me and his eyes completely averted from the hazards ahead. I longed to shout 'Look out' as another beetling crag seemed to hang above us but somehow I restrained myself and somehow he, at the last moment, neatly lobbed the plane over the top. In the end I thought it prudent to sit tight and say nothing as we circled round for an interminable third circuit of the area. It was a very shaken group which eventually disembarked at Charaña; the mad geometry of the terrain, the sight of the wreckage of the other plane below and the knowledge that we were surrounded by hundreds of gallons of inflammable fuel had combined to make it a very unnerving experience. Looking back now one marvels at the skill of Bolivian pilots; otherwise there would be many more accidents, and certainly there would have been one on that day.

The rest of the day was even more nightmarish. There was a grim greyness about Charaña. A mantle of nullifying dust blurred the contours of its few buildings so that their adobe walls were barely distinguishable above the earth streets, themselves mere extensions of the emergency landing strip. An hour or two later, the first helicopters arrived, bringing their macabre cargo from the top of the Andes. One or two trucks stood by to carry the bundles of sackcloth, no longer even vaguely reminiscent of the human form, to a large customs shed near the railway line for the heart-sickening process of identification. Somehow Charaña had contrived to produce forty or more rough wooden coffins which were laid out in the bare corral of one of the village huts, where passing llamas gazed incuriously over the crumbling earth wall.

By the end of the day one was numbed, one's senses mercifully bludgeoned into insensibility. Horror piled on horror could horrify no more. But my own search had been unavailing. It was late in the evening when a doctor brought news to me at the Panagra radio station where we were all crowded around the transmitter which unceasingly tapped out messages, thanks to the dedication of the radio operator and his wife who, after lonely months of exchanging laconic messages with aircraft

143

crossing the Andes, suddenly found themselves the focal point of high drama. The doctor said that he had personally identified the expert's body up on the mountain; since the helicopters could not fly after dark, it would be brought to Charaña by train from the nearest point on the railway line.

There was no point in staying longer as the plane in which we had come was already loaded with coffins, and would spend the next day flying between Charaña and La Paz. We had therefore to seek other means of transport for the return journey and ordered an *autocarril*—a small car running on the railway— from the station authorities. It had to come from La Paz so we spent the intervening hours in the railway bar, a cheerless room with mud floors and walls, where we had our first meal of the day.

At midnight, the *autocarril* clanked into the station. It was a very ancient and dilapidated automobile, which must have seen long and hard service on the *altiplano* roads before it was fitted with grooved wheels and given a new lease of life on the railway. Three of us sank into the sagging springs of the back seat which subsided on the rusty mudguards. During the next six hours we bumped and swayed our way back to La Paz to arrive at the 'Alto' just before dawn. The clatter of the metallic wheels on the iron rails made an ear-shattering din. The car itself bucketed and pranced like some half-broken wild animal, at times rearing up so that it left the ground entirely only to crash back on to the line with a jarring rattle that trembled throughout our bodies. Luckily I was wedged between two rather corpulent gentlemen who made up for the lack of shock-absorbers and provided some protection against the freezing draughts which rasped through the ill-fitting windows and the gaping holes in the fabric. We were still glad, however, to drape my sleeping bag around our knees and to take frequent swigs of fiery spirit from a bottle of *pisco* which one of my companions, a prudent Irishman, had purchased at the bar.

Late next afternoon I was up at the airport awaiting the last flight from Charaña. A large group of UN personnel was with me and the hearse was ready outside the airport sheds. When the plane came in for the last time, the load of coffins was lifted silently down and checked. Then there was consternation: the one we were seeking was not among them. A radio enquiry to Charaña elicited the macabre reply that one body had been found forgotten behind some bales in the customs warehouse, but this turned out to be one of the crew. Later still, the man in charge of the airlines rescue party, who had already worked several days and nights without sleep and with very little food, radioed to say that the American Consul from Antofagasta in Chile had claimed that one of the bodies awaiting shipment to La Paz was the American subject for whom he was searching, and had taken it by train to Arica, whence he planned to fly it back to the United States the following day. There seemed good reason to believe that this was the UN man. After feverish interventions with the American Embassy in La Paz and the Bolivian Consul in Arica, the coffin was opened again, and from the description of the man's clothes already given by the doctor who had first identified him, the mistake was proved beyond doubt.

And so the next day I flew off to Charaña once more in another dilapidated C–47—one with no seats this time—and over the cruelly spiked peaks beyond to Arica, sweltering in the late summer heat of the Pacific coast. Here there was more confusion. No one knew where the coffin was, messages had to be sent to the Bolivian consulate and the telephone wires hummed inconclusively. The margin of time for recrossing the *cordillera* before nightfall was running out and the pilot was already uneasy when a truck dashed up with no less than three coffins, all sent in error to Chile. All three were firmly nailed down and there was no time for identification.

Ominous storm clouds were pummelling the distant summits of the Andes and we were bundled aboard without ceremony, the three coffins lashed to the floor between the few silent passengers. It was not a pleasant journey. Already a week had gone by since the accident, in itself enough to cause nausea without any aid from the elements. But hardly had we crossed the *cordillera* when the storm broke, lifting us on to a surging

145

wave of air to fling us down in a seemingly bottomless trough. The plane doggedly churned its way on, tossed and buffeted by the wind and slashed by driving curtains of rain, while we clung to the metal bench as best we could. Below the dark cloudrack a strange yellowish light flickered over the *altiplano*, kindling a livid reflection in the glimmering pools of water left from the late rains of that year. It was an apocalyptic experience, a demonstration by the mountains and the forces of nature of who was the ultimate master. It seemed unbelievable when at last the wheels hit the ground, sending great jets of mud and water spurting up from the landing strip, now furrowed with deep runnels of water.

But the mountain had been persuaded to give up its prey. That night the poor human remains recovered with such difficulty lay lapped in the quiet light of candles and in the scent of many flowers. Next day they were buried in the English churchyard. We could at least be sure that that grave did in fact conceal what it purported to. Others were not so lucky. Many months later, graves in Bolivia and Chile holding victims of the disaster were being dug up and found to contain men instead of women, Chileans instead of Bolivians and vice versa, and the grief of relatives, lulled by the passage of time, was reawakened with a new and cruel sharpness. It would surely have been less painful for everyone if the bodies had been interred on the lonely peak where they had fallen, in a communal grave consecrated in the name of all the faiths represented by the victims.

But we digress from Tipuani. In so many parts of Bolivia human habitation wears a strictly temporary air: mud walls on the *altiplano* appear ready at any moment to subside into the earth which produced them; huts contrived from boughs and leaves in the warm valleys and plains seem likely to revert without warning to the forest. In Tipuani the tendency is accentuated by the gold-rush fever which entices people from one fortunate strike to the next or from one setback to a new and more promising prospect, lured on by the irrepressible hope of better luck. Tipuani village has been a centre for the area during two or three decades and boasts some buildings of a more permanent kind. We stayed in one of these, which had been rented by a small mining company giving assistance to the local goldminers' co-operatives in modernizing their methods of extraction. This was one of the few two-storey constructions and my three companions and I all slept in a large upstairs room from whose tiny windows one could glimpse the landing strip, the loop of the Tipuani river and the dark green hills beyond.

Tipuani is surrounded by a number of smaller settlements whose population fluctuates according to the success of the mining ventures carried out in their vicinity. The more important ones are linked by jeep trails hacked out of the bush and they are impassable when the rains are heavy, for the geological structure of the area is criss-crossed by huge faults and fractures. This is the last mad convulsion of the *cordillera* before it finally subsides into a more decorous slope down into the eastern plains. The valleys are steep and walled in sheer rock, making communication between them difficult. The jeep track is a switchback overhung by profuse vegetation, almost tropical in its density, which threatens to engulf the narrow trail again at any moment. As you pass, giant creepers brush the roof of the jeep, or grope along its sides in quest of new footholds, and immense flowers, vermilion and brilliant yellow, hang in an exotic frieze fringed with tendrils. The warm, humid air is heady with the scent of damp earth, of leaf mould allowed to accumulate untouched over centuries and of things growing.

But this green tunnel in which nature has been so prodigal of beauty and imagination leads to a scar-like clearing on the hillside which is a visual indictment of man and his so-called civilizing works. The village is a conglomeration of crumbling shacks crazily constructed of rusty sheets of corrugated iron and odd pieces of wood haphazardly thrown together. Refuse and excreta litter the earth street and a trickle of greenish water runs down a makeshift gutter on one side. In one of the bars a jukebox incongruously blares forth the sugary strains of a

147

remarkably recent sentimental hit from Paris and an equally unexpected kerosene refrigerator leans tipsily in one corner.

Yet even in these unprepossessing surroundings the people are kind and courteous. They ply you with large quantities of food and with the inevitable beer, consumed in such vast quantities here by a relatively small population. Life is lived at a feverish pace as if everyone expects to move on tomorrow or perhaps not to return.

Mining equipment is rudimentary and the whole operation breathes improvisation. Although the Tipuani river tumbles at break-neck speed down a deep boulder-strewn gorge, the ravine is already of respectable width. No bridge spans it, and you have to haul yourself across, sitting two at a time astride a flimsy plank, suspended from two rusty cables which blister and stain your hands. It is as well to be occupied, however, as you sway slowly across the ravine on this unsteady aerial cableway, for at least your attention is distracted from the boiling, white-frothed waters far below.

Some of the gold in the Tipuani area is obtained relatively easily from placers, though the terrain is not suitable for dredges. In many places, however, gold is found in the vein of the rock, often under the bed of the river itself. Crude shafts are driven down into the earth near the bank of the river and lateral passages and chambers are blasted at right angles beneath it. Tragic stories abound of miscalculations of the depth of the river, or mishandling of the Bolivian miner's old friend and enemy, dynamite, with the result that the explosion has blown through the river-bed and the Tipuani waters have surged in to drown those working underground. Even in the finished shaft the water flows incessantly down their crumbling sides. The miners clamber down into the darkness by a rope ladder or a rustic contraption of wood. They usually wear only a helmet and shorts or bathing trunks, for most of the time they have to work in water often as high as their waists, to emerge, hours later, dripping and mud-smeared. Primitive pulleys bring up the buckets of mud and stones which they dig from the shaft and the contents are washed and sifted nearby to separate the precious metal from the dross. Small boys pan the gold by the age-old method of shaking a shallow wooden or metal pan over a pool of water and by local tradition present the newcomer with all the gold found in the first pan.

Gold was mined here by the Incas and later by the Spaniards. In modern times the Aramayo company, one of the three 'Tin Barons', owned and worked a large concession in this valley. In recent years they have been supplanted by a co-operative of small miners who live a hand-to-mouth existence although they produce something like £800,000 worth of gold every year. Costs are high, especially for transport, the way of life induces bouts of wild extravagance when luck is with the miner, followed by periods of equally extreme frugality when business is bad, and such equipment as there is is decrepit and inefficient.

Since I had come with two geologists to try to work out a project in which the United Nations would help to introduce improved methods of exploration and exploitation, I was anxious to see what modifications had already been introduced. For most of one long, sweltering afternoon we scrambled down an interminable hillside to see a sluice that had been recently installed. After hours spent in the full heat of the sun, with no vegetation here to shade us, and after losing our way innumerable times, we were finally unable to see the sluice at close quarters, foiled by a sheer rockface falling straight into the river.

Next day we visited some small mining encampments farther downstream. Below Tipuani the river gouges its way so steeply between the mountains that there is no room even for a jeep trail along its banks. To reach the spots where gold is mined you have either to walk or else entrust yourself to a *balsa* raft, which is exhilarating but hard on the nerves. Down by the river bank the raft bobs on the turbulent surface of the water and strains at its moorings like some high-spirited filly. Shoes and socks are taken off and piled in an enormous plastic bag securely attached to the centre of the raft. The passengers roll their trouser legs as high as they can and stand braced on the flimsy *balsa* trunks, their feet wide apart, or, if they are greatly privileged, may have a narrow wooden bench lashed across the middle as a seat. As soon as the raft is unleashed it leaps forward at reckless speed, borne off on the seething current. The raftsmen pole feverishly with great dexterity. So flimsy is the craft that the slightest mishap or error seems bound to overturn it and deposit its hapless occupants in the maelstrom of water. But nothing of the kind happens. An almost nonchalant flick of the poles deftly twists the nose of the raft past the branch of a tree and other half-submerged hazards. At each of the sharp bends which speed the river's precipitate course down the mountainside the raft seems for endless minutes to be heading at breakneck speed for the rocky wall of the river bank; huge waves surge out from the shore and engulf the raft, creaming up as high as the braced knees of the passengers. When it seems already too late to avert disaster the polers, with superb timing, neatly deflect the raft back into the main stream of the river. The craft, which a moment before had seemed irretrievably submerged below the surface of the water, bounds up in a superb parabola like the flashing leap of a flying fish and once more skims the surface of the river. The raftsmen know every current by heart and exploit them skilfully. Borne on the swiftest of them one can travel many miles downstream in an unbelievably short time.

Reassured by their skill you are soon caught up in the exhilaration of speed and the beauty of the shimmering water. Tall cliffs, plumed high above with a sub-tropical profusion of trees and luxuriant undergrowth, tower upwards on either side and provide welcome shade. From time to time a narrow ledge of rock juts out from the shore. Though they are never more than a hundred yards or so long there are signs of abandoned workings at each one of them and at one there is even a pathetic ghost hamlet of a dozen dilapidated shanties strung out along the river-bank. Here, we are told, at the height of the gold-rush, there had been refrigerators, and pin-tables and beer, and even, as the ultimate in the artifacts of civilization, a jukebox moaning its plangent melodies across the river to echo back from the tall promontory on the other side.

The return journey upstream is a very different matter. On the raft it had taken us about twenty minutes to reach a wide bend in the river where a broad spit of land had sprung up and two or three families, living in rustic huts of boughs torn from the forest, were working gold placers. To return to the village of Cangallí whence we had started meant a walk of over two hours along a narrow and rocky path. The river was usually well below us as we toiled up and down the unending series of hills along its bank. Although it was dark and sunless under the thick overhanging growth of the trees, the noonday heat was at its height and the going very hard, so that before long we were soaked in sweat and labouring for breath. Once I observed far below something resembling a man's head bobbing among the turbulent waters and cried out, thinking that he was drowning. But I was told that this was the preferred way for hired labour at the mines to travel down the river to their work: they tied their clothes and belongings in a rubber bag which they clasped in front of themselves as a kind of float, and let themselves be carried down by the current. Compared with that hazardous passage even the forest path was preferable. All the same it was a great relief when we reached Cangallí and found the members of the co-operative waiting with the beer under the shade of a loofah tree. So thirsty were we that we did not even notice that it was as warm as the humid air around us; and we forbore to ask any more questions as to why so much beer is brought into Tipuani in exchange for gold.

9 BUT the principal attraction of the high valleys for the highland dwellers is as a gateway to new and less frugal lands, sub-tropical promontories breaking the headlong rush of the rivers down to the eastern plains. Wherever a road is built, no matter how rudimentary, the settlers pour in from the *altiplano*, in search of new land and an easier life. Even when the approach is only a mule track, it carries a continuous flow of spontaneous colonists, each group carrying their meagre household and personal possessions on their backs or on their heads. It is a movement reminiscent of the great pioneer treks westward in the United States during the latter part of the last century, except that here the geographical obstacles are, if anything, more obdurate, and the promised country lies to the east.

The readiness with which the prospective colonist faces the rigours of the journey, and the heavy work of the first few months when he has with his own hands to build himself a dwelling and hack out a piece of cultivable land from the virgin bush, is a measure of the even greater privations that he has suffered on the *altiplano*. The over-population of the arid highlands is a problem common to a number of Andean countries and international assistance has been given to their governments for the planning and execution of pilot settlement schemes in the valleys and lowlands. It was in this connection that I visited the Tambopata Valley in Peru with my colleague from Lima, an expert of the Food and Agriculture Organization and a Peruvian agronomist. Although this valley is in the Peruvian Yungas, just over the northern frontier of Bolivia, it is identical in aspect and conditions to the Bolivian valleys on the eastern side of the great watershed.

We started off early on a brilliant winter morning by jeep from Puno, the bleak, lakeside port on the Peruvian side of Titicaca. Most of the day we drove across the Peruvian *altiplano*, the *puna* as they call it here, so high and remote in places that just below the white peaks of Anane we saw a flock of vicuña silhouetted against the snows. Late in the afternoon, the flat highlands ended abruptly and the road began to spiral down beneath a skyline notched with jagged peaks. Farther down the hillsides were ribbed with terraces dating from Inca times. The people here were warm and friendly, softened by the influence of a gentler climate. Real flowers garlanded their round felt hats, and in a stone-built village which did not seem to have changed much from Inca times, a hump-backed Inca bridge still crossed the stream; village belles in long red embroidered dresses and flat-topped hats smiled engagingly from ancient archways; and in the patios chickens scratched among the warp and woof of primitive handlooms on which wizened old women, squatting on the bare earth, were weaving colourful cloth and shawls.

Dark had fallen by the time we reached Sandia, a prosperous market town which until recently had been the end of the road. Now a jeep track was being built towards our destination, San Juan del Oro, and had penetrated 15 kilometres beyond Sandia. We therefore decided to press on and to spend the night at the last hamlet on the roadside, in order to save as much time as possible the next morning, when we would have to start walking the remaining forty-odd kilometres. We had not gone far, however, before we were brought up short by the inevitable landslide. Though the *altiplano* was in the throes of winter drought, rain was falling heavily in the humid valleys. A brief reconnoitre with a torch convinced us that the slide was impassable. Several tons of soft wet earth had collapsed on the trail from the hillside above, obliterating it for a distance of a hundred yards and, in some places, to a depth of fifteen feet or more.

We agreed not to return to the hotel in Sandia but to spend the night at some roadside huts we had passed a couple of kilometres back on the road. This was a transit station for the colonists and for the merchants who carried supplies to San Juan del Oro and beyond. The huts were temporary affairs of boughs and twigs haphazardly arranged on wooden frames, for the air was already much warmer. Small yellow lights flickered on all sides like glow-worms; the place seemed full of people, crouching in the huts or lying outside on the ground where one had to step over the sudden dark shadow of their bodies; under the nearby trees, groups of tethered mules occasionally stamped their hooves; and from far below came the roar of a small torrent, magnified by the echoing mountain wall ahead.

Stumbling around in the moonlight, we found an open bank covered with straw that seemed fairly clean and dry, and stretched ourselves out to sleep. It was not to be a restful night. Before long, an inquisitive pig came rooting through the straw to which he clearly considered he had prior claim. Then, at about three o'clock, the sky clouded over and soon afterwards rain began to fall. We sheltered for a while beneath a corrugated iron roof nearby, but since it had no walls we were soon wet through and forced to make a run for it to the jeep where we huddled, shivering, until the dawn came.

Taking stock, we found that we had survived the mishaps of the night fairly well, although our plentiful stock of hard-boiled eggs has not taken kindly to being used as a pillow by one of the party. We were more concerned about the weather for a steady, penetrating drizzle had set in and the clouds lay low on the hilltops. We had not come prepared for rain but the problem was solved by the Peruvian agronomist, who went to the tumbledown store set up on the roadside by some enterprising capitalist, and bought several sheets of brightly coloured plastic which he pinned around our necks as makeshift capes. This we soon discovered was uniform rainwear for all colonists.

The agronomist also came back with a porter whom he had hired for the two-way journey. Mariano Cruz was a typical *altiplano* Indian from the Ayaviri area. He wore the usual shapeless felt hat, well-weathered, a rough homespun jacket with no sleeves, and breeches frayed off just below his knees. His footwear was the classic *altiplano* sandal, botched together from old motor tyres, but he was still better off than many others who made the trip unshod. He spent his time as a porter, carrying building materials or other necessities into San Juan del Oro and bringing out coffee and sub-tropical produce. He was either too poor, or had no desire, to settle in the lowlands himself and the pittance he earned with his legs and the strength of his back helped to eke out the meagre living his family obtained from a small plot in the highlands. His life was indescribably hard, yet he radiated cheerfulness and his furrowed brown face was constantly wrinkled in smiles. However heavy the burden, he seemed always to move at a sharp trot rather than a walk. But I believe he regarded portering for us as a sinecure compared to his usual work. Our various bits and pieces were laid out on the ground and rolled up together in one large cloth. It was a bulky bundle, but he swung it easily on to his back and set off with a grin.

It must also have been a novelty for him to work with *gringos*, but he did not take long to adapt to our strange way of going about things. Very early on there was a characteristic incident, after we had scrambled along the rock wall above the landslide which had barred our way the previous night. A pick-up belonging to the road-builders had remained on the farther side and the driver offered me a lift to the end of the trail. I declined, because there was only one place and I did not want to abandon my companions. Mariano found this incomprehensible but did not waste time brooding on it. When the pick-up passed us a little later it was he who waved an ecstatic greeting from the vacant seat, his bundle comfortably resting on his knee.

We did not see him again until over two hours later when we came to the last village along the jeep trail where we should have spent the previous night, a poor affair of squalid hovels sagging over the last kilometre of the new jeep trail. We had breakfast in one of these, squatting on the earth floor, and drinking coffee from blackened cups dipped into a cauldron over a wood fire, which were refilled and passed on to the next customer without any nonsense about washing up. The coffee was at least hot, and the fire warmed our chilled bones and drew steam from our clothes, already sodden in spite of our plastic capes.

The jeep trail ended at the river. There we clambered up on to a narrow, rocky footpath which hugged the contours of the hills for miles, several hundred feet above a deep river gorge. The path, though not difficult, was treacherous, and a false step or a momentary lapse of concentration might easily send one crashing far below. Mariano and the Peruvian agronomist cheered on our faltering steps with a series of stories about men and mules who had met a premature end in this way. When these were exhausted, they embarked on some scarcely more heartening anecdotes illustrating the prevalence of rattle-snakes in the neighbourhood, their viciousness and fatal efficacity.

After some hours of circling round grassy hillsides, still masked in drenching rain, we came to a hilltop where many muleteers and their trains of mules had made a halt. Before us a deeply cleft valley lay gashed in the hillside. As the crow flies the distance between the peak on which we stood and the one opposite was probably not more than a mile or so, but many hours passed before we finally flung ourselves, panting, on its crest. First we had to scramble hundreds of feet down to a decaying wooden bridge, crossing an impudently small tributary of the big river we had already left, and then make our way laboriously up the opposite slope, a notorious hill known as Wari-Wari, which at times seemed to have a gradient of one in one. Narrow and difficult as the path was, it was thronged as thickly as if it were a broad thoroughfare. Already from the halting place on the opposite side of the valley one could descry, through the trees that thinly clothed its sheer face, an unending stream of men and women passing up and down, looking, in their incongruous plastic coverings, like a column of

156

above, left: View of Potosí.
below, left: San Felipe Nery, Sucre.
above: Cerro Rico, Potosí.
below: Milluni Mine.

left: Devil dancer
before the miners
monument in Or
below, left: The
Archangel Micha
below, centre: The
Condor.
below, right: Devi
dance.

multicoloured ants, while the bells of the mule trains sounded a melancholy diapason across the canyon between.

Once on the Wari-Wari, those bells bore down on you around every corner, giving you only just enough warning to flatten yourself against the steep bank before twenty or thirty loaded mules came careering down the path. Men and women were loaded too; many of the men, bound like ourselves for the Tambopata, were often bent double under two or three heavy sheets of corrugated iron for roofing and yet they overtook us at a spanking pace that caused me shame as I struggled to catch my breath and overcome the stitch in my side. Most exhausting of all was the convention which required each and every individual, no matter in which direction he was travelling, to pass the time of day with us. With endless repetition the greeting became an antiphonal chant slowly ascending the mountainside:

'¡Buenos días, señor!'

'¡Buenos días, señor!'

'¡Buenos días, señor!'

'¡Buenos días, señorita!'

In vain, we tried to save our breath for the climb by giving a group greeting in return; their gentle but unrelenting courtesy obliged us to reply to each one. Since we must have passed hundreds and hundreds of people as we toiled on upwards, it meant that we were engaged in an almost non-stop exchange of formalities. One man was so overcome with emotion at meeting a European woman on the trail that he dropped everything, rushed forward with both hands outstretched and embraced me warmly. I thanked my lucky stars that no one else followed his example or we should never have got to the top at all.

Whether as a result of our exertions or from constant speech, we were plagued with thirst, for Mariano had bounded nimbly on ahead with the pack containing our few precious oranges and bottles of water. When finally we scrambled to the top of the last of many deceptive slopes which had promised to be final, we found him peaceably contemplating the view, looking as if he had been there for hours.

As we ate and drank, Mariano cast an appraising eye over us and decided that we were in need of comfort.

'Not far now,' he said encouragingly. 'We shall spend the night at Yanacocha.'

We looked gratefully at the trail which now led round hills of wind-rippled grass with little variation of altitude. Soon after we started off again the rain stopped, which seemed a good omen, and our clothes began to dry on our backs. To keep our spirits up we mingled our greetings to the unending stream of travellers with enquiries about the distance to Yanacocha.

'*Aquicito, no más*'—literally 'Just a little here' or 'Just over yonder'—and '*A la vueltita*' 'Round the next little bend'—chorused back the heartwarming replies, giving new strength to our weary legs.

It must have been three hours and many little bends later—certainly dusk was falling—when we at last struggled glumly into Yanacocha. I had long ago decided that I would use such remaining strength as I had to despatch the next porter who blithely announced that our resting-place was just ahead. In my anxiety to be reassured, I had forgotten that you have to be on your guard against that other endearing but infuriating law of Andean etiquette, according to which it is better to give an enquirer the kind of reply he probably wants to hear, rather than upset him with the unpalatable truth.

Yanacocha was rather a grand name for two huts perched athwart the trail, one for the porters to sleep in and the other a cookhouse and dwelling for the grimy and ragged family who provided the food. We slept, fully-dressed, on home-made wooden bunks arranged end-to-end round three walls of the hut. There were no mattresses but a few soiled blankets were provided. Some soldiers passing through shared the hut with us, and Mariano curled himself up on the floor at our feet, his hat still firmly on his head—I never saw him take it off during the whole trip—and the pack underneath as a pillow.

The next day's stint was almost worse. We washed in a nearby stream and started out early. At first the path was broad and even, though muddy from the previous day's rain, but after an hour or two we came to a stretch of five kilometres which was a permanent marsh. It was called the Marroncunca and was to prove as memorable as the Wari-Wari. Logs had at some time been laid at regular intervals to make a permanent path but it was not in good repair. To walk along it was an acrobatic feat. Every yard or so you had to leap over a yawning gap of squelching mud from one slippery, mud-slimed log to the next. It was a nightmare of mud from which there was not even the release of waking up. If you tried to leave the path and walk higher up the hillside, you sank into another morass of mud churned up by the preparations for the jeep road. I slipped and fell so many times that I almost ceased to care. My back, always troublesome, had reacted badly to the exertions and the soaking of the previous day and I almost despaired of getting out. Each footstep required a superhuman effort; at times I was stuck in the quagmire up to my calves and often the suction was so strong that I left my boot behind. Several times I sat down abruptly, covering the seat of my jeans in slime and causing my companions a good deal of unnecessary amusement. The Quechua porters were more respectful and continued to salute me with admirable gravity but it was galling to see them scurrying past under their heavy loads while I continued to flounder.

Though the rest of that day involved no more than a hard footslog, I think we had all been worn out by the Marroncunca. It was a fine day, and at this altitude of only seven or eight thousand feet, the sun beat down strongly, awakening a ravaging thirst such as I have never experienced before or since. Settlements were so few and far between that we were not even able to buy oranges in this sub-tropical paradise.

The last part of the trek was mercifully downhill, but it was one of those interminable hillsides in the style of the Wari-Wari, so steep that your toes stubbed painfully on the toecaps of your boots at every step. When, at the bottom, we came to stepping stones across the river Tambopata, we tore off our boots and sat for some time without speaking, bathing our feet in the swift water.

159

We had only a few yards farther to go. San Juan del Oro—
Saint John of the Gold, as it is romantically called, for gold was
to be found in placers in the river, though not in such quantities
as at Tipuani—was a pioneer township, a close-knit community
struggling for self-improvement against great odds. We drank
pisco that night with the locals in the fusty little bar of the one
and only *pensión* and slept on real beds with sheets in the community centre. The resources of the place were astonishing.
I had been dismayed to find that I could no longer squeeze my
swollen feet into my boots but willing messengers went off to
the local shop and brought back a selection of canvas basket-ball
boots, from which I was able to find a suitable pair—the largest
in the place they admiringly announced, to my chagrin.

In the morning, we had a long meeting in the municipality
with all the community leaders, during which we discussed the
progress of the project and the further assistance they would
require for their health service, their school and their agricultural projects. After lunch, we were already back on that horren-
dous trail, returning the way we had come, and managed to
scale the first enormous hill by nightfall. At one of the few
hamlets along the wayside we obtained permission to spend the
night in the schoolroom, using the trestle tables as beds. We
were all feeling exhausted and I at least secretly wondering
whether I could hold out physically until we reached the jeep
trail again. As we sat on the tables eating some tinned meat and
bread by torchlight, the door was thrust open and in came three
husky young American boys, Peace Corps Volunteers, straight
out of college. Compared with our rudimentary preparations,
their equipment was magnificent. Folding beds emerged from
their rucksacks, inflatable mattresses complete with a miniature
hand-pump, and warm, light sleeping-bags. They had special
iron rations, whose vitamin, protein and calory content had
been carefully calculated, and even some sultanas and nuts
which they generously passed round. But they were dropping
with fatigue to the point of no longer speaking to one another.
They too were on their way to San Juan del Oro but were to
spend a few days there carrying out a nutrition survey. The

news that we had arrived there only the night before and were already on our way back seemed to increase their exhaustion by sympathetic reaction. Perversely, we felt stimulated by the realization that even people much younger and physically fitter than ourselves found this an ordeal and that we were at least in better spirits than they.

The three boys did not stir next day at dawn when we eased our cramped limbs off the table tops, packed up our things and left. It was certainly a forced march and, as far as I was concerned, was accomplished by willpower alone, for my legs and feet seemed no longer to belong to me. A mule had been hired for me, but it was a particularly temperamental one and slipped so often on the stones that I felt I would rather trust my own feet. The decision was clinched for me rather dramatically by a bull which appeared suddenly round a bend, blocking the narrow path, and throwing the mule into such a frenzy that it reared on its hind legs, very nearly throwing me down the steep hillside. After that I walked, and Mariano loaded his pack on to the mule's back without surprise, no doubt regarding it as quite consistent with the strange ways of foreigners to hire a mule and then not ride on it.

It was eight o'clock at night before we finally staggered on to the jeep trail by the river, and sank to the ground. There we sat, by the light of two candle-stumps stuck to the road, until the jeep reached us from our halting place of three days previously. The last part of the walk had been gruelling. Somehow we had survived the swamps of Marroncunca, the descent of the Wari-Wari, which was almost as tiring as the ascent, and the long drag up the opposite side of the valley. After that, however, the trail round the hilltops had seemed interminable. I had developed an outsize blister on one big toe, which later turned out to be as large as the toe itself, and made every step agony. Dusk was creeping up rapidly between the hills and many groups were already encamped for the night, the fires alight under their cooking pots. The temptation just to throw oneself down by the side of the path and sink into sleep was overwhelming. In just over three days, we had covered about one

161

hundred kilometres in very difficult conditions. Somehow, however, Mariano kept us plodding on, leading the way with his laden mule and stopping from time to time to shout back words of encouragement. The worst part of all was negotiating the most dangerous stretch where the valley narrowed towards its head, and the precipice, down which so many men and mules had crashed to their death, if our local companions were to be believed, dropped sheer away from the rocky path at our feet. In two or three places waterfalls cascaded across the path and the going became even more difficult. At last, however, we saw a wavering torch-light ahead of us. One of the party, with greater stamina, had reached the road ahead of us and came back to help us along the rest of the way which we accomplished without incident.

Mariano, who had spent every night at our feet, said to me with great feeling for the mournfulness of the occasion, if not for the proprieties, 'This is the last night that we shall sleep together, señorita.'

However, even that was denied him. Since the landslide had been cleared, we reached Sandia by jeep that same night and slept in the only hotel, a very modest establishment which nonetheless seemed the height of luxury compared with the rigours of the previous nights. Poor Mariano was left standing by the river, holding the hired mule that must be returned across the mountains, and the brim of the hat that was so inseparable a part of his person seemed to be drooping more disconsolately than ever.

A few months afterwards, the jeep trail reached San Juan del Oro. By now, it may well have been pushed on to the flat plains of the Madre de Díos, more suitable for settlement and cultivation than the high valleys where handkerchiefs of land are tilted at such impossible angles that it seems both ploughman and oxen must lose their balance and fall, and every furrow turned spells incipient erosion. But there are many who will still be walking that trail today, while thousands of others will be toiling up and down the steep valleys in eastern Bolivia and Peru, where no jeep trail has yet reached, performing daily miracles of endurance and courage in their search for a new life which will be only a little less unbearable than the one they have left behind them on the *altiplano*. And Mariano perhaps is still tramping anything up to a hundred miles a week up hill and down dale, carrying in stores and bringing out produce.

Not all the intermediate levels of the Bolivian Andes are so steeply canted as the Yungas, and settlement in these more accessible places is older in origin. The descent to Cochabamba and Sucre, though rugged, is more gradual, and the towns themselves repose in broader valleys which make cultivation and habitation easier. Both were established soon after the Conquest, for their gentler climate no doubt recalled to the Spanish invaders the delights of Andalusia. The gentleness and gaiety has left its imprint not only on the climate and the landscape but also on the inhabitants. This is Quechua land, inhabited by the descendants of those outposted settlers whom the Incas sent beyond the limits of the conquered Aymara areas, to guard the fringes of the Empire. Smiles respond more swiftly here, and the music loses some of its harshness, taking on a lingering plaintive lilt. One feels that the language, slow and reflective, exists for the sake of its poetic cadences alone. No one is in any hurry to get to the point. Once, when we stopped to ask a Quechua Indian the way, we were treated to a ten-minute speech during which his eloquent arms repeatedly embraced the horizon as if pointing out the road. Patiently, we heard him out. When at last he fell silent with a quiet smile, we asked the driver what he had said, but were quite unprepared for the terse reply:

'He says he doesn't know.'

Even when they speak Spanish, the Quechuas manage to temper its angularity with frequent diminutives, giving it an archaic, sixteenth-century flavour.

The blander air of the countryside makes itself felt with every passing minute if you make the descent towards Sucre from the stony moorlands of Otavi, in the department of Potosí. Such a journey is best made in crisp winter weather, and started before

163

dawn, when the chill dark is stippled with the fires of other travellers, dim, pinched figures, stretching limbs frozen from a night in the open with only a poncho as protection against the upland frost and stoking a fire of peat-like *yareta* under the blackened cooking-pots in which they heat a glutinous porridge-like mixture of *quinua*, probably their only hot meal for the day. Beside them the llamas also stir, craning their long necks and fixing the coming day, now faintly breaking, with a stare of infinite and crushing disdain. They say that llamas weep every morning until the sun rises, lamenting their ancient Inca masters, the sons of the Sun; and it is true that one can hear them groaning softly to themselves, though the cold is likely to be the more mundane explanation.

These llama caravans and their drovers travel for many weeks at a time, often carrying salt down into the valleys from the salt-flats of Uyuni, each animal carrying no more than two of the greyish-brown blocks of crystal, strapped on either side of its back. Progress is slow; they cover only a few miles each day and at night encamp in the open, wherever nightfall catches them.

This is a landscape littered by boulders, bleached white by the weather, an ossified land where, in winter, the dried-up watercourses that cross and re-cross the road, and the dry stone walls, which tortuously dissect the hillsides, create a skeletal geography of their own, seared into aridity by sun and wind and frost. The lane that threads through its contorted anatomy, with its water-worn slabs and flints, seems a case of lost identity, a river that in a moment of aberration became a road.

Almost absent-mindedly that road leads down to Betanzos, a bustling market town linking valley and mountain, crowded with lorry-loads of country-folk who come from many miles around for the renowned Sunday market and for splendid, colourful *fiestas* where the dancers twirl in endless serpentines, lubricated by gallons of beer and *chicha*, and the guitars and *charangos* twang tirelessly for hours, or even days, on end. For ten kilometres or more on the other side of Betanzos you will meet people trudging to the fair, driving before them a loaded donkey or a small huddle of sheep. Not for them the drab attire of the *altiplano* where man tries to pass unperceived by making himself indistinguishable from the land around him. Here the ponchos are a jaunty red and are flaunted with panache by their owners who come, in groups or singly, each one strumming his *charango*, a small, stringed instrument traditionally hollowed out from the spiny shell of the armadillo, but sometimes copied more cheaply in wood. Even the lone travellers play to keep themelvses company as they walk, to get fingers and feet into trim for the *fiesta*. The air vibrates with the high-pitched sound and staccato rhythms of hundreds of *charangos* converging on Betanzos from all directions, until its seems as if the music flows from the earth and permeates the atmosphere, while the never-ending procession of bright figures winding along the hillside road, or making their way towards it across the neighbouring fields, resembles, in its colour and fantasy, some rich and motley pageant.

Music is the stuff of everyday life here, the medium through which the countryman uninhibitedly expresses his joys and cares, his hopes and fears; it is an art, cultivated with exquisite care and formality, but it is also the humdrum companion and confidant of each day's labours. There is a certain Elizabethan quality in the vitality which throbs through the haunting Quechua songs and melodies, and in the lyricism which translates lived experience with such directness, ease, and grace into popular expression.

Except for a brief rainy season for two months or so each year the countryside here is dry. Though it is much lower already than the *altiplano* you do not find the green, dense valleys of Yungas. It is a sun-soaked, tawny land of broad vales and sweeping downs, stretching itself secretly and luxuriously in the tepid warmth like some large and somnolent animal. But the impression is not one of passivity but rather of hidden, tensile strength, strong muscles flexed beneath the quiet flanks of the hills, of a quality essentially feline and tiger-like. Where deep river beds have chiselled a ragged course between the ridges the dusty road coils down between brindled hillsides splashed with fields of golden stubble. A bronzed and ochre country, it is unrelieved by green except where the delicately-fronded acacias crowd alongside the scant watercourses or where, on the roadside banks, the agaves loom like sentinels picketing the distant horizon.

As you draw nearer Sucre the signs of long settlement, and of a certain degree of ease and comfort, so conspicuously absent in the rest of Bolivia, begin to multiply. Over the Pilcomayo, forging its broad way down towards Paraguay and the River Plate, you suddenly come to a bizarre bridge slung between two portentous towers bristling with crenellated turrets in a profusion reminiscent of Victorian Gothic architecture, or perhaps intended by its ambitious designer to recall the splendours of the Rhineland. Alas! in its functioning it inclines rather towards the tradition of Bolivian bridges: the pretentious construction with its intricate struts and wires suspends nothing more solid than a narrow passage of slatted wood, part of which is more often than not dangling forlornly in mid-air, so that you have to make your way through the fast-flowing channel below, with a small boy wading ahead to find the shallowest and firmest parts where a vehicle may pass. Farther on, the road is bordered by high, moss-grown walls, crumbling through age and neglect, affording glimpses, where the stones have fallen away, of dilapidated mansions, once magnificent, and now marooned in the midst of their ruined Italianate gardens and pleasances, where the trim box walks are overgrown, the pseudo-Grecian forms of the pillars and the statuary are obscured by a luxuriance of rank rose growth and the mildewed gazebos genteelly decay on top of their artificial eminences under the encroaching fingers of the undergrowth. There are orchards of aged fruit trees that have not felt the pruner's knife for many years and a few spreading cedars cast a mournful shade over the forgotten elegance of a lost age.

It is a fitting prelude to the entry to Sucre, which seems perennially bewildered at finding itself in the twentieth century. Although it is the legal capital of Bolivia, and the Supreme Court is located there, it has none of the other trappings of government and seems to relapse thankfully into being a quiet backwater. Not that it was always so. Since its foundation in 1538, one or other of its four famous names—Charcas, La Plata, Chuquisaca and Sucre—has reverberated through the annals of Bolivian history at all its most dramatic moments. In colonial times Chuquisaca was the seat of the rich and powerful Audiencia of Charcas within the Viceroyalty of Lima and later of La Plata, and held sway over most of modern Bolivia and, at various times, over Paraguay, much of Argentina and the coastal region of Atacama now incorporated in Chile. Nor was its leadership merely political and economic; its reputation as a centre of culture and learning earned it the title of the 'Athens of America', in competition with Bogotá, and its University of San Javier, founded in the sixteenth century, became the centre of advanced liberal ideas on the continent. It was there that the first cry of freedom from the Peninsular yoke rang out on 25 May 1809.

There is not much of a revolutionary swagger about Sucre today, and it is doubtful if it was ever very revolutionary by modern standards. Gabriel René Moreno, in his book *The Last Days of the Colony in Upper Peru*, describes it as a centre of constant polemic, but his references to scholasticism and the duplicity of society convey an atmosphere of sterile argument rather than intellectual ferment; and Simón Rodríguez, Bolívar's tutor, sent to Chuquisaca in 1823 to try out his new system of education, had to confess failure and close his school in the face of traditional opposition.

'Only you understand,' he wrote to Bolívar, 'because you see things as I do, that to make a new republic you must first make a new people.'

Sucre was the home of the Bolivian aristocracy, the *criollo* families who had amassed their fortunes in the New World, surrounding themselves with wealth and comfort and *objets d'art* brought from Europe, and who wished to have freedom to enjoy these privileges and direct their country's destiny without interference from a mother-country whose interests were felt to be increasingly alien. The standard of freedom which they raised for the first time in the Americas threw a very short

167

shadow: it did not embrace the rights of the Indians who slaved in the mines or of the peasants dispossessed of land in order to provide the broad acres of their *haciendas* and well-proportioned gardens. Though the centre of power had been translated to the Andes, Sucre continued to look towards Europe; it is no accident that the two main hotels today, long past their prime, are called nostalgically París and Londres. Life continued very comfortably during the nineteenth century and the early part of the twentieth. The names of several well-known Sucre families figure on the admittedly long list of Bolivian Presidents. Children were educated in Europe and most families travelled there regularly, despite the difficulties of the journey, or contrived to be posted there on diplomatic missions. Some of the wealthiest even purchased titles of nobility and there was a brief flowering of counts and marquises and even princes, described by Arguedas as 'the cult of aristocracy'. Everyone brought back collections of porcelain and pictures and fine French furniture which, added to the colonial treasures handed down as family heirlooms, made Sucre an oasis of culture and elegance in a rugged, uncouth age.

By a strange paradox, the town which sparked off the rebellion against Spanish rule has confirmed and deepened its own intrinsic Spanishness in the century and a half that has elapsed since then. Once the tides of nationalist feeling and of a revolutionary zeal to redress the wrongs suffered for centuries by the Indians swept across the country, Sucre closed her gates, and the new currents flowed round her, leaving her as an island of tradition. As a result, Sucre seems to have turned in upon herself. It is an enchanting town that somehow falls short of reality, like a film set carefully designed in every detail that yet fails to create the impression of life. The paved square at the top of a hill above the town commands a view of the cobbled streets that ramble down to the main *plaza* and of russet roofs clustering round the towers and belfries of many churches, and the large bulk of the cathedral. There are some imposing buildings, such as the Palace of Justice and the University, and ecclesiastical architecture of a rather florid type predominates.

168

In contrast, the houses present a deceptively simple exterior to the passer-by, a long immaculately white wall under the overhanging tiled eaves, anonymously blank, pierced infrequently, if at all, by a high iron grille, and at street level only by an unobstrusive door. Beyond the door, however, one enters another world of colonnades and patios paved with worn flagstones, a dim, walled world, fretted with the delicate tracery of ferns, enhanced by the dark gloss of the leaves of orange trees, and threaded with the sound of water tinkling from small fountains. The smell of jasmine hangs in the air. One might be in Seville or Granada. The houses are rambling and old, with flower-shrouded balconies from which bougainvillea and geraniums tumble in profusion to the patio below. They are houses that have been lived in for three or four centuries, built haphazardly to accommodate the needs of succeeding generations. One passes from one treasure-laden room to the next where riches of the colonial epoch rub shoulders with *objets d'art* brought back from Europe. Yet nowadays, the unmistakable smell of poverty hangs over all this wealth. One sits in a carved high-backed chair sipping tea out of delicate porcelain that has crossed the Atlantic and the Andes, fingering the exquisite contours of an ivory triptych or admiring the tooled leather of an old colonial travelling chest and listens to the sad tales of elderly people who find the world different from the one they knew when they were young but who still try to cling to its outward trappings. As one looks at these proud, disillusioned faces, one feels sure that they would rather forgo a meal than dispose of a single one of their treasures. They are loud in their strictures of the new order and it is useless to contradict. There do not seem to be any young people in these houses any more, only the shuffling footsteps of the old, echoing along the flagged passages. A museum-like atmosphere pervades these homes, for all the exuberance of their blossoming balconies. It is a world in eclipse, waning inexorably into the yellowing twilight of its own dim patios.

As one would expect, Sucre is a conservative town. You are more conscious of religion here than in the rest of Bolivia, though nowhere is it as immanent as in Bogotá or Quito, where the streets are thronged with black-robed priests. Here one seems to come across a church at every corner, small baroque churches with dark interiors, fusty with the incense of centuries. Sucre is rich in ecclesiastical treasures. They include a miraculous Virgin, the Virgin of Guadalupe, who has been the object of so many votive offerings that her jewels and ornaments are said to be of fabulous value. She is heavily guarded in a revolving iron case but if you are privileged you may be allowed to see her. It is a disappointing experience for she is so cluttered with precious stones, huge emeralds, and diamonds and rubies, jewelled watches, brooches and pendants pinned on to her brocade gown wherever there happened to be a space, that the beauty of individual ornaments is overshadowed to the point of tawdriness and the total effect is unaesthetic. The story is told that, not so long ago, a progressive archbishop suggested that the wealth of the Virgin of Guadalupe might be sold and the proceeds used to succour the many poor of the dioceses. There was an immediate public outcry and the loudest and most outraged protests came from those same poor, who were scandalized that their revered Virgin should be desecrated in this way. The great majority of them were Indians but the gesture was unmistakably Spanish. So the Virgin of Guadalupe continues to preside over new miracles in a gown encrusted, like that of some *nouvelle riche*, with the incongruous gems of wealthy penitents.

Two or three hours away, over the burnished hills beyond Sucre, you come to the village of Tarabuco where the men still wear foreshortened ponchos and black felt bonnets painstakingly moulded into the shape of the breastplates and helmets that the Spanish conquistadors wore as part of their armour when they first fought their way here over four hundred years ago. The helmets are decorated round the brim with brightly-coloured embroidered braid and sequins but the likeness is unmistakable and one may still recognize the Indian from Tarabuco anywhere by his black and red striped poncho and his archaic headgear.

When I came back to Sucre once after visiting Tarabuco and

170

was dining at the Hotel Londres (contrary to one's expectations, it is deemed best to eat at the Londres and stay at the París, though the cuisine at the former is not noticeably European, while the plumbing at the latter is unmistakably of French inspiration) when an American acquaintance from La Paz rushed up exuding concern and ominous predictions.

'Tarabuco?' he said. 'Didn't you know that they've got an outbreak of bubonic plague?'

One might really have been back in the sixteenth century. But though I could not find a chemist open to make up the antidote kindly prescribed by my friend, I did not, luckily, contract the disease. However, when I arrived in New York a few days later, it provided a good riposte to the health officer monotonously reciting the interminable list of dread maladies to which I had exposed myself by living in such outlandish places, and on the first sign of any or all of which I must immediately present myself and a bilious-looking card to the nearest doctor.

'*And* bubonic plague,' I added helpfully when he had finished his dreary catalogue.

He gave me a distinctly odd look, as if wondering whether to rebuke me for being facetious, and passed on to the next person.

The road from Sucre to Cochabamba follows a roundabout route, probing its way across the mountains through linking valleys. In part it cuts across the edge of the region which, farther to the south-east, merges into the hot lands of the Chaco where the Bolivians lost the disastrous war with Paraguay thirty years ago. Even here, on its farthest margin, the earth is already sandy and barren, covered only by a vegetation of thin scrub and a weird forest of outsize, monolithic cacti.

Rivers are troublesome here too. Once, when a new bridge had been swept away by the current, we had to send our Land-Rover back on the three-day détour to La Paz, via Sucre, Potosí and Oruro, and continue ourselves in a bus which was waiting on the other side, packed with people and squawking chickens. Travelling on a bus in Bolivia is fun, except that most of the drivers tend to drive alarmingly fast on the dangerous mountain roads. But one's comfort, if not one's safety, is a matter of communal concern, as are one's destination, business, country of origin and even the members of one's family. At mealtimes the bus draws up at some pre-appointed wayside inn where thick steaming soup is already being put out on long trestle tables and the hot spicy smell of *aji* tickles the nostrils from afar.

The last part of the journey recalls the forgotten luxury of a paved road, for it covers part of (what was until 1965, at least) the only stretch of macadam in Bolivia, the highway between Cochabamba and the tropical town of Santa Cruz de la Sierra. But we turn back up into the mountains, and emerge on the long, fertile valley of Punata, a rich agricultural land scattered with dark clumps of feathery eucalyptus and yellow fields of maize. Yet this peaceful, bucolic aspect is illusory, belied by the long history of bloodshed and cruel feuding between the villages of Cliza and Ucureña.

At the far end, under the lee of the bare ochreous hills leading back to Oruro and La Paz, lies Cochabamba, the second city of Bolivia, enjoying a climate that is not unjustly described as eternal spring. Flowers grow everywhere in Cochabamba, all the year round. Bougainvillea wreathes the ugliest iron lamp-posts, and cascades over every available wall. Gardens and public squares float in a pervasive violet cloud of jacaranda blossom and pink and white oleanders march primly along the edge of the pavements.

Cochabamba is opposite in temperament to Sucre. This is the Bolivian equivalent of the bustling commercial city. There is industry here, small but growing, based mainly on the processing of the agricultural produce from the rich surrounding area. This is not an introspective town like Sucre, turned in upon itself in endless contemplation of a glorious past. Here everything is modern and externalized. There are many houses of recent construction with neat gardens laid out in front instead of the interior patios. Life is lived in the street here and not behind closed walls: in the Avenida Ballivián, where the pretty

172

left: Road to Yungas.
below: Sorata.
bottom: Market above Sorata, with
the Illampu in the background.

left: Cochabamba market woman.
above: Women from Arana, near Cochabamba
below: Harvesting maize in the Cochabamba valley.

girls stroll up and down the tree-lined centre of the street, and the band plays on Sunday; in the cafés, where men sit hunched over plastic-topped tables discussing the latest turn of political events; in the *chicherías*—bars or simply private houses, where the white flag hanging on a stick outside beckons with the welcoming message '*¡Hay chicha!*'—the sweetish, cloying maize beer, which is the staple drink of the *Valle*. If you see how it is made, they say—by toothless old Indian crones patiently chewing the grains of maize before they are fermented —you will never touch it again.

But there is intellectual ferment here too. In contrast to Sucre, wrapped in the chrysalis of history, and to La Paz where, by some curiously stultifying effect of the altitude and the cold, ideas, though in constant ebullition, yet seem to conform to well-defined trends, Cochabamba leans towards modernity and is always in the *avant-garde*. It is hard to imagine that as recently as 1906 the authorities had to intervene to prevent a Protestant preacher from being burnt alive on a pyre of his own evangelical books, but could not stop the angry mob from stoning the infidels.

Today, the University of San Simón seethes with new and startling ideas which, though often badly assimilated, act as a catalyst on the life of the nation. It is no coincidence that the seeds of many of Bolivia's revolutions have germinated in Cochabamba. The *cochabambino* is in any case a byword in the country: he is the go-getter, the entrepreneur, the meritocrat who gains all the best positions in the government, in business or in politics, comparable to the *antioqueño* in Colombia, or, in continental Latin-American terms, to the Chilean. The *cochabambino*, if you like, plays the same rôle in the life of Bolivia as the Scotsman does in England.

There are some who say that the capital should be transferred to Cochabamba and once or twice, in deference to the failing health of visiting heads of state, whose medical advisers have not wished to expose them to a heavy official programme at four thousand metres, the seat of government, epitomized in the President, the Cabinet, the Presidential car, the state silver and plate, and the Diplomatic Corps, has creaked down to Cochabamba by train, or battled its way through the spiralling dust of the road over the mountains. A permanent transfer seems improbable, however. La Paz remains indisputably the centre of the state, although Cochabamba provides much of the driving force.

One always feels that Cochabamba is about to erupt, that restless passion constantly throbs beneath the apparently normal exterior of everyday life. Even in the Cochabamba Hotel, the rural peace of a garden wreathed in bougainvillea and climbing geraniums is shattered at an unbearably early hour each dawn by the strident bells of the neighbouring church, remorselessly banging in the dawn; while at the Capitol, in the centre, you will be jerked awake, after an evening with Cochabamba friends during which the conversation has turned unrelievedly on the inevitability of imminent public disturbances, by wild cries conveying to a half-wakened and apprehensive mind the impression of a massed and angry crowd forging through the town, of the heavy wheels of tumbrils already grinding past, only to discover, when you hang out of the window, half-dressed, over a placid lamp-lit street, that it is the cinema disgorging its late-night audience after the triumphant finale of some Wild Western, transmitted by acoustic excess into the neighbouring hotel bedrooms.

It is somehow in keeping with this brashness that Cochabamba should boast the Palacio Portales, a magnificent mansion built by Patiño, with no thought for expense, taste, or aesthetic harmony. The interior of this monstrosity is so liberally provided with pseudo-classical statuary, and designed in such a variety of styles, from austere marble halls, to the ultimate fantasy of a billiard room, heavily decorated and tiled in the Morisco style and seeming almost to have been transported, as it stands, from the Alhambra, that the senses are quite confounded. It is the *nouveau riche* gone almost beserk. Less startling but hardly less deplorable is Patino's country mansion, built a few miles out in the valley, in the midst of a rich agricultural estate, and in a splendid position under the lee of the hills. I was not able to go

174

inside, but was taken round the grounds by an old retainer well-versed in stories of the thirty or forty European artists, Italian architects, Japanese gardeners, and the like, who had been commissioned to build something that would dumbfound Bolivia. The result is certainly staggering, though not perhaps in the way its originator intended. According to my guide, the house, which had then been built just over thirty years previously, had been inhabited perhaps for a total of three or four months in the intervening period. A vast marble mausoleum occupies a large area in front of the house, dominating the Cochabamba valley, and marked by a boulder said to contain part of the first vein of tin discovered by Patiño, which laid the foundation of his colossal fortune; it speaks eloquently for itself as the self-dedicated monument of the 'local boy who made good'. But it seems that Bolivia is the preferred residence only after death.

And yet there is a certain anomaly about the brashness and modernity of Cochabamba, set in the midst of a pastoral region where tradition, too, remains deeply-rooted. Often, the first sight to greet you, as you emerge from the compact little airport on the outskirts of the town, is a peasant woman gracefully riding her panniered donkey side-saddle as she makes her slow progress to market along the dust-laden road outside, her skirts decorously draped around her. They are stately and beautiful, these Cochabamba women, women of character, like those who defended the city against the loyalist Spaniards in 1811, heroically led by Juana de Padilla, and who are commemorated by a rather bleak memorial on the San Sebastián hill above the town.

The *campesina* of Cochabamba today wears her tall white wide-brimmed hat, neatly encircled by narrow black ribbon, at a provocative angle. Not that there is much scope for subterfuge, for one is assured that the discerning male can tell by a glance at the number and form of the loops of ribbon round the crown, whether the wearer is single, married or a widow. These same hats bob incongruously on the backs of lorries, crystal-white in the sunshine, an emblem of constancy in the midst of rapid change. In the backstreets of Cochabamba and of Potosí the manufacture and repair of these hats is a flourishing local industry. From a distance, they appear to be made of hard straw but in reality the basis is a hand-crocheted material, so finely worked that it takes one person about a month to complete the fabric for a single hat. This rather floppy article is then starched and shaped, and finally stiffened and whitened to the consistency almost of shiny white-painted board by the application of white oxide. In spite of their light colour and generally fragile appearance, these hats last for years, and can often be refurbished by a fresh coat of oxide and a new ribbon.

At least they do not have to be discarded prematurely because fashion in millinery in Bolivia is a regional characteristic rather than a matter of changing public taste. With a little practice it is soon easy to distinguish where a woman comes from by what she wears on her head. In and around La Paz the severe bowler, usually black, is regulation headgear for the Aymara women. As one moves further south and east into Quechua country, the bowler gives way to the tall stovepipe hat, broad-brimmed, and slightly narrower at the flat-topped crown than at the base, a sort of Andean imitation of a Welshwoman's traditional hat. In the warmer valleys, as in Cochabamba, it is a glistening white encircled in black ribbon; in the colder uplands of Oruro (where there is still a considerable intermingling of bowlers) and Potosí it is in dark brown or black or even bottle-green felt. For *fiestas* very weighty and elaborate styles are worn; they also vary according to the region, but are usually made of brightly-coloured silks and velvets, heavily embroidered in sequins and pearls. Less sophisticated ladies in the rural areas wear greasy round felt pudding basins, indistinguishable from those of their menfolk. But however poor they are, they never go bareheaded, for the hat is a status symbol in Bolivia as well as a protection against the bleak highland winds.

By a strange convention, perhaps not so distant from the social shibboleths of more advanced communities, a man's wealth and standing are judged by the number of hats his wife possesses. I remember once visiting the house of a chauffeur

176

working at a rural development base. His salary was not large, though it must have seemed enormous in comparison with the poverty of the *campesinos* living round about, and he and his wife lived in one room, with almost no furniture whatsoever apart from a bed and a couple of rough-hewn chairs. The floor was of bare earth, the walls of adobe, and their few clothes were slung on a cord stretched across the room. But every available space on the wall was occupied by a bowler hat, hanging from a nail. There were perhaps twenty of them, all identical in shape, which is dictated by tradition, and varying only in colour; there were black ones, brown ones and fawn ones, but that was about the extent of the differentiation. One wondered when their privileged owner had time to wear them all and how on earth she chose between them.

The Foreign Office in La Paz bears one striking resemblance to its English counterpart in Downing Street: it, too, is full of bowler hats but the difference is that in the Andean capital they are sported by female suppliants rather than by aspiring diplomats. Little girls are no exception: almost as soon as they can start to toddle they are dressed in an exact replica of their mothers' apparel. The hat is usually a faded affair, turning green round its curling brim, that has been handed down from an elder sister or even from mother herself, so that it often lodges unbecomingly on the young wearer's ears, to the partial, if not complete, detriment of her vision. But in spite of this inauspicious start, she will, like her sisters, develop a faultless ability to tilt her hat at its most alluring angle. Somehow this charming coquetry, so out of place with the grim surroundings, epitomizes the unfailing resilience of both Aymara and Quechua women.

The Spanish quality that still pervades some aspects of urban life in Bolivia is especially strong in the larger valley towns, and in the villages clinging beneath the lowering crags of the Eastern Cordillera. Cochabamba is an exception, impregnated with a sense of industry and a desire for commercial gain that are rare in other settlements dozing in the warmer climate of the high valleys. In Tarija you will find the same pattern of patios and blossoming balconies as in Sucre, the same manifestations of pride in the past, and contempt for the present, the same individualism which no one seems to find incompatible with the profound conviction that life is a predestined and circumscribed affair in which each has his appointed place and his appointed rôle. The roots of feudalism are still deep here, despite the cataclysmic changes of recent years. They help to explain the typically Spanish attitude towards manual labour, a peninsular concept fostered by the continued availability of cheap or even gratis, labour. In these towns it is not difficult to understand how Bolivia lived for so long behind its mountains, breathing the musty, confined air of Spanish traditionalism.

Regionalism is also inherited from Spain and has been reinforced by the geographical barriers which made travel even between relatively highly-populated areas of the country a matter of high adventure until only a few years ago. Even today the regional traits ascribed by popular belief to the inhabitants of various areas often have some basis in fact. While the *cochabambino* is the ambitious and industrious go-getter, and the *chuquisaqueño*—from Sucre—is the conservative intellectual still living in the stiff, high collars of the nineteenth century, the *tarijeño* is the gentle laughing-stock of the rest of the Republic, pictured as lounging on the banks of the Guadalquivir, rather like the Mexican typically portrayed with his large straw hat slumped over his eyes, slow of speech and thought, and too lazy to bestir himself even in his own interest or protection. Whenever a joke in Bolivia relates the antics of a buffoon or of someone rather slow in the uptake, you may be sure that the individual will be dubbed a *tarijeño*. Not even the fact that one of the most active and hard-working of Bolivian Presidents came from Tarija has shaken this particular myth. More authentic is the *chapaco* music from Tarija, wild, harsh singing, often commenting on events of rural life or on love, which, in its passionate intensity and the number of tones produced by the singer within a small compass, is reminiscent of *cante hondo*, an echo of Andalusia and of ancient Moorish and

178

gypsy influence strangely transposed to the Andes and quite unlike any other Bolivian music.

For there is at the same time a curious variety about these valley towns. On the sun-drenched hill-slopes of Camargo, to the north of Tarija, vines are cultivated. Sorata, in the Department of La Paz, also has an indefinably Mediterranean air as it sprawls down a steep escarpment beneath the snow-covered hulk of the Illampu, but its jumble of weathered tile roofs is Italianate rather than Spanish, recalling those compact Etruscan hill villages that began as mediaeval forts.

At the other end of the Royal Cordillera the long valley winding down to Quime from the jagged, triple-peaked summit of Quimsa Cruz could be a Scottish glen, suffused with the pink spires of foxgloves and loud with the noise of its rushing trout-brown streams. Quime is again different, tucked away in a thickly-wooded valley, where the young stands of eucalyptus veil the hillsides in a tender mist of blue and purple. Yet it stands out in my memory chiefly because of an encounter with a young American Peace Corps volunteer, the only foreigner in the small town. It was he who sought us out in the only inn, with its inevitable cobbled patio and outside tap, overjoyed to find English-speaking company. Over a glass of whisky he told us that he was working as sanitary inspector on the strength of a six weeks' course in public health after graduating in political science. This poor young man had been isolated for nearly a year in this enclosed valley, without even a national team of doctors and nurses to work with him. One had to admire his dogged persistence in the face of many frustrations. To encourage him I remarked that I had been impressed to see, on a walk earlier that evening, that the town actually boasted a public lavatory—a most unusual facility in Bolivia—decorously divided into *varones* and *mujeres*. It turned out, however, that this civic monument was the young man's despair and obsession for its cement floor contained no drainage whatsoever and was hardly less of a health hazard than the street corners and walls of buildings used before it was built. The young man had got it into his head that the solution was to cut a number of triangular-shaped holes—no other form would do—into the floor, although this would merely dump the excreta into the river below. This however, was the recurrent refrain of his conversation and the burden, one gathered, of his daily, fruitless negotiations with the mayor and other dignitaries of the town, all, alas, equally slow to grasp the significance of these magic triangles. It was almost ludicrous and yet one felt desperately sorry for this young man, trying so hard to justify his presence and the sacrifice of a year of his life in this enclave of settlement, sealed away for centuries on the far side of the mountains.

You can see the innate conservatism of most of the valley towns reflected in the decorous precision and almost military regularity of their *plazas*, all built to the old Spanish formula, with the church or cathedral along one side of the square and the temporal power, in the form of the Prefectura, or the mayor's office, on the adjacent side. The resistance to change symbolized by this rigid adherence to the old forms is one of the greatest obstacles to Bolivian development, especially when it occurs in these outlying towns on the eastern side of the *cordillera*, which ought to be the spearheads of development towards the untapped natural wealth of the *Oriente*.

La Chaskañawi, a novel written in the 'twenties by Carlos Medinacelli, describes the stultifying monotony of these small towns in San Javier de Chirca, where the only distractions were alcohol, *fiestas* and politics and the hero, Adolfo Reyes, a young man of good family who has come from his legal studies at Chuquisaca University to collect an inheritance, seems to spend his days dancing and drinking *chicha* beer or *yungueños* (cocktails of *singani*, the grape brandy, and orange juice, in a self-defeating attempt to cure the *ch'aqui*, or hangover, of the day before. He is saved from complete decadence only by his love for the *Chaskañawi*, a beautiful *chola*, full of the resolution and energy which he lacks, and with whom he settles down to a simple and hardworking life upon a farm. There he reflects that his intellectual, Western European education has done him irreparable harm, and has broken his will without putting anything in its place; there is a terrible gulf between the metaphysical formation of his mind and the wild countryside about him, which can only be bridged by *La Chaskañawi* who, being *mestiza*, represents the harmonization of the Spanish and the Indian heritage.

The thesis and the symbolism are somewhat forced and full of contradictions since they are themselves impregnated with the European *fin-de-siècle* ideas rejected by the book, being in the Rousseauesque and Romantic tradition of 'the noble savage!' But the picture of the *tedium vitae* in the towns of the high valleys, the conflicts between the Spanish and the Indian heritage, and the need to adapt the Bolivian educational system to the requirements of everyday life, is still valid today.

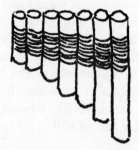

10 BOLIVIA descends in a trio of steps from the high *cordillera* in the west of the territory, down through the high valleys to the eastern plains, which they say were discovered by the Inca Emperor, Tito Yupanqui, who, however, preferred to keep the knowledge secret, lest his peoples be tempted to leave their austere highlands.

But it is a capricious kind of staircase that as often as not makes you climb up again to new heights before you reach a lower level. Over the valley of Cochabamba broods the Tunari, a tall peak scarved at all seasons with the faintest tippet of snow. Even though you have toiled over the interminable mountain road from La Paz and Oruro, where the stark moorlands alternate with vistas of steep valleys and tangled crags, piled pell-mell upon one another until the farthest point of the horizon, in a welter of every conceivable colour from deep red to slate blue, you still have to surmount new barriers before you come to the tropical *llanos*.

If you wish to go to Santa Cruz de la Sierra you must ascend first into a weird petrified forest, permanently cloud-hung and eerily garlanded with fronds of lichen which transform the trees into menacing spectres glimpsed through the gloom. This place, where the upkeep of the road becomes an almost hopeless struggle against the elements, is called, with some reason, Siberia. If, on the other hand, you wish to go down into the lush valleys and forests of Chapare then you must once more cross the snowline. On this high ridge a sudden fall of snow may block the road with drifts, and two ascetic log huts have been built at the top of the pass to shelter the stranded traveller.

Travellers' tales in Bolivia need few embellishments to sound like bravado. Near Cochabamba the eastern slopes of the *cordillera* careen down into the plains even more steeply than in the Yungas of the Department of La Paz. Here there are no intervening, temperate valleys. From the crest of the pass your gaze plunges almost straight down, to the flat lands, miles below, paled by distance into a faintly opalescent sea, and veined here and there by the brighter threads of tropical rivers, slug-gishly winding towards the Atlantic. The narrow road descends almost as perpendicularly as a spiral staircase, and with every labyrinthine bend the vegetation and the quality of the country-side change before one's eyes. A thin, skeletal scrub struggles into life almost immediately beneath the bare crown of the mountain, and this becomes perceptibly more abundant and varied until the steep cliff from which the track is hewn re-sembles a botanist's paradise. One can almost see the sap run-ning more freely, just as one feels the additional oxygen flooding into one's lungs with every yard of the descent. Nature burgeons in exuberant growth, in a profusion of thickly-entangled creepers that straggle down the hillside, spreading a canopy of shade beneath which countless varieties of small plants flourish. Ferns spread out their damp tendrils in search of the moisture which hangs almost as droplets in the air and begonias and orchids blossom wild as in some exotic hothouse. Most of the plants are thick and fleshy, with waxen leaves and succulent stems and the ground is carpeted with thick, damp moss. On all sides tiny rills tumble down the mountainside like crystal icicles towards the river foaming deep in the gorge and the valley reverberates with the sound of falling water.

The pitch of the hill is too sheer even for the most intrepid colonizer and it is only near the bottom that one finds a quaint wooden bridge humped over the creaming waters of the main river or a path twisting up to a bluff where a wooden homestead

183

stands in a circle of felled trees. Yet there is plenty of traffic, for the flat rich area between the Chapare and Chimoré rivers is a favourite place for new settlement. Because the road is so excessively steep and narrow only one-way traffic is allowed, exclusively upwards or downwards according to the day of the week, more days being allowed for the upward journey. Even so, some of the elderly and heavily-laden lorries will quite often overrun their time and as you zoom down, carefree because nothing can be coming in the opposite direction, you suddenly come upon some laggard, delayed by a breakdown, chugging relentlessly towards you on a bend, regardless of the careful highway regulations.

Down below, the limpid water of the mountain streams merges into the pewter-coloured rivers of the *Oriente*, the beginning of a great network of waterways which covers the whole of the eastern and northern tropical lowlands, and drains away into the Amazon basin. There are no more roads here and the rivers are the chief means of communication. When I visited the area a few years ago, in connection with some tropical agricultural experiments being undertaken with the assistance of the Food and Agricultural Organization, the trail did not even reach Todos Santos. You drove to the banks of a broad-flowing river, and sat on a tree-trunk until a boatman came and ferried you across to the other side, where you walked the rest of the way. Even that was impossible on my visit, however, as the river was in spate and had changed its course. So we turned back and drove to Villa Tunari where one is slung across the river, jeep and all, on a platform swinging high above the water, and manipulated by pulleys between two towers on either bank. Like most contraptions for crossing rivers in Bolivia this mechanism has an alarmingly makeshift and casual air about it, but even large trucks are ferried across in this way and the only accident of which I heard was caused by a helicopter cutting one of the overhead cables.

All this level area at the foot of the *cordillera* is forested with tall trees and thickly covered with undergrowth. On the other side of the river from Villa Tunari colonization is in full swing.

184

A narrow track of red earth runs through a swathe of open land where the jungle has been cleared. Settlers of a year or two's standing have wooden huts thatched with dry grass, but more recent arrivals live in rough wigwams of twigs and straw, known as *pawiches*. The earth is blackened and littered with scarred tree stumps where the forest has been burnt and hacked down. Young maize sprouts like green spears from earth that has been crudely tilled between the torn stubs of the forest, banana trees spread the large fans of their leaves over the makeshift dwellings, and on squares of beaten earth in front of them great mats of *coca* leaves are being turned in the sun to dry. The children here run about almost naked, with only a ragged vest to cover them, but the highland women still cling to their bowler hats, their tight bodices, full skirts and many petticoats. Usually several years pass before they make concessions to the hot, steamy climate.

The road ends at the Chapare, in a clearing where the few trees on the bank overhang a bend in the river. It had been euphemistically described to us as a 'port', and sure enough there was one battered motor-vessel tied up to the bank. It was small and did not look very seaworthy, nor was the river very impressive, for, though evidently deep, it was narrow and closely roofed with trees. There was not a soul in sight. Yet this for the moment is the main surface link with the eastern region of the Beni and motor-launches of the kind we saw come up from Trinidad carrying cargo as far as the mouth of the Chapare on flat-bottomed barges known as *remolques*. Like most Bolivian rivers, the Chapare is not easy to navigate, and is usually passable only in the summer months when the rains are heaviest. Even so, it is littered with submerged tree-trunks which may impale the bottom of the boat, and is constantly changing its course so that even the most experienced pilot may have difficulty in finding the right channel or the craft may go aground on shallows formed by recent silting. This is the great problem confronting the development of the thinly-populated and potentially rich plains of Eastern Bolivia: they are cut off from the main centres of population and consumption in the country by the almost impenetrable wall of the Andean mountains, as yet traversed only here and there by narrow roads so prone to dislocation through landslides during the rainy season as to be uneconomic. The length of the journey, and the extremes of climate and temperature cause high percentages of loss to perishable tropical fruits, while expensive trucks have a short life owing to the steep gradients and poor surfaces of the roads. In a way it is not surprising that Bolivia has jumped one stage of development, as it were, and that much of the produce of the Beni is carried by air. But the cost is exorbitantly high, particularly for the bulkier and more valuable products such as meat and timber.

Until recent years the obsession with extractive mining deflected attention from the possibilities of the area. So little had things altered since the early years of the Republic that the advice which Alcide d'Orbigny gave to the government of Santa Cruz in 1830 could have been repeated almost word for word a decade ago. Now this is changing. All-weather trails are being built between the navigable ports on the rivers and the expanding network of main roads in order to link the tropical agricultural areas to the main centres of production. Hydrographic studies are being made of the main river arteries and dredging operations undertaken to clear them of obstacles.

It is a slow business because resources are inadequate and the problems immense. But the enthusiasm and excitement in an outpost of settlement like the Chapare are so infectious that you really do feel that you are watching a country on the move and are given new hope for the future. One sometimes thinks that this is a people which thrives on difficulties. The great diesel trucks lumber along, stacked high with people and their sacks of produce or belongings, churning up great ruts in the embryonic trails through the forests and sometimes grinding to a stop. Then everyone leaps off and with great energy and cheerfulness piles stones and tree-trunks under the wheels, pushing and shoving with a great will, in spite of their fragile physique, until at last the ponderous caravan is on its way again.

The river crossings are great bottle-necks where queues of

lorries may wait for hours or even days before they can be ferried across. The one near Villa Tunari is no exception. When we returned at dusk from our short excursion to the Chapare it was to find that the pulleys had stopped working for the night. The passengers on the long string of vehicles straggling down to the river bank were already crowding into the row of wooden bars or *boliches* by the side of the trail looking for food and drink, and somewhere to doss down for the night. We had found part of an upper floor which we were to share with other travellers, when the message came that a last journey was, after all, to be made across the river especially for us.

Villa Tunari, which we reached after dark, is the prototype of the frontier settlement, the town that has sprung up at the end of the road. It is only a few wooden huts, dotted among the banana and the papaya trees, but it bristles with life and movement. Its muddy street is choked with lorries about to make the river crossing or pausing before the long haul back up to the highlands, and the bars and stores which occupy almost every hut along the roadside do a roaring trade. To walk along the road in the dark is to be conscious of life in ebullition on either side. By the flaring light of tapers and candles small boys are running backwards and forwards to the lorries balancing trays of coffee. Beneath the lorries every space is crowded and life goes on with supreme disregard for privacy or what, in other places, might be called the proprieties. Some are sleeping, worn out by the long day's travel; women are giving the breast to their babies, while their menfolk consume beer of *chicha*, some of them already to excess; other couples are making love, procreating new life to people the rich new lands they have come to discover. Over it all hangs the smell of frying oil and the spicy tang of *ají* from the *boliches*, and the heavy odour of excreta and stale urine from the street corners. It is a harsh, crude town, where life is lived in the raw. And yet, though your senses are constantly repelled, you cannot fail to be moved by this display of fortitude and vigour in the face of unutterable privations. The vital flame of life burns very strong in Villa Tunari.

The one hotel is for the élite. It has a large dining-room, open-sided, except for a low wall running round to a height of about a metre, and two separate lodging houses, one for men and one for women. Both of these are full, but we are promised a meal and told that we may afterwards sleep in the dining-room. Besides ourselves there are some young Bolivian social workers carrying out a survey for the Government in the settlement areas. They will spend several weeks living in conditions not much better than those of the people they are investigating. This is another thing that gives one hope in Bolivia, that many of the educated young people do not quail before the prospect of dirtying their hands or facing privations, unlike many of their predecessors—or even their colleagues in other countries today—who preferred the comfort of an office desk to the realities of rural life.

There is also a noisy table of local people, men of some substance who have settled in the region for several years and made a go of it; one of them is a dentist, surely the only one in Villa Tunari. They are drinking prodigious quantities of beer, and presently ask us to join them. We are regaled with the time-honoured tales of the region, the tall stories of snakes and crocodiles and *pirañas*, and of miraculous escapes from death. Mostly, however, the conversation turns—as long as it is lucid—on the problems of the locality, the need for a bridge across the river, for certain social amenities in the town and so on, and we are pressed to take these petitions back to the proper government authorities.

Later, the talk becomes less intelligible, the pronunciation slurs, the voices rise and the plaints against an ungrateful and inefficient government multiply. The dentist puts a scratched record of an Argentine tango on an ancient, wheezing gramophone and insists on playing it over and over again. There are, of course, no sanitary facilities, and from time to time people stagger out into the night, picking their way uncertainly between a flock of sheep cropping the coarse grass outside. We decide that it is time to sleep and stretch out my sleeping-bag on the dining-room table. To our chagrin we run into

188

difficulties trying to hang a couple of hammocks for my male colleagues from the rafters and have to seek help from our local friends, whose fingers, even when fuddled with beer, prove nimble in unravelling hammock strings. We clamber ostentatiously into our makeshift beds, hoping that our companions will go home, for it is after midnight. But Villa Tunari has a constant, if somewhat bizarre, night life from which it is impossible to escape. The gramophone continues to wheeze out the banal story of an abandoned lover in the River Plate, the voices at the nearby table increase in shrillness and whole armies of mosquitoes begin to swarm in for the kill. Outside one is conscious of the more distant buzz of activity in the street. It is impossible to sleep.

Suddenly I am shaken violently by the shoulder. I open my eyes to find the dentist bending over me, breathing great gusts of stale beer into my face. Not content with listening to the tango, he has now decided he wants to dance it, and I am the only available partner. With difficulty I persuade him that I am not in a dancing mood, and anyway dislike tangos intensely. Five minutes later he is back, perching on my table-bed, and launched into a cosy chat about the 'problems of the region'— a phrase which has now attained the status of a popular refrain through constant repetition—and the prospects of persuading the Minister of Agriculture to come down personally and see for himself. Diplomacy deserts me, and I roll over in my sleeping-bag growling 'Go away'. This time the message has at last got through. The last of the group disperses and for a while a blissful near-silence ensues. I am just dropping off to sleep— by this time it must be two or three o'clock in the morning— when I am jerked into cursing wakefulness again by the most monumental snoring, which seems to shake the whole fabric of the dining-room. So far as I can tell it comes from the colleague suspended in a hammock two or three feet above me.

'Such a nice man,' I thought. 'Who would have imagined that he could be afflicted with this terrible defect.' At last I can stand it no longer and raising myself on one elbow, give the hammock a hefty shove.

'What are you doing?' enquires an injured voice.

'I'm sorry, but I must get some sleep and I can't if you snore so loudly,' I reply.

'But it isn't me! It's *your* snoring that's been keeping me awake. Only just now I was thinking what a pity it is that a woman should have such an aggressive, masculine snore.'

At this point in the argument I realize suddenly that we are both shouting, not in anger, but simply to make ourselves heard above the clamorous snoring which thunders on unabated somewhere nearby. The source is not hard to find: some other exhausted traveller from one of the diesel trucks has dossed down on the ground, not a yard from us, outside the half-wall of the dining-room and now slumbers on in noisy oblivion.

So there is little sleep for anyone except him and the hour before dawn finds me wide awake, sticky and uncomfortable from sleeping in my clothes during a heavy, tropical night. I get up, but can only wash myself rather sketchily with the chipped enamel bowl of water and dipper provided for guests outside the door of the blackened kitchen. Deciding that I might at least change my underwear and shirt, I make my way in the near-dark to an open space near the river bank. I had forgotten that the light breaks quickly in these equatorial latitudes, a grey miasma that detaches itself slowly from the sluggish brown waters of the river, first outlining the trees and other objects on the bank in vague silhouette, and then suddenly brightening to reveal them in every detail. It is thus that the dawn and a rather startled Scandinavian gentleman surprise me, clinging half-clad to the disconcertingly slim trunk of a papaya tree. It is hard to know which of us is more embarrassed when he is introduced to me at breakfast as a visiting missionary, but I console myself that we are, after all, in Villa Tunari.

Santa Cruz in its way is a frontier town too, but very different from Villa Tunari. This is no brash settlement hurriedly constructed at the gateway to new lands, but a respectable borough

with three centuries of history behind it, founded in 1651 by
Ñuflo de Chaves. For most of those three hundred years Santa
Cruz was isolated from the rest of the country, a small island
of Spanish settlement surrounded by forests inhabited by
primitive Indian tribes and vast plains where, with the help and
guidance of Jesuit missionaries, the people of Mojos enjoyed
a brief period of prosperity.

Santa Cruz kept itself very much to itself. Contrary to what
happened in the rest of the country, there was little inter-
marriage with indigenous tribes and the Spanish stock maintained
itself almost totally unmixed down the centuries, true to the
concept of *limpieza de sangre*—the purity of the blood—by
which the Spaniards set so much store in the Golden Age.
Even today the *cruceñas*—the girls of Santa Cruz—are famed
for their Andalusian-type grace and beauty. Like most other
things, they did not escape the appraising eye of Alcide
d'Orbigny, who one feels would be a delightful travelling companion, lively and gay, dismissing hardship with humour. To
do justice to the women of Santa Cruz, he said, it would be
necessary to create 'a superlative of superlatives', and himself
paid them the compliment of breaking his endless journeyings
there for several months.

Until just over ten years ago, there was no all-weather road
between Cochabamba and Santa Cruz. Even in the dry season
the only way to travel on the old trading route was by heavy
lorry or horseback and the journey of just over three hundred
miles might take anything between one to three weeks. When
the paved road, begun in 1945, was at last finished, private cars
were able to do the journey in between eight to ten hours. The
new highway was a triumph of engineering, forging through a
twisted maze of mountains. It was also very costly and has been
criticized as uneconomic because even today traffic is not heavy.
Yet it has transformed Santa Cruz from a sleepy backwater into
the hub of a rapidly developing region which still has enormous
untapped potential. The benefits, moreover, are not only material
but also political, social and psychological.

For all that, d'Orbigny's description of Santa Cruz as a town

191

with an 'entirely provisional' air still holds good today, though I would not go as far as he does in singling it out as 'the most rustic of all those I have seen in America'. But you might well take it for a wild western outpost on the American prairies some time in the middle of the nineteenth century. The atmosphere is thrust upon you as soon as you arrive, when the macadam of the paved highway stops abruptly on the outskirts of the town and you bounce on to one of the main thoroughfares, rudely jolted into the realization that you have reached Santa Cruz. Again d'Orbigny's description still applies. The streets, he says, 'are covered with moving sand into which one sinks up to mid-calf, both in dry weather and in the rains.'

The addition of motor traffic has simply added to the hazards and only the sturdiest vehicles survive, for during the rains they flounder in a morass of mud, while in dry weather it is difficult to get a purchase on the drifted sand without a four-wheel drive. One is not surprised to find that the town's fleet of taxis is exclusively composed of jeeps, zigzagging wildly about in defiance of all traffic rules in their efforts to miss the larger potholes. The passengers are mercilessly flung about from side to side and in wet weather unwary passers-by are bespattered with mud and the dirty water spurting up from the wildly gyrating wheels.

The truth is, of course, that Santa Cruz was never designed for motor traffic at all, or even for pedestrians, but was custom-built for horsemen. The brick-floored, arcaded pavements running along both sides of each street are at just the right height for mounting a horse at one leap and galloping off into the distance in the best cowboy tradition; nothing could be less convenient for the tight-skirted, high-heeled belles of modern Santa Cruz who struggle up and down them on their way to the daily parade of local beauty and fashion in the main square. Each street corner has its hitching-post, many of them so old and gnarled that they might have stood there since the town was founded. Every other building seems to be either a bar or a barber's shop where men have leisurely haircuts, or, bearded in froth, spend hours contemplating the comings and goings in the street, and gossiping about local events. It is still quite common to see horsemen coming in from the vast hinterland of Santa Cruz, rider and horse coated with mud or dust according to the season. Produce is brought into market by ponderous ox-carts, lumbering along behind plodding oxen; it is their solid wooden wheels, wobbling like those of a badly-made souvenir, which help to keep the streets in their characteristically churned-up state.

Much of Santa Cruz is unrepentantly archaic and many of the signs of progress seem out of place. Sometimes there is a touch of sheer fantasy. Flowering cacti sprout at unlikely angles from the mossy tiled roofs, whose long eaves cover the high brick arcades, leaning on tall pillars at the roadside, and the telegraph wires that cross and re-cross the street are tasselled with orchids and greenish-grey lichen like the mouldering decorations of some forgotten carnival.

It would be misleading to conclude that Santa Cruz is an apathetic backwater. The *cambas*, as the *cruceños* are styled, are as ebullient as the *kollas* of the highlands when the mood takes them. The leap from siesta hammock to machine-gun post may be very sudden, and one can leave the sleeping city at dawn, as I once did, to find one's return obstructed a few hours later by hastily-erected barricades and the crossfire of disputing factions of the same political party.

Material progress is not lacking nowadays, although much of it seems to be in the *reculer pour mieux sauter* tradition. Streets never designed for anything so banal as locomotion have been gashed across by deep trenches and rendered totally impassable by great gaping holes, all necessary adjuncts, it seems, of laying the water supply and the sewerage system. Other improvements are more immediately obvious. There are new hotels so that one no longer has to trudge the streets late at night, as I did on my first visit in 1960, fruitlessly seeking a bed. One of them even styles itself as a 'motel', regardless of its almost complete inaccessibility to motor traffic in a heavy downpour. Nowadays there are reasonable eating-places and there is not likely to be a repetition of the incident during one of my

193

early visits when an indifferent dinner was followed by exe-crable coffee, surely an unnecessary penance in a country which grows some of the most delicately-flavoured coffee in the world. One of my companions could stand it no more:

'What on earth do you make the coffee from here?' he asked testily.

'¡Maíz, señor!' ('Maize, sir!') came the answer pat from the beaming waiter, effectively disarming all retort.

Little by little Santa Cruz is becoming more sophisticated and less remote from the outside world. Apart from the highway to Cochabamba, it is linked to the Brazilian frontier at Corumbá by the quaint, narrow-gauge railway on which legend would have it that passengers are required to fuel the engine. A shorter, paved highway leads to a rich sugar-growing area and to the sugar-mill at Guabirá, and from there a rough-surfaced, but all-weather road, cuts through the forest to Puerto Grether, where settlements are beginning to encroach on the jungle. But it is probably the discovery of new oil-bearing structures that has most contributed to Santa Cruz's development in recent years. Camiri, farther to the south-east, has for some time been the main centre of oil production, but the recent strikes at Bulo-Bulo and Naranjillos are nearer Santa Cruz and pro-duce large quantities of natural gas.

Proximity is a relative concept in Bolivia. Distances lose their significance in such a vast, unruly and under-populated territory and ease of access is a surer yardstick than any spatial measurement. This is why, when contemplating a journey, it is always safer to ask how many hours it takes rather than the number of kilometres. The best way of getting to Bulo-Bulo is to fly by one of the State oil company's Cessna planes from the small airfield at Santa Cruz. From the air one sees the immense monotony of the grassy plain, studded with low trees and scrub stretching away eastwards to the Brazilian frontier, and perhaps even, in the blue haze of distance, to the end of the world itself. Westward lie the sand-coloured foothills of the *sierra*, which gives Santa Cruz the second part of its name, mottled with darker patches of bush. But the plane swings northward, where the jungle springs tall and dark green, seamed with the sluggish coils of turbid rivers, oozing between the trees as if they were themselves some vast seepage of oil. It is an enigmatic landscape; seen from above its canopied trees form an impenetrably matted green floor, shrouding the ground from sight. Yet suddenly, there are signs of human activity: a broad causeway slashed through the forest for many miles, no one remembers when, or for what purpose, and now fast being gathered back into the insidious, octopus-like embrace of the jungle; the Yapacaní-Puerto Grether road, gaping like a raw red wound and bordered by neat homesteads, whose *chacras* or small-holdings, stretch for a mile or so on either side, until they are brusquely curtailed by the uncompromising palisade of the forest; and, in small clearings on the river banks, the plane swoops low over a scattering of thatched huts, a makeshift port with a boat or two bobbing on the water. By their very rareness these islands of habitation in a billowing green sea appear almost insolent, an impudent challenge to the exuberant supremacy of nature.

Bulo-Bulo lies in one of these clearings snatched from the jungle. The trees crowd in on the narrow landing strip and on the jeep trail leading up to the drilling site; there the flames flare strangely against the tropical sky, glimpsed only briefly above the clearing. Although the biggest trees are a hundred feet or more high, the space between their straight tall trunks is choked with smaller species grappling for light and air, intertwined and fettered together by their implacable struggle for survival. Even dead trees cannot fall down, for their bleached skeletons are held erect by the tangled vegetation. From the topmost boughs immense lianas, long since dead, writhe downwards like many-headed snakes. Creepers still alive are matted together in an arras of greenery linking tree with tree and enclosing the vision with an impenetrable leafy wall. You can almost sense the silent fight for existence going on around you and the hot, thick air tastes stalely as if it has been breathed a million times before. Once you leave the wooden huts and rigs of the camp a pall of silence envelopes you. There

195

is not much movement or life in the jungle: an occasional clatter and twittering of monkeys, unseen in the branches, the comic 'wolf-whistle' of a bird hidden deep in the thicket, the slither of a snake, perhaps, through the long foliage of a bank, the high-pitched zing of a cicada sounding almost like a circular saw.

It seems strange to come back afterwards to the clearing to play ping-pong and then sit outside under a filtered moon, listening to a radio excitedly blaring forth the results of a British election which rebound from the indifferent wall of the forest. Did one ever belong to such a world, and can one ever go back? Later the moon disappears and you sleep to the noise of torrential rain beating down on to a tin roof.

The workers here do not have any easy life. There is an oppressive, almost threatening atmosphere about the jungle which easily breeds claustrophobia. The work is hard and the obstacles very great. None of the heavy drilling equipment can be brought in by air, but has to be dragged inch by inch over an uneven track gashed out of the jungle and hoisted by pulleys and wires over the innumerable rivers which loop back and forth across the trail. The camps are comfortable enough, but one is not always able to reach them. When I was returning from a visit to Bulo-Bulo with a group of United Nations and Bolivian geologists who had carried out the original survey work, we were caught by night at a crossing of the River Yapacaní and although we managed to reach the other side in a native canoe, roughly hollowed out from a solid tree trunk, our Land-Rovers had to wait until next morning.

On the far side there was at least a *boliche*, a crude bar, where we could get something to eat. It was only a thatched room with open sides, covered in better days with mosquito netting that was now sagging into holes, but there was beer, and some very tough meat purporting to be steak and spiced with the inevitable *ají*. Afterwards we sat outside on the sand, in the moonlight, listening to the tribulations of a foreman who had been stuck there for several days, waiting for the river level to fall so that he could transport a heavy drilling rig to a new site on the opposite side. As always, his story was well laced with highly-coloured tales of the dangers and discomforts of his métier, meant to impress the squeamish and uninitiated, ranging from lethal snakes to the singularly unpleasant *borro* which lays an egg under your skin that develops, three weeks later, into a thick, squirming larva, half-an-inch long. Soon we were on to politics, the perennial theme, and everyone's spirits brightened visibly as tongues warmed to the task of tearing the Government of the day apart. From there it was only a step to music and before long I found myself invited to a spirited *cueca*, danced barefoot in the sand, with muddy jeans rolled knee-high.

After such an evening's entertainment it was something of a come-down to deal with the banal business of where to sleep. Finally, at my suggestion, we dossed down at the edge of the clearing on the river bank. It seemed to me a romantic spot, as I lay listening to the quiet sound of the water at my feet and watched the dark fringe of trees silhouetted enigmatically against a moonlit sky. But I had, of course, forgotten to allow for the plentiful population of mosquitoes, who converged on this unexpected fresh fare with enthusiasm, or of the toxic brume which rose from the surface of the river at about three or four in the morning, enveloping us in a fitful white mist that chilled the bones to the marrow despite the tropical latitude. One by one I heard the Bolivian geologists creeping away into the *boliche* until there were only the three *gringos* left to rise, bleary-eyed, an hour or two later and try vainly to refresh ourselves with the tepid, soupy water of the river.

I had the usual harvest of bites on that trip, mysteriously acquired through high leather boots, trousers and long sleeves. I did not pay much attention to them until I woke up one morning three weeks later to find that I could not put my foot to the ground and that I had a swelling on my right leg, hard and round as a ping-pong ball. It seemed a heavy forfeit to pay for my scepticism over the foreman's moonlight tales; in my case the larva of the *borro* had died inside my leg and caused an abscess which had to be cut away in hospital that same day in order to prevent septicaemia. By one of those strange Bolivian

197

paradoxes I owed much to an incipient revolution, but for which I should already have been away on another field trip, far from medical facilities. But I still bear the scar on my leg to remind me of the *borro* and my night on the banks of the Yapacaní.

11 IN THE long run the discovery of oil may well become the decisive factor for the future of Santa Cruz and the region around it. Already the American Mid-West atmosphere that has always permeated the town is accentuated by the tough, hard-drinking oil men who now frequent its many bars when they come in from the jungle. But for the moment the oil is in isolated pockets and in the immediate future the influx of colonists and the spread of agriculture over an area formerly given over to grazing or jungle is likely to alter the face of the landscape much more drastically. Wherever there is reasonable access the jungle has been felled, and small green oases of cultivation have sprung up among the charred tree stumps. Often the people do not possess even the rudimentary kind of housing used in the warmer areas of the country, but live in a *pawiche* hastily put together on the edge of the plot. Their pioneer existence involves much hardship and some danger. As the tentacles of settlement gradually encroach farther and farther into the primeval forest, the original inhabitants, primitive tribes so shy that they rarely emerge from the dark glades of the jungle, are gradually being forced into a smaller and smaller area, like animals on the move. I was once shown the spot where, only the previous week, a group of workmen felling trees to build an access road, were showered with arrows, which could only have come from a few yards away.

A few years ago none of this settlement would have seemed possible, so great was the scepticism with which it was regarded. The Indians would never descend from the highlands to the tropical lowlands, it was said, or if they did they would succumb to disease and die, or else fail to adapt to the new environment and return to the *altiplano*. The two or three pilot settlement projects which the Government has started in the area during the past decade, though they have suffered many setbacks and some errors, have proved that, with proper organization, there is no reason why the Andean-Indian should not adapt perfectly well to life in the lowlands. One class of settlers must be excepted, however: the miner, who, as in most parts of the world, finds it difficult to accustom himself to any other way of life.

In Bolivia, however, not even peaceful rural pursuits are without their hazards. In 1963, I had to visit Cotoca, a settlement which has received some assistance from international organizations under the Andean-Indian programme, in order to supervise the transfer of some vocational training equipment, which was not being fully utilized, to the site of a new rural polytechnic school in the Cochabamba valley. It was an apparently straightforward task, for the Government favoured the transfer, and on that very day was to sign the relevant agreement in Lima, the Peruvian capital. After nearly four years in Bolivia, I ought to have known better.

Besides the relatively recent settlement of migrants from the highlands, there is also a long-established village at Cotoca, famed for its miraculous Virgin, the object of many devout pilgrimages, and celebrated in popular folksong. Certainly either faith or music is needed to distract your mind from the state of the road to Cotoca. Though only twenty-five kilometres from Santa Cruz, it is so deeply rutted and riddled with pot-holes, made by the solid wooden wheels of the ox-carts, that it has been known for the journey to take up to eight hours in the rainy season. The first time that I went, we had ferried a two-stroke Citroën down from La Paz for the settlement. The little car had struggled gallantly over the backbone of the Andes, but had subsided with a protesting squeak in the sandy streets of Santa Cruz and had to be loaded on to a lorry for the rest of the journey. We lurched through the night, holding on to the side of the lorry with one hand and supporting the car with the other, since it threatened to topple over on us as we negotiated one yawning pothole after another. It was a weird experience across a moon-drenched, empty countryside, which swayed up and down in harmony with our own erratic progress like some shadowy, tempestuous sea.

In 1963 we were better equipped. We had set out very early from Santa Cruz in a jeep leading the convoy of lorries on which the equipment was to be loaded. There were seven or eight of us, Bolivian officials, a couple of experts of the International Labour Organization, a young UK volunteer and a distinguished academic from Cambridge, who was anxious to see as much as possible of the country. A few straws in the wind on our arrival should have told us that all was not well. First the man in charge rapidly evaporated on a bicycle with a plea that he had urgent work elsewhere, then the key could not be found and we had to force the door to the workshop.

But a little later I had quite forgotten these initial setbacks and was watching the rapid loading of the first lorry with some complacency. Suddenly I felt an unaccustomed current of air ruffle the still, sultry heat. I swung round to find an enormous settler, quite the largest Amerindian I had ever encountered, breathing heavily and brandishing an equally outsize axe over my head. It was evident that he had been drinking and he was having some difficulty in articulating his thoughts. However, there could be no doubt about the burden of his message and I retreated hastily. Soon he was joined by others, including some women. One of the Bolivian officials was detailed to listen to their complaints and to explain to them that the transfer of the equipment would benefit them, since their children would be offered scholarships to study at the new school, where it would be better used. Bolivians are never lacking in eloquence and this particular official was particularly well-endowed—the uncharitable claimed excessively so—with the gift of oratory. He certainly came into his own on that day and was soon holding

201

forth from the vantage point of a wagon, while the protesting settlers crowded around his feet and heckled lustily. Meanwhile, in the background, the loading of the lorries went on unhindered.

An hour perhaps passed like this and then the distinguished academic, who was acting as treasurer and wandering around clutching a Gladstone bag bulging with cash for the labourers we had brought with us, pointed ominously to something moving on the horizon. It looked at first like the proverbial cloud no bigger than a man's hand, and indeed it was a cloud of dust, through which, as it drew nearer, we glimpsed a contingent of a hundred men or more moving towards us very fast indeed. Any doubts about their intentions were quickly dispelled. Angry shouts began to reach us, and we could see that the men were flourishing a motley collection of weapons, ancient rifles, machetes, axes and heavy sticks. Before we could recover from our surprise they had burst into our midst.

The crowd of settlers, till then absorbed in listening to the Bolivian official's harangue, melted away and for a moment, before he realized what was happening, he was left addressing the empty air. The rest of us were, however, in no position to enjoy his expression of pained surprise as we were being lined up against the machine-shop, which suddenly and alarmingly began to resemble an execution wall. Evidently this impression was shared by the ILO expert next to me, a Frenchman who had been in the *maquis*, for, with a 'those-who-are-about-to-die' look, he implanted a kiss on my left cheek with such panache that it was positively an act of defiance to our attackers. We were completely outnumbered and I hoped desperately that none of our group had a gun. This would have been fatal provocation for our assailants had spent the whole night plotting their attack and drinking to keep their courage up, so that they were in no mood to tolerate opposition or argument.

At that very moment, the main bulk of the men swarmed on to the lorries bellowing '¡Abajo los equipos!' and suiting the action to the words by hurling down the machinery we had so carefully loaded. After a while I could stand it no longer. I had singled out one man who seemed to be some sort of leader, and who looked more reasonable than the rest, though the situation had clearly passed beyond his control. To him I explained that the equipment was being moved with the government's consent and appealed to him to ask men not to damage it, since then it would be of no use to anyone and there were bound to be reprisals from the government. At that time there were splits in the governing party, which had regrouped itself in factions each known by the name of a prominent politician. It had occurred to me that perhaps our attackers, who were a mixed collection of settlers and of the original inhabitants of the village of Cotoca, might belong to one of the rival groups in opposition to the President. When I ventured to question their affiliation, however, the answer was unequivocal:

'But of course we are *pazestenssoritas,*' he declared staunchly.

All the more reason, then, I said firmly, why they should take my advice, as I could not imagine that the President would be very grateful to them for that day's work.

My words had some effect, and the leader, for such he was, at least gave orders to his men to handle the delicate equipment more carefully. By now, however, the euphoria of victory following on a night's drinking had carried them beyond the pale of discipline or common sense. The leader, looking distinctly anxious, said that he could not be responsible for our safety if we stayed longer, and that he would try to keep the people back if we made our getaway immediately. It was then I realized that we were even more of a minority than at the outset for the whole convoy of lorries, with the exception of the one receiving the none too gentle attentions of our assailants, had taken advantage of the general fracas and confusion to creep away, together with our deceptively tough-looking labourers. In a trice we had all leapt into our jeep. At once an angry group surrounded us banging on the roof and the windows, but the driver already had the car in gear, and off we shot leaving a forest of brandished fists and machetes behind us.

But our troubles were not over. When we reached the main trail to the village, enclosed on one side by the embankment of the Santa Cruz–Corumbá railway and on the other by a line of trees interspersed with dense bush, it was to discover that our attackers had had the foresight to block our escape completely by felling seven or eight large trees at intervals over the narrow track. Fearing that they might already be in hot pursuit across a short cut through the cane fields, we took the only immediate solution possible and pushed and heaved the jeep up on the single track railway line. Fortunately it is not much used, but as we bumped over the sleepers for several miles I found myself nonetheless keeping my fingers crossed lest we were unlucky enough to meet one of the once-weekly trains to and from Brazil or one of the rare fleet of goods-wagons and hoping that, if we did, their progress would be as snail-like as malicious public report would suggest.

However, we reached Cotoca without incident. Only a few women and children witnessed our precipitate flight through the village, most of the able-bodied males being at the scene of the battle, and we were soon speeding towards Santa Cruz. I do not imagine that notorious road has ever been covered so fast or with so little concern for the springs of the vehicle. We bounced straight up to the headquarters of the provincial government where news of our arrival and the imminent approach of trouble had evidently preceded us, for we found the Prefect already out in the street with one foot on the step of his jeep, a harassed look on his face and an apology on his lips: predictably, he had been called away on an urgent matter that would brook no delay. I quickly reassured him; all we needed was the use of his radio in order to speak to the President in La Paz.

An hour or two later, when the President must have been in the midst of his Saturday afternoon siesta, the radio conference came through. Meanwhile, I had already sent a cable to Lima suggesting that the signing of the agreement should be postponed until we had regained possession of the equipment. I learned afterwards that this message had arrived as a bomb-shell to explode among the tinkling champagne glasses celebrating the conclusion of the agreement, on which the ink was still scarcely dry. To the President I rapidly outlined the

above: Santa Cruz.
below: Pots being prepared for Santa Cruz market.

left: River scene in tropical Bolivia.
above: Oil rig in the jungle.
below: Crossing the Yapacani river.

dramatic happenings of the morning. His reply, of which I still have the text, was a masterpiece of understatement. It began: 'But you, señorita, understand the *idiosyncrasies* of this country better than anyone . . . ' and advocated patience.

It would perhaps not have been a very reassuring message had I not still been at the radio station a few minutes later when a peremptory presidential message was received, instructing the local authorities to retrieve the equipment without fail the next day and transport it to Cochabamba.

While I was speaking to the President, local journalists descended on the hotel and interrogated the academic and the UK volunteer, whom we had left behind because they had no official connection with the operation. So laconic were their replies that the reporters had to fall back on their imaginations which they deployed to good effect, if not exactly in the service of truth. Next day the two local papers—no more than four pages apiece—blazed forth in the largest print they could muster: 'Attempted theft of valuable equipment from Cotoca: mysterious agents of Point IV implicated.' The mysterious agents of Point IV—the American aid organization—were identified by the names of the two British citizens who had been no more than innocent bystanders. However, it did not seem to be the moment to issue a *démenti* or put the record straight and deciding that discretion was the better part of valour we prudently fell back on Cochabamba ourselves, where we learned a day or two later that the President's instructions had been carried out without further incident.

Santa Cruz may have primitive streets and anachronistic customs but it is still the largest town in the *Oriente* and appears an advanced modern metropolis compared with other townships in the vast tropical regions of Eastern Bolivia. Camiri, well to the south of Santa Cruz, is the main oil producing centre in the country, connected with Oruro, La Paz and so to the Chilean port of Arica by a pipeline which traverses the Andean *cordillera* from east to west; yet it seems to cling precariously to the jungle-covered foothills of the Andes, in the marginal region where these disintegrate into the scattered scrub and, eventually, the semi-arid desert of the Gran Chaco. As one flies over the jagged green hills in one of the small planes used by the state oil company, or grinds up the corkscrew roads hewn out of their steep escarpments, the oil installations, emerging like startled giraffes from the tangled dark undergrowth, seem less an anomaly than an act of bravado flung in the face of an inimical nature.

Man's hold on this landscape is ephemeral. You can easily understand how, more recently, the primeval forests of these twisted valleys could have harboured, undetected for several months, the guerrilla bands led by Ché Guevara. There is a desperation about this countryside which gives the key to the almost predestined tragedy of Guevara's campaign, doomed to failure from the outset in the eyes of anyone knowing this region and its people well, and compellingly described in the terse, everyday language of his diaries: the forced marches, hacking a trail through the jungle with machetes and fording torrential rivers; the execrable food and the frequent hunger and illness; the daily tensions and personality clashes; skirmishes with the army, causing dead and wounded on both sides; the constant fear of encirclement; and then, at last, silence in the Quebrada del Yuro.

The very confusion of the narrative, threaded with references to shadowy people and places, somehow heightens the reader's perception of the group's own predicament, marching back and forth over unknown country in conditions of incredible hardship, vainly seeking the support of a peasantry that was not in any case numerous and whose attitude was ambivalent, unaware of the fate or whereabouts of their companion group and constantly misled about the degree of political support which they might obtain in other parts of the country.

Violence, war and death are no strangers to this landscape. Even the music in Camiri, slower and more languorous as befits the dry, hot, enervating nights of the Chaco, throbs with the melancholy of the lost lands, the lands that were fought over thirty years ago and steeped in the blood of countless Bolivians and Paraguayans. The Paraguayans themselves won only a Pyrrhic victory, for their male population was decimated and the supposed deposits of oil, for which they died, have still not been discovered in the area ceded to them. As in so much of Bolivia, life here oscillates between two extreme poles of gentleness and cruelty, of romantic love and paranoid hate. There is no paradox in the fact that, only a few yards away from where I was once awoken from the first sleep of a warm night by the sound of guitars, and a serenade of the lilting, languid, sensuous love songs of the Gran Chaco, the young French writer, Régis Debray, should have undergone trial for his life a year or two later. Love and death, those old inseparables, the doctrine of whose indivisibility has been handed down since the time of the old Spanish conquistadors as carefully as that of Catholicism itself, walk hand in hand here too.

The sense of dramatic contrast, of a great destiny half-glimpsed and only half-achieved, constantly recurs. You see it again in the rolling pampas of the Beni, northwards of Santa Cruz, in the land of Mojos. Several times in the sixteenth century the Spaniards invaded this region, lured on by rumours that here was yet another site of the elusive and illusory El Dorado. Later, there was a more peaceful infiltration by the Jesuits and in only a hundred years the lowland tribes of Mojos had become prosperous and cultivated, excelling in their own native handwork and in the new craft which the Jesuits taught them, growing tropical fruits, yucca, sweet potatoes, tobacco, rice, sugar-cane and cotton, and breeding horses and cattle which thrived on the unlimited pasture lands of the eastern plains. For a while the population increased, encouraged by the Jesuit's policy of forbidding men and women to grow their hair until they had had children. This is the origin of the term *pelado* and *pelada* (literally 'the bald ones'), still a common term in the Santa Cruz area for describing young people.

Bolivia is only now painfully recapturing the self-sufficiency in rice and sugar which she enjoyed then for, after the expulsion of the Jesuits in 1767, the area fell into a decline from which it has never recovered. Their marvellous churches with their gold and silver-laden interiors were handed over to parish priests who within fifteen years allowed to fall into decay what they did not steal. Such treasures as escaped were later borne away during the wars of independence to defray the costs of the campaigns. But some of the arts taught by the Jesuits survived longer, and d'Orbigny movingly describes how sixty years after they had left he heard a High Mass sung in the denuded Church of San Javier de Chiquitos to an orchestral accompaniment of European and indigenous instruments unsurpassed in all his travels.

Ever since, this part of Bolivia has been the shuttlecock of individual whims and enterprise. In the late nineteenth century the search for quinine and rubber brought more adventurers into the untrodden forests of the Departments of Beni and Pando and another brief blaze of prosperity. Then the firm of the Suárez Brothers became the ruler of a virtually independent empire, controlling vast tracts of lands, having its own army and using English sovereigns as currency. London, reached by riverboat along the network of rivers in the Amazon basin and then by ocean steamer, was in fact nearer in time than La Paz and in the heyday of the rubber trade the night life of Guayaramerín, today a fading town on the Brazilian border, was as gay and expensive as that of Paris. But the prosperity was short-lived. Even while it lasted it might have happened on another continent for all the benefits it brought to the country as a whole. To the people of the region it meant only exploitation and forced labour.

Suárez Hermanos had their headquarters at Cachuela Esperanza—the Waterfalls of Hope—below Riberalta, near the Brazilian frontier, which breaks the natural communications system of Bolivian waterways. A hundred years ago this was unknown territory, inhabited only by wild tribes, and it was only after the travels of explorers, especially Edwin Heath, the American, that others ventured there in search of rubber, cocao, vanilla, ipecacuanha and cinnamon. Heath travelled down the River Beni by boat in 1880 and made the first perilous descent of the waterfalls, thus linking up with the earlier explorations of Palacios, who had been Prefect of the Beni, and proving the existence of a navigable outlet to the east. It was a hazardous expedition in a fifteen-foot boat caulked with maize leaves and mud, with only two Indians for company, and one of those was ill.

Heath recounted his experiences in a laconic diary interlaced with meteorological observations and with occasional flashes of humour, as when he described before the journey started the reactions of one Indian tribe who considered the descent of the Beni impossible.

'How can *you* think of such a thing when we, who are men, cannot do so?' they enquired.

Asked why they were men and the others not they explained to a Bolivian companion of Heath's:

'Because we see that you have only one wife, while the most incapable man in our tribe has at least four!'

Heath was equally unmoved by the premonitions of another tribe which despatched the tiny expedition with chants of 'Death, death', and dressed in mourning for a month, convinced that they had been in contact with death and would surely die themselves. Only the insects aroused emotion in him:

'Certain flies of the river banks, the *marigüis* and the black and yellow horseflies make the days unbearable, while the mosquitoes at night prevent all rest.'

Anyone who has been there can sympathize, for in some respects the Beni has not changed at all.

One of Heath's Indian companions, Ildefonso Roca, was a man of great valour and dedication, and it was he who gave Cachuela Esperanza its name by asking:

'So there is hope after all that we shall not lose our lives?'

They had to launch their boat over the rock-spiked rapids as their machetes had been stolen and they had only one small knife which was quite inadequate for cutting their way through the jungle, and even this they later lost in the turbulent waters. Their food was reduced to what they could hunt, eked out by dried bananas and worm-riddled yuccas.

It is interesting that Heath writes much more graphically and emotionally of these events in letters sent twenty years later from Garfield Avenue, Kansas City, an address which has a comfortably suburban ring, far removed from the crocodiles and cannibal tribes of the Beni River. Poor Ildefonso was less fortunate: he was drowned in 1885 at the Cachuela Esperanza, in the Waterfalls of Hope that he had named.

Today, as one flies over the vast expanse of the savannahs— for there are no roads whatsoever in a region comprising almost half of Bolivia—one has the impression of a land without past or future, searching for a solution that has always just eluded its grasp. Below there is an endless succession of prairies, wind-silvered grass broken only by occasional thickets of trees or scrub, and scarred by dark-brown surly rivers, dispiritedly meandering as if they too seek an outlet that they have long since despaired of finding. They trickle over the land like torpid streams of half-molten chocolate.

Once over the snow-covered barrier of the *cordillera* the plane stops everywhere, for the DC-3 is the country bus of Beni and Pando, landing with a sickening thud on rough grassland and trundling up to the island of settlement, a circle of grass thatched houses in the middle of nowhere, surrounded by a wooden palisade. The whole of the scanty population gathers to greet the plane, for its arrival is a weekly event, the source of news and gossip and of provisions and beer. Usually half their number is travelling in one direction or another. Most of the people who clamber aboard with great aplomb, hung around with straw bags and sacks, and clutching squawking hens and other small livestock in their arms, have seldom, if ever, travelled in a car or a lorry.

Here air and water are the only elements offering communication with the rest of the country, and still today the journey by boat is slow and hazardous, for the rivers are spiked with submerged driftwood that can rip the bottom out of a small craft, and the water level fluctuates greatly, either shrinking to a trickle or flooding wide stretches of the countryside. Their channels may also capriciously change course, and there is at least one instance near Santa Cruz of a bridge built at great expense over what is now a dried-up bed. This is why most of the products of this potentially rich area have to be flown out, including the meat and tropical hardwoods which are the region's greatest potential wealth. Costly and precarious communications, on the other hand, are the greatest obstacles to their development.

It is hard to imagine the utter isolation of life in these small settlements. On every side the savannah undulates endlessly to the horizon, dulling the gaze by its sheer monotony and devitalizing the imagination. It is an enervating landscape beckoning only to inertia and indolence. Here too one is assailed by the overwhelming impression that man is an anachronism, an intrusion only marginally tolerated by an all-powerful Nature, in whose hands all the cards are stacked. The horses and the troupes of half-wild cattle which have roamed these grasslands since the Jesuits introduced them three hundred years ago have staked a more valid claim to be the natural denizens of the Beni. Just how precarious man's tenancy is was shown in recent years when a strange and virulent disease swept through the township of San Joaquín like the black death and in two or three years reduced it to a fragment of its former size, despite the heroic endeavours of the American scientists brought in to find an antidote; indeed it nearly cost two of them their lives.

Even in the larger towns the sense of impermanence is strong; you feel that some vital stages in development have been omitted and that the whole structure of such civilization as exists rests on flimsy foundations that may at any moment subside. It is not merely that the aeroplane has come before the car. In Trinidad you may find yourself and your luggage being transported to the airport on a fleet of motorcycles instead of by taxi. Further north, in Riberalta, the streets are made of grass, broad lawns stretching from one end of the town to the other, and are lined with one-storey wooden huts with thatched roofs. I scarcely saw more than one four-wheeled vehicle—a jeep—during the two visits I made there. All the green roads in Riberalta lead down to the river, because the river is the

211

main artery of the town. Muddy though the slack waters are, the body of the water is so immense—it is here nearly a thousand yards wide, though still thousands of miles from the Amazon and the Atlantic—that it imposes with a kind of decadent majesty. In the northern part of the Beni the pampas give way to Amazonian forest, and the jungle marches straight down to the shores opposite Riberalta. In contrast, the river bank nearest the town surges with activity and is cluttered with craft of every description, from small canoes hollowed out of a single tree-trunk to motor cruisers.

A mile or two above Riberalta two of the greatest rivers of northern Bolivia, the Madre de Díos, which drains the southern part of the Peruvian sierra, and the Beni, which rises in the Yungas of the Department of La Paz, join in one great water-way. It was Heath who discovered the confluence, but his curt prose gives no hint of its beauty: the two rivers flow majestically together round a small wooded island, their shores thickly jungled with magnificent tall trees, and at evening the setting sun transmutes the turbid water into burnished copper and sets the forest aflame.

Afterwards, as you slither ashore on the muddy banks of Riberalta the dusk throbs with the syncopated chorus of cicadas and frogs. In the grassy square in the centre of the town a hundred fires glow secretly, flirting with shadowy figures that merge in the fast-gathering darkness. As your eye becomes accustomed to the gloom, you realize that most of the populace must be gathered here. Tapers glimmer warmly at small tables where one may eat spicy *empanadas* or even a *sajta de pollo*. Riberalta is a gregarious town where people are perhaps drawn together by the almost physical presence of the encircling jungle and the sense of their own isolation. It seems as if life has hardly changed since the beginning of the century, despite the advent of the aeroplane, and that the town might at any moment slip quietly back into the jungle. As you walk back through the dark streets afterwards, where even the heaviest footfall is silenced in the grass, and the mosquitoes and *jejenes* nibble at your ankles, the languid Amazonian heat enfolds you in its close embrace, warm and soft as a layer of woollen clothing.

The sense of timeless well-being does not usually long survive the encounter with the hotel, where the tropical fragrance of the night is transformed into a foetid stuffiness and as likely as not you will be offered a hammock rather than a bed in an already overcrowded room. I speak from experience, for in Riberalta I learnt once again that Bolivia is undoubtedly a man's country: the male members of the party were borne off to the relative luxury of the Maryknoll Fathers' mission, and the women left to make the best of the exiguous resources of the town.

As over so many other things, Bolivians can never agree about the *Oriente*. It has its enthusiasts, men whose eyes gleam at the very mention of the tropical lowlands, seeing there the whole future prosperity and expansion of the country, because of its rich resources of wood and livestock, its enormous productive potential for the cultivation of food crops, its vast expanse of untilled and virtually uninhabited land awaiting development. Others are less sanguine; they cite the monumental geographical barriers which inhibit communication and integration, the disease problems of a tropical region, the supposed inadaptability of the Andean-Indian to this strange environment, and they cast doubts on the fertility of the soil and on the richness of the area's natural resources. Compromise has little appeal for the Bolivian mentality, which tends to see things in mutually exclusive shades of black and white, yet the best solution would surely be a joint and complementary onslaught on the problems of both the *altiplano* and the tropical lowlands, in preference to the exclusive, or unbalanced, development of one or the other. Even if the Government achieves its declared objective of transferring some 100,000 families— about half-a-million people in all—to the lowlands by the early 1970s, this will do no more than siphon off the expected increase in population during the same period, if the current estimates of population growth, admittedly rather haphazard, come anywhere near the truth. This means that the excessive population pressure on the highest and most arid land in the country, already acute in many places, will merely be prevented from becoming worse, but will not be relieved.

The development of the *Oriente*, the achievement of closer links with the western, mountainous part of the country, through better communications and the transfer of greater numbers of highland peoples to the plains is not an alternative, but the necessary concomitant of the improvement of agricultural productivity and standards of living on the *altiplano*. In the last few years significant advances have been made and even though they are unobtrusive in relation to the size of the problem they are nonetheless an important element of unification in a country formerly divided against itself by the idiosyncrasies of nature and history.

12 WHEN you return to the windswept roof of the country and see La Paz crouched below its eaves, like a fugitive, or a miser mourning the spent gold of the Choqueyapu, it is difficult to believe that this is the centre of government for so vast and varied a country, that it is from this unlikely collection of buildings, threatened, it seems, with imminent extinction by the mountains which loom over it, that the fortunes of all those rich lands, with their untapped resources, are decreed. La Paz makes no concessions to easy popularity. It is a city without charm, austere, take-me-or-leave-me and this is perhaps why it exerts a strong hold over those who come to love it. There is nothing nondescript about La Paz; you can almost see the sinews that have forged its strange destiny exteriorized in the straining rocks buttressing the gully in which it lies.

La Paz does not have the cultural aura of Sucre, the delicate refinement of flower-hung patios betokening a safe, enclosed world of ease, of long, drowsy afternoons devoted for centuries to books and music and beautiful *objets d'art*. Nor does it have the brisk gaiety of Cochabamba, although it, too, is a commercial city; and it is certainly not blessed with the same soft climate or fanned with zephyrous valley airs: the wind that rasps off the *altiplano* cuts down to the bare bone. Nor, yet again, does La Paz share the brash, frontier-town atmosphere of Santa Cruz, that sense of being poised on the edge of the unknown and the incalculable, of having one tremulous foot already in the future. La Paz is solidly embedded in its origins. It is the prototype of the self-made city and there is a kind of terse, unshakeable confidence about its dowdy buildings.

Its origins were, after all, very humble, for it began as a staging-post on the silver route from Potosí to Lima. Its first site, in 1548, was on the *altiplano* where the village of Laja now stands, but it was almost immediately transferred to the more sheltered ravine of the Choquepyapu River, where the llama and mule trains loaded with precious metal might find protection at night from the searing upland winds on their long, slow journey across the Andes to the coast. Even today one quarter in the upper reaches of the city is known as *La Garita de Lima*. Later, it became the centre for another trade, that of *coca*, brought up from the Yungas valleys and sent to the mining camps in Potosí.

La Paz has made its way in the world by sheer tenacity of purpose and independence of spirit. It is no coincidence that the revolutionary cry first heard in Sucre in 1809 only achieved its true significance, that of outright secession from the Spanish monarchy, when it was echoed in La Paz a month or two later by Pedro Domingo Murillo, who died in its utterance, or that the main fighting during the 1952 revolution, which changed Bolivia's future, took place in her streets.

Yet La Paz wears her history lightly and almost carelessly. Murillo's home in the quaintly cobbled Calle Jaén houses a frowsty and not very imaginative museum, seldom pointed out to visitors. The house where Bolívar stayed in 1825 after his triumphal entry into La Paz, and the final rout of the Spanish royalist forces at Ayacucho, is marked by no memorial save local tradition. It leans sadly over the steep paving stones of the Calle Colón as if its worn wattle and daub might at any moment collapse and crumble into dust like the continental dreams of the *Libertador*. Only a few ragged flowers and a desultory sentry encircle the prosaic lamp-post outside the presidential palace where the body of the luckless Villaroel was strung up to be vilified by the mob in 1946.

But, as the very mention of Villaroel's name would remind one, it would be a mistake to think of this as a passionless city. Passion here runs deeply if unobtrusively; tightly leashed, from time to time it bursts forth uncontrollably. These, after all, were the streets where Melgarejo, the megalomaniac dictator of a hundred years ago, prowled during his drunken orgies, striking fear into the hapless passers-by whom he pitilessly assaulted, and down which Queen Victoria's emissary was unceremoniously bundled, on a donkey, tied to face its tail, because he refused to be a boon companion to the President in his excesses. The taut air here is charged with emotion that when least expected explodes into flame. For the individual the explosion may take the form of some inexplicable and contrary act; when I had only been in La Paz a couple of days a woman walking down the main street was killed because a man in a bar, on a sudden whim, had fired his pistol out through the door, presumably into the empty air. Again Melgarejo provides a precedent: when he received a present of a rifle from the President of Peru, he is said to have wished to try it out on the first person who walked into the Plaza Murillo, below the Palace balconies where he stationed himself in readiness. Bloodshed was only prevented by the prompt action of his mistress, Juana Sánchez, who posted sentries at the four corners to prevent anyone entering.

Collectively, this pent-up emotion resolves itself into one of the street demonstrations or *manifestaciones* which are a regular feature of civic life in La Paz.

Nor is La Paz devoid of beauty. If you arrive back from a journey across the *altiplano* at night the first sight of the city as you cross the lip of the ravine dumbfounds even more than in daytime. In the town the harsh lights and the neon signs may seem tawdry but from above they look like a sparkling necklace of crystal beads, tumbling down the valley. Seen from below, from one of the rough cart-tracks that meander up into the hills from Calacoto, the city hangs glittering in the sky above you, like some gigantic candelabra or a bejewelled portent of the Andean gods. And if you wander down the worn cobbles of

217

the Calle Jaén on a moonlight night, glimpsing through half-open doors the lamplit courtyards, with their pots of geraniums and their decaying balconies, it would seem the most normal thing in the world, in this one corner where the savour of the old colonial town still seeps from aged beams and masonry, if Murillo were to come out from the house just down the road, in a black cape and a wide-brimmed hat, and swing away down the alley, bound for some rendezvous with his fellow-conspirators, perhaps in a café off the *plaza* that now bears his name.

Next day, by contrast, the town appears drabber and work-worn. Poverty makes scant attempt to conceal its traces here but one is spared the distressing contrasts of wealth and destitution that mar other Latin American capitals, usually deemed more advanced. Except in the centre of the city by far the majority of the buildings are made of adobe, genteelly concealed behind a layer of plaster in residential houses of a certain standing. I lived for years in the house of an ex-President before discovering, when the plaster began to flake off a wall behind the chimney, the tell-tale sprigs of straw sticking out from sun-baked mud. This is why, in the upper reaches of the city, where most of the poorer people live, whole rows of houses are washed away every year in the rains; and a friend of mine once told me how a house in which he had been staying had just slipped quietly into the ravine in the course of a single night.

Most places could do with a coat of paint and there are practically no new buildings at all. A few windowless and roofless silhouettes stand like tombstones commemorating the frantic building boom that took place during the galloping inflation of the middle nineteen-fifties and as swiftly petered out when stabilization measures were introduced in 1956, and for a time stamped out all growth. During the first half of the sixties I never saw so much as one brick added to these sad memorials.

The modern buildings that have been completed bear a seedy air. If they belong to the government the windows more often than not are gaping holes surrounded by splintered glass, for they are the preferred target of the dissident multitude which

218

every so often marches the streets giving vent to its frustration and discontent. It is lucky that there are few buildings more than six or seven storeys high, for most lifts in the city ceased to work years ago and their rusted doors are no more than a status symbol; even those that do function are put out of action by lengthy power cuts during the dry winter months. Running up and down innumerable flights of stairs every day in the altitude of La Paz is no joke, even to the acclimatized, but physical strain is not the only risk. In the Ministry of Labour an aged wooden staircase used to creak and groan piteously under the packed hordes of workers seeking redress or assistance, so that one thought twice before entrusting oneself to its rotting steps; while in the Ministry of Rural Affairs the grimy, finger-marked corridors and stairways were so choked with Indians from all parts of the country, exuding the heavy smell of *coca* intermingled with sweat, that one risked being trampled underfoot.

Though the wheels of government turn anything but smoothly, at least these people straining to move a foot nearer the office of the Minister or some other official have felt for the first time in history that the government bears some relation to them personally and that their interests are cared for, however slow or inefficient the process. *Trámites*—official transactions—are in any case an inescapable fact of life in La Paz even for its more fortunate citizens, and consume an unconscionable amount of time, temper, ink and indelible rubber stamps. According to the dictionaries the Spanish word comes from the Latin *trames* 'way, road, or means' but anyone exposed to the process in Latin America would be more inclined to believe that it originates from the word *trama*, meaning 'weave' or 'plot', so intricate and devious is the mechanism involved.

It is not that people mean to be unhelpful but simply that the human impulse and official procedures work at cross-purposes and end by cancelling one another out. The result defies all logic and cloaks every transaction in an impenetrable fog. When I had been only a short time in La Paz a very grubby small boy rang the bell at my gate one Sunday afternoon and presented me with a moth-eaten piece of yellow paper that looked as if it might have blown in from the gutter. Deciphering it with difficulty I learned that an express letter had arrived for me. A faint stamp on one corner disclosed further that this urgent communication had been received no less than three weeks previously. There was no house-to-house delivery in La Paz but even so such a long delay seemed inexcusable. Next day I went in person to the post office and stood in the queue before the window dealing with registered letters. When at last my turn came I explained the situation very slowly and carefully to the girl in charge: someone had paid extra so that this letter would be given priority and instead it had inexplicably been held up for three weeks. Listening courteously, the girl took the tattered piece of paper and examined it with infinite care. She read the front, then turned it over and looked at the back, and finally perused it upside down with a deepening frown of puzzlement, as if sustained concentration would reveal some secret explanation hidden from the normal gaze—written perhaps in invisible ink. At last she raised her eyes to mine:

'But this arrived twenty days ago!' she exclaimed.

'Yes,' said I, elated that the essential message had sunk in. 'What do you think of that?'

But the answer routed me completely.

'Then why,' she asked severely 'did you not come to collect it long before this?'

The signs of poverty are not confined to the buildings. At every street corner you will be accosted by a ragged urchin trying to sell two or three packets of cigarettes, boxes of matches, or tubes of sweets, a sure sign of under-employment. Many a time I have left my office, in the dark—for here the equatorial night falls soon after six-thirty all the year round— to find one or two ill-clad children with scabby, chapped faces, huddled in the doorway opposite, fast asleep, in the glacial cold, and evidently settled down for the night. For a large majority life is lived in the streets. Many a *cholita* will sit on the pavement in a main thoroughfare, her back propped against

220

above: Folklore festival, La Paz.
below: Carnival in La Paz.

above: Erosion near La Paz.
below: The Valley of Cristina and Juan.

the wall of a building, feet splayed in front of her, unconcernedly breast-feeding her baby; afterwards, equally oblivious of the pedestrians swirling past her, she will lay the baby on top of an *aguayo* spread out on the stones, roll the infant up in it expertly and with a deft twist heave it on to her back again.

The terrace of my house commanded a magnificent view of the valley sweeping down to Obrajes and Calacoto and of the gaunt hills beyond, and once, when I was out early to see the dawn-flush on the Illimani, I heard a faint but frantic mewing sound from the direction of the road. It sounded like a cat or small dog in difficulties and I hurried round the house to find the cause of the trouble. At first I could see nothing, and then, through the iron railings of the small gate set in a thick pine hedge, my eyes were suddenly riveted on an *aguayo* lying bundled up on the opposite pavement, a bizarre splash of colour on the grey stone. Even as I gazed the bundle began to squirm and cry again. It could only be an abandoned baby. Hardly had I realized this, however, and begun to grapple with the padlock on the gate, than there was a flurry of steps round the corner of the deserted street and a *cholita* rushed into view and snatched the squawling child to her breast. In her hand still swung one of the ineffectual besoms with which they profess to sweep the streets in La Paz; she was a street cleaner, and had no option but to take her baby out with her at dawn and leave it sleeping on the pavement.

Many of those who successfully weather such perils in childhood—and mortality rates are high—survive to become little more than beasts of burden. It is an all too familiar sight to see some unwieldy object, a wardrobe, say, or a heavy table with its legs pointing skywards, staggering up one of the steep streets, apparently under its own propulsion, only to discover on closer inspection that it is roped to the tattered, homespun back of an Indian porter, humped so low that one has to bend almost to pavement level to see his wrinkled face, twisted almost out of human semblance, yet bearing the stamp of all human misery since the world began. In many respects the status of the Indian has improved but too often economic realities have defeated the best-intentioned political and social philosophies.

These streets are difficult enough to negotiate even for the unburdened. Crazily tilted at impossible gradients, they strain heart and lungs during the ascent, and require prodigious feats of balance when you come down. The streets themselves are cobbled but the pavements are made of granite slabs which multitudes of feet, bare and shod, over many years have rubbed to the deadly smoothness of polished glass. Periodically notches are chipped in the stone with pickaxes but they are ineffectual and the descent from the Plaza Murillo is still rather like walking down a sheet of sheer ice inclined at an angle of forty-five degrees. Native *paceños* sprint down at a great rate, but the uninitiated stranger totters along, clutching at the wall or his companions as his foothold threatens to elude him at every step.

Still, the steeply canted streets have one advantage: combined with the excessive altitude, which takes its toll of the combustion engine as well as of the human body, they impose a natural speed limit on traffic. But for this, road casualties would be much higher, for the *paceño* is not to be outvied in recklessness by any other Latin American once he gets behind a steering wheel. Usually he thrusts an authoritative arm out of the window and proceeds to execute a series of hieroglyphics in the air. They may mean that he intends to turn left, right or to stop abruptly. There is no way of knowing unless you have a gift for thought-reading, but woe betide you if you guess his intentions wrongly.

'But I put out my hand,' he will cry indignantly, as soon as the crash of crumpled metal has ceased to reverberate through the thin air, and no amount of arguing will wipe the aggrieved expression from his face or convince him that a less esoteric form of signalling might have staved off disaster.

By and large, driving a car in La Paz is an unnerving business. Grinding up one of the steeper streets in first gear behind a snorting, overloaded bus that looks as if it is nearing its last gasp and at any moment will expire on top of you is a harrowing experience, second only to that of travelling in the bus yourself. There is only one rule about the capacity of these battered vehicles, which get by on faith and the inspired application of odd bits of string and wire, and that is that the passengers should be packed in until not so much as a baby can be fitted into the remaining crevices. For some unfathomable reason the Bolivians, like the Chileans, refer to these ungainly, lumbering vehicles as *góndolas*, though whether this is intentional irony or nostalgia for their lost seaboard is hard to say. Adjured to 'take the *góndola*' the bemused newcomer conjures up a vision of some forgotten Andean Venice, or perhaps a romantic excursion on Lake Titicaca, but his dreams are soon dashed. Nothing could be more inexorably earthbound than the Bolivian *góndola*.

Then there are the dangers of theft. Every conceivably removable object on a private vehicle has to be firmly fixed, or taken off if it is not essential. Hub-caps must be tortuously attached with screws and wires to foil the nimble fingers of a thief with only a few moments at his disposal. Outside mirrors and emblems have to be solidly riveted to the body of the car and windscreen wipers must be meticulously removed and kept inside the car even during the drenching storms of the short rainy season. Once a strip of nickel plating was torn from my car in broad daylight under the eyes of the sentries at the main garrison opposite my house. The ultimate indignity was to be told by the local agent the next day that their stock of replacements had long since been exhausted but that by a happy chance the exact part required had come in that very day . . . But irritating as it is to have to buy back one's own property, minor thefts like this are inevitable in a poor society in which many people have only their wits between them and starvation.

The occasional theft of whole vehicles comes nearer to being organized crime, of which there is happily no very great evidence in Bolivia so far, one of the few advantages of underdevelopment. Car-stealing is not in any case so easy as, say, in Uruguay, where in a matter of hours a stolen car can be whipped over the Brazilian border and start circulating again with a new coat of paint and a changed number plate. There is nowhere you can escape to from La Paz, unless you are prepared to chug for days across the *altiplano*, in imminent danger of detection. Instead, the stolen car is coasted downhill to one of the eroded gullies of Obrajes, and there stripped of everything saleable. If you are not swift in pursuit you will find your erstwhile automobile dismantled down to the chassis. I speak from personal experience, for I once emerged from a dinner to find that my official car had disappeared into thin air. By dint of chivvying the police and purchasing petrol for their jeeps and motorcycles we managed to catch up with the culprits before they got very far. They abandoned the car at our approach, taking with them only the cigarette lighter and, for some strange reason, the United Nations flag, though whether this signified devotion to the United Nations ideal or desire for international protection remained an unsolved mystery.

But for the most part, *paceños* are sturdy, honest folk. Self-reliance and resilience are the common denominator, from the street market women who squat on the shelving streets in the upper reaches of the town, with their wares neatly piled on the ground before them, to their more sophisticated colleagues in the indoor markets in the centre, females of imposing size and demeanour who sit enthroned on top of monumental mounds of fruit and vegetables and grain as if personifying the bountiful Pachamama herself and wearing their bowler hats like crowns. Rumour has it that most of these redoubtable ladies have considerable sums of hard cash tucked away under their mattresses. Regal they most certainly are, though they are not averse to some pretty stiff haggling and, indeed, will despise you if you accept their first price unquestioningly. Their language has the traditional pithiness of a street-cry. 'Buy my choice oranges, *casera*', they wheedle after you as you pick your way down narrow, slippery alleys, high-walled on either side with produce, and step over the odd sleeping infant tucked away in a handy crevice between the melons and the cabbages. Any illusion that you may have got the best of the bargain will be dispelled when, at the end, they throw in an extra orange for your supposedly beautiful eyes.

This is not only salesmanship or commercial calculation. The *paceño* is naturally affectionate and gregarious. Two friends who meet almost every day will yet stand entranced in one another's company, enquiring minutely after the health and well-being not only of themselves but also of every relative, near or far, on both sides. Externally, this solicitous concern is epitomized in the *abrazo* or embrace with which they greet one another. The *abrazo* is by the way of being a solemn ritual and is practised indiscriminately between members of the same sex or between the sexes. I remember my own horrified alarm when, shortly after my arrival in Bolivia, I went to the Foreign Ministry to bid farewell to an official who was being posted abroad and found myself suddenly clasped to him in a bearlike hug. My previous contacts with him had been of the slightest and most formal kind and as I struggled, with more energy than diplomacy, to free myself, the wry thought crossed my mind that perhaps, after all those years of disproving popular scepticism about the survival prospects of a working woman in Latin America, Nemesis had at last caught up with me. In the context of these fevered thoughts it was a trifle dashing to discover that I was being surveyed with gentle amusement and then indoctrinated into the technique of the Bolivian *abrazo*. In fact it has all the sedate propriety of a minuet: you shake your right hands, then merge in a clinch, right arms over left shoulders, left arms tucked under right arms (men at this stage often thump one another heartily on the back, presumably to give a touch of virility to the proceedings), then break apart and solemnly shake right hands again. Nowadays there are no barriers of class either; this gravely affectionate salute comes as naturally to the Indian peasant or miner as to the Cabinet Minister. Not infrequently, therefore, it is a somewhat pungent experience, but infinitely preferable to the genuflection and hand kissing to which I was once subjected in an out-of-the-way village.

The café society so beloved of other Latin American countries does not enjoy the same vogue in La Paz, perhaps because of the lack of facilities and perhaps also because the climate is not very propitious for pavement café life. Every day at noon in the winter time, however, when the sun is at its brightest, the rusty tables outside the Copacabana hotel in the Prado will be packed with people—almost exclusively men—enjoying a lunchtime drink and gossip. On Saturdays and Sundays it is the custom for whole families to congregate there to eat *salteñas*, spiced meat pasties, oozing with soupy liquid which spurts out at the first bite and liberally sprays the inexpert or unforewarned with greasy fluid. On Sundays, when the people stream out from Mass, at the church opposite, there is the weekly parade of beauty. The young girls stroll self-consciously up and down, in groups of two or more, between the emaciated palms and scrawny flowers of the Prado, ogled by young bloods from the Military Academy, who are dressed to kill in resplendently archaic uniforms, reminiscent of the wars of independence against Spain. In the distance, a band laboriously thumps out martial airs and half-hearted waltzes.

Here, as in Spain, 'the fine appearance' is held in high esteem and one finds the same paradox between the frugal, sober nature of the people, and the extravagant love of display revealed in their brilliantly coloured folk costumes, sparkling with embroidery and sequins, and in the baroque adornments of their carnival disguises, especially the accoutrements of the devil dancers. Most of the girls sauntering with demure seductiveness down the Prado on Sundays, beautifully turned out in their crisply laundered dresses, come from shabby homes, where they may have to pick their way carefully between pools of dirty water in the unevenly flagged courtyard before they reach the street. There is not much luxury left in La Paz since the 1952 revolution. The great houses of the Aramayos and the like have been let out to Embassies, and most of the so-called *rosca*, the moneyed upper class whose entrenched privileges were most affected by the advent to power of the National Revolutionary Movement, have lived abroad since and rented their homes to foreigners. But in a curiously Spanish style, in this ex-Spanish colony which impatiently threw off the Spanish yoke, much of the social life takes place in the street and this is the main place of entertainment. For this reason, however cramped the circumstances may be at home, all but the very poor will take pains to dress well when they go out.

The street, too, is the main source of information and the forum for much of the political activity and speculation which occupies so many of the waking hours of the *paceño*, whatever his walk in life. Provided you are reasonably well-connected you have only to walk once or twice up and down one of the principal streets on any day of the week to glean some enticing titbit of information, the latest iniquities of the President (for to all self-respecting Bolivians the government in power, whatever its complexion or their own political affiliations, is by definition wrong, inefficient and, probably, they hint darkly, corrupt into the bargain) or the stop-press rumours on the next reshuffle of the Cabinet. A judiciously-timed stroll along the right route, combined with the perusal of the newspapers, will keep you abreast of events.

There has been much criticism of lack of freedom in the Bolivian press over the last fifteen years, causing regional bodies to pass censorious resolutions. Yet I must say I found Bolivian newspapers remarkably outspoken. Given a basic knowledge of the personalities and the political interests involved (not easy, I admit, for a foreigner, but installed into all Bolivians with their mothers' milk) plus a few well-informed street contacts, and you know everything that is going on. Indeed, many of the comments and strictures I have seen published would, in my opinion, have been considered little short of libellous had they appeared in print in an English context. The Bolivian delights in gossip, a predilection fostered by the relatively small scale of La Paz society, for although the population numbers around 300,000, business and official life of any consequence is probably confined to no more than 50,000. While some project is still half formed in your mind, news of your intentions will be relayed back to you, and you may be sure that the tale will have lost nothing in the telling. There is a certain village-like quality about life in La Paz and the Spanish obsession with the '¿Qué dirán?' (What will the neighbours say?) looms large in the lives of all but the most rebellious.

227

Their concern is well-founded, for the Bolivian, as long as he is on the side of the omnipotent 'they', rather than the hapless object of comment, has a pithy, sardonic kind of humour, which strips things to their essentials just as centuries of erosion have worn the hillsides round the town down to the bare rock. He is the born sceptic ;'¡No me diga!' ('Don't tell me!') he will cry in delighted disbelief when you regale him with some juicy piece of intelligence that has escaped his notice. Perhaps this is the secret of his survival and his unrepentant cheerfulness in the face of difficulties and setbacks that would have over-whelmed most people.

All of this gives an unmistakable tang to life in La Paz, the almost imperceptible quiver of a snake's tongue in the cut and thrust of everyday life, just as the sharp, dry air flickers like a fang at the back of one's nostrils.

Survival may be difficult in every sense but, just as the plants which survive the extremes of frost and hail and burning sun achieve a stunted but sturdy growth in the arid gardens of La Paz, so do the people acquire a robust, immutable strength. You can depend on them in big things, if not always in small. My cook, Pancha, was a temperamental creature, a roly-poly of a woman, with a nutbrown face and snapping dark eyes that belied her deceptively acquiescent chubbiness. Her progress through the house was punctuated by a series of crashes and bangs as she fell over large objects or let my most precious possessions slip between her fingers. Her temper, to say the least, was uncertain and her relations with other members of the household tempestuous. One weekend jaunt very nearly had to be sacrificed when loud screams from the kitchen brought me scurrying to a scene of dreadful carnage: a dispute over which picnic basket should be used had ended with Pancha seizing the housemaid by the hair. The housemaid had retaliated in kind and they were now locked in deadly combat. Great tufts of black hair strewed the kitchen and it was only by thrusting Pancha in the larder, locking the door and threatening to leave her there for the rest of the weekend that I was able to restore calm.

Yet at the time of the 1964 revolution, when the maid had fled because the house was too near the main garrison, Pancha proved a tower of strength. She produced, out of nothing, lunch for about twenty people stranded at my house when the fighting broke out. That evening she asked for permission to go home because she had heard that her son, who was connected with the railwayman's union, had been taken prisoner. I did not expect to see her back until everything was over, for all that night mortars and bazookas kept up the combat and the roof of the house was peppered with bullets intended for the garrison. But soon after dawn next day I heard a familiar raucous voice shouting at the gate and demanding entrance (for of course there was no electricity). There was Pancha, round and dependable and irascible as ever, having scuttled down the several steep miles from the top of the city on her stubby little legs—for there was no transport of any kind either—because she thought I needed her.

Víctor, the office chauffeur, a man who prided himself on driving a smart bargain, proved no less devoted. When the outbreak of fighting caught us in the Prado he did not for a moment demur when I told him to drive me back to the office to fetch the other people cut off there but drove straight through the municipal flowerbeds and fought his way back against a tide of vehicles streaming down both sides of the avenue, in their drivers' panic-stricken haste to leave the centre of the city where shooting could already be heard. Later with equal alacrity, he drove me to the Palace when fighting there had only just ceased, though not a soul was moving in the deserted streets, and I believe that he would have charged a machine-gun emplacement had I asked him to do so. Whenever I went out on field trips Víctor appointed himself as my bodyguard. 'Who will look after you if I am not there?' he would demand if there was ever any question of leaving him behind, and together we survived any number of adventures.

There is not much outside entertainment in La Paz. For the relatively more affluent and sophisticated there are a few night-clubs, whose respectability is judged in direct proportion to the amount of light allowed to play on the scene. Not that this is ever very considerable, since a judicious penumbra can also conceal a seedy décor or the splinters and holes in the floor which unwary feet will find soon enough. But the bands are usually first-class, though it is only on Fridays and Saturdays that they have the satisfaction of playing to capacity. Even here the note of melodrama sometimes intervenes: a political quarrel will suddenly flare up between drinking companions, pistols may be brandished and sometimes even fired.

Football is the abiding passion of most *paceños*. On Sundays and holidays the stadium is packed to capacity and the food-vendors outside do a roaring trade with *salteñas* and *humintas* wrapped in maize leaves. The occasion when Bolivia won the South American championship in La Paz caused more rejoicing than a successful revolution, and was not at all diluted by the realization that the rival teams were at a disadvantage because they were unaccustomed to such extreme altitude. A day's holiday was declared and people drove deliriously round the streets sounding the victory sign on their horns for hours on end.

Local folklore and tradition permeate everyday life, however. La Paz has its devil dancers too, though they are fewer in number and less organized than those of Oruro. Local feastdays and saints' festivals are celebrated with music and dancing: every *barrio* seems to have its own brass band, and on any pretext the nearest open space or square will be a-swirl with brilliantly hued skirts and petticoats, flashing emerald, blinding blue and heliotrope.

It is not only the popular *barrios* which maintain the folk tradition. At more sophisticated parties in the homes of professional people, the guests eat *fricassé*, a deliciously spiced stew of pork, and dance popular rhythms from all over the country to music played perhaps by the finest *charango* player in the country, who works, improbably enough, in the barber's shop opposite the Ministry of Finance: *huayños* from the *altiplano*, *bailecitos*, *taquiraris* and *carnavalitos* from the valleys and the tropical lowlands. But most popular of all is the *cueca*—the graceful courtship dance inherited from Spain and found in varying forms in all the neighbouring countries, as the *marinera* in Peru, the *samba* in Uruguay and Argentina and the *cueca* again—though subtly different—in Chile. It has the grace of a stately dance, nostalgically remembered perhaps from some courtly revels in Spain, and given new zest by the coquetry of the flirting handkerchiefs in the dancers' hands and the interplay of seduction and pursuit; and the *zapateado* with which each movement ends faintly recalls the *flamenco* tradition of Andalusia. Sometimes, there are folk dance festivals and then the stadium becomes an exotic garden aflame with brilliant costumes displaying the inexhaustible wealth of the Bolivian popular imagination, from the nodding *suri* plumes of the headdresses rising three feet above the heads of some of the performers to the macabre masks of the devil dancers.

Once a year, on 24 January, the traditional *Alacitas* fair takes place in La Paz. Several streets are closed and crammed with stalls selling all manner of traditional articles, all made in miniature. *Alacitas* means 'buy me' and, according to popular belief, whatever you buy at *Alacitas* you will come to possess during the coming year: if you want a house, you buy a diminutive chalet; if you wish to travel, you buy a tiny doll's suitcase; and if you hanker for wealth you may even buy vast quantities of *bolivianos*, exact replicas of ordinary currency, except that they are a fraction of normal size. Here too, there is the familiar synthesis of religious and pagan beliefs: 24 January is the feast of Our Lady of La Paz, the patron saint of the city, but the presiding genius at the fair goes back far beyond the advent of the Spaniards: it is the guffawing, rubicond dwarf known as the Ekeko, the genial household god, loaded with all kinds of goodies in miniature, whom you have to keep supplied with new provisions each year if your home is to remain happy and prosperous.

The ancient *kollas* paid homage to the Ekeko at the summer solstice, offering him the fruits of the harvest, pottery, woven cloth and clay figures and this ceremony continued into Spanish

231

times. On 24 January 1782 Don Sebastián Segurola, the Governor of La Paz, inaugurated the feast of the Virgin of La Paz, in gratitude for the victory over the Indian uprising of two years earlier, and ordered that the day should be set aside for the sale of miniatures, which had originally taken place throughout the year. The Indians could hardly be expected to enter wholeheartedly into the spirit of these festivities and one cannot help thinking that they had their tongues in their cheeks when they followed the Governor's instructions to the letter but turned the occasion into worship of the Ekeko. And it is they who had the last word for, two centuries later, the Ekeko is to be found in every Bolivian household.

The same ambivalence surrounds the festival of the winter solstice in June, when the Inti Raimi of the Incas, nine days of ceremonies and sacrifices dedicated to the worship of the Sun and to fertility rites, blends with the ancient European midsummer festival, brought here by the Spaniards. The sacrificial fire which the Inca priests struck by holding a sacred bracelet up to the Sun, and which had to be preserved throughout the year in the Temple of the Sun if the omens were to remain propitious, is indistinguishable now from the bonfires of St John's Eve. These are lit after dusk at the gates of every house in the city and the surrounding bowl of the hills is speckled with the answering fires of the villages and hamlets outside as if an immense swarm of glow-worms was hovering in the sky above. Oblivious of the cold, people eat outside and dance round the blaze and for days afterwards a thick pall of smoke hangs over the city.

But although thousands of fires are lit practically on the doorsteps of the houses, there is no fear of conflagration because of the low oxygen content in the air. Until very recently La Paz had the distinction of being the only capital city in the world without a fire engine. When, soon after my arrival, a small paint factory went up in flames, the sight was so novel that the whole city turned out to see it. I have, however, a wry memory of an ill-fated UN Day exhibition which we had set up in the middle of the Prado in a tent loaned to us by the Bolivian Air

Force, which had held a display in it the previous week. We had worked feverishly through a weekend of mounting political tension, deafened by the loudspeakers of the Federation of Mining Workers' Syndicates, blaring forth the militant views of some housewives from the Catavi mine, whose aptitude for strident oratory seemed quite unimpaired by a hunger strike. When at last I had left the exhibition ready for inauguration on the following day the situation was worse. There were demonstrations against the authorities in the Prado and by an unfortunate confusion of identity an angry crowd set fire to the Air Force tent with a petrol flare and so burnt down the United Nations exhibition. By the time I arrived back on the scene, pushing my way through the troops and the clouds of tear-gas, only a few blackened tatters of canvas remained.

When the Municipality eventually acquired firefighting equipment it was more often employed in dispersing demonstrations—*manifestaciónes* as they are called—by squirting coloured water on the crowd—or simply plain water, for high in the Andes a douche of icy water is sufficient to quench the enthusiasm of all but the most ardent revolutionary. This is the preferred pastime of the *paceño*—the *manifestación*.

Though cynics may claim that the inextinguishable torch lit by Murillo was the perpetual flame of revolution, and make sarcastic play with the full name of the city—'La Ciudad de Nuestra Señora de La Paz', the 'City of Our Lady of Peace'—they often confuse the street demonstration with real revolutions which of recent years have been less prevalent. I am rash enough to think that I can by now tell the difference between a serious *manifestación*, bound to lead to some more profound upheaval, and the kind that is meant for a lark as much as anything, signifying some discontent but mostly an overwhelming desire to find an outlet for boredom and the claustrophobia bred from living in the maw of a chasm high up in the Andes. As often as not, the *manifestación* seems to be a substitute for a national sport, playing the same rôle, say, as cricket in an English village life. There is no bull-fighting in La Paz, perhaps because the lack of oxygen defeats even the bull's stamina to charge, and

233

football is an imported passion. The *manifestación*, on the other hand, is a wholly indigenous phenomenon, having, like cricket, its own rules and taboos, inexplicable to any but initiated enthusiasts. Window-breaking, for instance, is a time-hallowed part of any self-respecting *manifestación*, and, whatever the original object of the demonstration, you always end up protesting against the government of the day. Some apprehensive Chilean colleagues whom I attempted to console with this theory when the agitation for an outlet to the sea was resuscitated a few years ago, found this hard to believe on the eve of a demonstration against Chile. Events vindicated me, but very much to my cost, for I happened to be sitting in the President's office, at a meeting of the National Economic and Social Development Council, when the dynamite began to explode outside, an angry mob burst into the ground floor of the Palace, and tear-gas started to seep through the closed windows, making us shed real tears over the economic prospects of the next ten years.

La Paz has a tradition of the barricades. The rickety benches in the Prado have reached their present state of honourable decrepitude not from bearing the weight of generations of aged and worthy citizens but from constantly being flung into the breach, or used as battering rams. A state of siege was so much more often in force than not that one came to regard it merely as a useful excuse for escaping home to bed early from official dinners. True, I had to carry on a running battle with the garrison sentries opposite my house who would never let me stop my car in the street while I opened my garage doors, but commanded me to drive straight in, presumably to a resounding crash of splintering wood; but I was never really scared until the night when a covey of men jumped over the wall and encircled me with a palisade of bayonets before I had so much as one foot out of the car. They looked as if they had orders to shoot first and ask questions afterwards so I considered myself lucky to be given the chance of stammering out my identity and business.

The reason for this worrying innovation became clear next day when Adlai Stevenson arrived. I was among the group waiting to receive him at the airport, and when the official cortège was ready to move off I told my chauffeur to wait until all the important people had driven away before returning to the city. Hardly were the words out of my mouth when I was astonished to see a portly figure imperiously waving us into a position only two or three places behind the head of the procession.

'He's obviously confused us with someone else,' I said to Víctor. 'Stay where you are.'

But the gesticulations continued and became almost menacing. Víctor did not seem eager to tarry for explanations.

'That's the chief of the secret police,' he confided in some awe and alarm, 'and I must do what he says.'

Off we sped, therefore, in the vanguard, but had not got very far when we were stopped by two young officials, acquaintances of mine, whose car had sprung a puncture. From them I learnt the secret behind the elaborate precautions of the previous evening and of the unwonted pre-eminence given to the United Nations now. The Government, which was encountering a good deal of overt opposition at the time, had been warned that a bomb attempt was to be made on the life of Adlai Stevenson on the way down from the airport. As there was only one road down the mountainside, he was to be driven off unobtrusively later in a nondescript saloon. To foil the supposed conspirators a dummy cavalcade had been organized, complete with outriders and sirens, and a luckless high government official had been designated to impersonate the distinguished visitor in the first car. It was in this bogus procession that we had the doubtful privilege of occupying a leading place. According to my companions Mr Stevenson's stand-in (who could not have looked more unlike him) was feeling understandably nervous and they were anxious to set his mind at rest by taking his place. With these antecedents, no one was gladder than I to swing out of the line of cars, which seemed more akin to a funeral cortège with every passing moment, dash to the head, flag down the leading car and extricate the perspiring impersonator, depositing the two young men in exchange. As we sped down the hill leaving the official cars far behind I was unchivalrous enough to extract a *quid pro quo* from my willing captive, a promise that he would speak to the commanding officer of the garrison about the alarming way in which I had been accosted on the previous evening.

As with most such incidents in La Paz, it all turned out very well. There was no bomb attempt. I had no more trouble with officious, trigger-happy sentries at the garrison. And the only calamity suffered by Adlai Stevenson during his visit was to get stuck in the lift at the Hotel Crillon.

13 Y o u breathe in politics with the air in Bolivia, almost as if this was the vitalizing element introduced to eke out the exiguous oxygen. Augusto Céspedes begins his book *El Dictador Suicida*, which gives the background to the tragic death of General Busch in 1939, with the description of a popular election, which he witnessed in Cochabamba as a child. All the elements of the turbulent Bolivian political scene are there: a man advancing alone against the multitude, revolver shots, stones flying; the man helped away from the scene with his face bathed in blood. In a phrase Céspedes reveals the secret not only of himself but of the great majority of Bolivians:

'The Colombian, Eustacio Rivera, writes that in his youth he gambled his heart away and it was won by Violence. I would say that in my childhood my heart was won by Politics.'

Alcides Arguedas said the same thing more harshly. For him, politics are the *fruto archiprodrido*—the rotten fruit—of Bolivian life; this is the only activity, and a sterile one at that, which arouses the enthusiasm of everyone.

Bolivian politics are as intricate and convoluted as the mountains which encircle the *altiplano* and divide one region from another. Almost a lifetime's novitiate is necessary before one can trace the shifting shades of influence, the constant ebb and flow of power and personalities, with anything approaching confidence. Subjectivity and personalism are the keynotes.

Until 1880, when two reasonably well-defined parties, the Liberals and the Conservatives, were formed after the initial disasters of the war with Chile, Bolivian political life had been dominated by petty, warring factions, identified only by the date of their rise to power or by the names of their *caudillo*, or leader, who varied the group's policies according to his personal whim. Even with the more developed political structure of today traces of *caudillismo* still persist, and exercise a more directly individual influence than would be the case in more sophisticated countries. Thus one hears the different tendencies described, for example, as *pazestenssorista* or *barrientista*, according to whether they follow Paz Estenssoro or Barrientos. It is a trait reminiscent of Europe of the Middle Ages, or Spain at the time of the Reconquest.

The same subjectivity runs right through the body politic. Sometimes it is hard to keep abreast of the affiliations of one's Bolivian friends, so swiftly do they veer round. Often these changes are not unrelated to considerations of personal interest. Such a statement will not sound pejorative or unduly critical to anyone who has spent some time in Bolivia and has observed how far politics impinge on everyday life. This is a common Hispanic tendency, but is more marked here than elsewhere. The man in the street, whether he likes it or not (though, if the truth be told, most of them do, for the reason suggested by Augusto Céspedes), must take an interest in politics if he is to get on with the ordinary business of living, be it only to facilitate those endless *trámites*, in which the most simple and necessary transactions, such as, for example, obtaining a driving licence, can become inextricably enmeshed if one does not have direct and easy access to the official responsible. Good personal relations are a first precept for any kind of business in Bolivia and the wheels are infinitely better oiled by common political interests.

One Bolivian lady was famous during the 1950s and early 1960s for her flagrant and impassioned support of an opposition party which was in constant and open conflict with the ruling party, then the National Revolutionary Movement (MNR).

She suffered for her beliefs, distributed pamphlets, and took part in *manifestaciónes*. Discreet enquiry was always necessary in order to ascertain whether she was, at the moment, behind bars or not. When the 1964 revolution took place, and the party she had so long and loyally supported was among the victorious rebel forces, I remarked to a friend that now, at last, the tribulations of Doña X would come to an end and she would be rewarded for her devotion.

'Not at all,' came the astonishing reply. 'You see, a couple of months ago she joined the MNR.'

'However could that be?' I asked, flabbergasted at such an inexplicable volte-face at a time when the waning power of the MNR had been obvious to all.

'Well, she only joined the other party in the early 1950s because she believed they had a good chance of coming to power at that time. She thought that they would help her with a legal case over a block of apartments she owned. After ten years of supporting them fruitlessly, however, she gave up and went over to the government party. Unfortunately for her, they were at last really on the decline. So now she is back where she started.'

The example is, of course, an extreme one, and one could not imagine a person entering the political arena with such dedication for material reasons alone. Like Augusto Céspedes, Doña X must have lost her heart to politics at an early age.

The extraordinary fluidity of party politics in Bolivia illustrates the same pragmatic approach. Take for example the Nationalist Revolutionary Movement—the MNR—which grew up in reaction against the tragic fiasco of the Chaco War and which, after its success in the 1952 revolution, broke the old moulds for ever. At the time of Villaroel, just before the end of the Second World War, the MNR was accused of being Nazi-Fascist; after the 1952 revolution, because of its Marxist inspiration, it was suspected of being Communist; and not so many years later, when the country's fragile economy was bolstered by large-scale American aid, including direct financial support of the budget, some of its opponents branded it as sold to the Americans. Many of these extreme variations existed in the eye of the beholder, of course, but there is also no doubt that the MNR's ideology was flexible and adapted itself to the changing demands of circumstances. Two threads, however, remained constant: the need to find national solutions to the country's problems; and the determination to give the indigenous majority their rightful place in national life. One reason for the MNR's pliant approach is that it never aspired to being a party in the strict sense of the word; rather, as the name implies, it was a movement, a loosely-knit group made up of many subsidiary associations, some of them differing greatly in outlook. A broad base of this kind was made possible by the lack of any well-defined divisions of social class in Bolivia today. Divisions naturally do exist but they have not found any significant expression in individual political parties.

To understand the fluctuations of political life in Bolivia, one must go back to her history. Politics are less tense in other countries because the existence of a historical collectivity has already been established. This is not yet the case in Bolivia, where the struggle towards a national identity still continues, in spite of the many achievements of recent years. When the Spanish conquerors who swept into the mountain fastnesses of the Andes in the sixteenth century ruptured the old traditions and the old social, political and economic framework so carefully devised by the Incas, they erected in its place an administrative structure that was not too dissimilar in form, for it too was a pyramid, but which was vastly different in essence. The apex of the pyramid now lay across the Atlantic ocean, instead of in the heart of the Andean highlands, and the whole operation of its far-flung network of Viceroyalties and Audiencias was designed to plunder every last item of booty and carry it across the seas to swell the riches and grandeur of Spain. It was an administration harnessed to the needs of the Imperial Court in Madrid. Although some administrative innovations have been introduced, the effects of this distortion continue to this day and explain why much of the country's institutional framework is ill-suited to the development policies and programmes which it is trying to carry out.

One might have thought that the formal severance of the Spanish connection and the setting up of the new Republic in 1825 would have provided a remedy, but this was not the case. Social conscience and progressive ideas were not far advanced in Europe at the time when Latin America obtained its independence. This is one reason why comparisons between the struggle against colonialism in Latin America in the nineteenth century and that of our own day in, say, Africa, are totally misleading. Little thought was given in the early nineteenth century to the welfare or aspirations of the original, indigenous inhabitants of the newly-independent territories. Indeed, the revolution was sponsored and praised by some of the greatest liberals of the age, although the Indians were still regarded as an inferior race by the revolutionaries, who continued to treat them as slaves.

Bolívar's ideas had been different but they were eclipsed by the commercial and political interests of the *criollos*. The first constitution which Bolívar sent from Lima to the new Bolivian Assembly not only enshrined his libertarian and humanistic ideals, but has been described as one of his most important political pronouncements. It seems to have owed much to the First Consulate in France. The President's appointment was to be for life, and carried with it the power of nominating a successor, though there were specific limitations on the Head of State's powers.

'The authority of the president must be perpetual,' said Bolívar, in a curiously prescient phrase, 'because in countries with no social distinctions it is necessary to have some fixed point around which everything revolves.'

He himself saw this constitution as combining the advantages of a limited monarchy and of a republic, without the drawbacks of either. A more sardonic observation by a French diplomat described it as 'a throne draped in republican colours.' Whichever may be the more apt of the two, in practice the Constitution was doomed to a short and not very glorious life and was never much more than a dead letter.

The Republic which had taken his name hardly fared better.

241

Throughout the tempestuous course of Bolivian history in the nineteenth century, marred by internecine struggles between different *caudillos* and their factions, and a succession of megalomaniac dictators, each more colourful and more disastrous than the last, the search for a national identity was subordinated to individual interests. The country meandered on, ever more divided against itself, until it was on the brink of disintegration.

It was the Pacific war and the loss of the littoral which brought this disruptive process to a halt. The national disaster of losing such large areas of territory, including the whole of the seaboard, brought some semblance of unity to Bolivia's troubled political scene, and it is no coincidence that the creation of the Conservative and Liberal parties, and the development of more orderly government, stemmed from about this time. Yet the stability which marked the end of the last century and the first two or three decades of the present one was deceptive. Though Bolivia had been forced to search within herself for unity and strength, the search had not yet gone deeply enough. To all practical intents and purposes, the country was still governed from outside, its policies determined by interests far removed from, and sometimes alien to, the country's own advantage, and the main bulk of the population—the Aymara and Quechua Indians—were still ignored, except by a few. This complete blindness to national values affected every aspect of political and cultural life, as well as social attitudes. In literature it reached the point almost of absurdity: the predominant theme in Hispanic literature was the cult of the exotic, yet Bolivian *modernistas* were laboriously seeking their themes in Nordic sagas and Greek myths, completely insensitive to the exotic quality of their own indigenous tradition. The counter-movement towards national themes led by Franz Tamayo was not, however, merely a literary fashion; it also had far-reaching political effects.

1932 was the great dividing line. It was the beginning of yet another disastrous territorial war, this time waged against Paraguay for control of the barren and largely unexplored region of the Chaco, which lies across the frontier of the two countries.

The struggle over the disputed area had been going on for some time, mainly for political reasons, backed up by Bolivia's desire, after the loss of her Pacific seaboard, to retain a navigable outlet to the Atlantic along the Paraguay river. Open hostilities finally broke out in the late twenties after the discovery of petroleum in neighbouring areas. The fully-fledged war which followed later was little short of cataclysmic for Bolivia. The exacting climate, the hard terrain, the long lines of communication and supplies with the centre of the country and the prevalence of disease all taxed the endurance of the Bolivian armies —mainly composed of Indians from the *altiplano* who had never lived in such conditions before, much less fought in them—to breaking point. Tremendously high casualties—some sixty thousand men killed—were suffered in relation to the size of the population. Although the war petered out in 1935 when both sides were exhausted, the Bolivian army had lost a considerable amount of ground and, as a result, the greater part of the disputed territory was conceded to Paraguay under the terms of the peace treaty eventually signed in 1938. Thus Bolivia was shorn of another sizeable area of her territory, in addition to her population losses.

The economic effects of the Chaco war are still felt today, for the enormous cost of the war in relation to the country's exiguous financial resources set in train an inflationary process which continued unchecked until it reached galloping proportions in the nineteen-fifties and had to be restrained by a stabilization programme of equal severity.

The moral consequences were even more far-reaching: the new generation of educated young men who had gone to fight in the Chaco came back filled with revulsion at the carnage seen there and at the corruption and ineptitude of the governing classes which had led to such ignominious defeat. They were appalled at the low repute into which Bolivia had fallen internationally and fiercely determined to rethink national policies and build new values. After this the search for a national destiny, which had previously been diffused among many small groups, gradually began to crystallize.

The Chaco war showed beyond any shadow of doubt that national policies had been based on false premises, and so completed the gradual awakening to reality that had begun with the Pacific war and the later loss of Acre to Brazil. In the catalytic effect it had on Bolivia socially, politically and intellectually, and in the stimulus it gave to a group of writers and thinkers, the Chaco defeat has something in common with the Spanish experience at the end of the last century, when the loss of Cuba and the Philippines led to an upsurge of creative writing and thinking by young intellectuals—the famous generation of 1898—analysing the causes of the defeat and aiming to build a new nation based on purer traditions more in keeping with the country's true interests and background.

The Bolivian sense of nationhood has been forged in adversity. The moments of triumph and euphoria in the country's history have done little to enhance the national destiny or strengthen the national character; on the contrary, they have tended to be debilitating and divisive in their effect. The aftermath of the achievement of independence was marked by personal feuds of the basest kind. On the other hand, the successive limitation of her frontiers through the loss first of the Arica and Antofogasta ports, then of Acre, and, finally, of the Chaco seems to have fortified the consciousness of a national identity. Bolivia was forced to withdraw behind her embattled mountains to seek and develop her own values and look to her own resources for solutions. During the years between the end of the Chaco war and 1952 Bolivia showed the first signs of coming to grips with her problems, albeit clumsily, with many false starts and setbacks. The abortive governments of Busch and Villaroel, with their tragic dénouements, still marked irrevocable milestones along the road towards a more integrated national approach, which culminated in the MNR's accession to power in 1952.

Over the next twelve years a new kind of stability reigned in Bolivia. Many will consider this a controversial judgment, pointing to the innumerable upheavals and the economic decline which occurred during much of that period. Yet, for the first time in many decades, three successive presidential periods were completed and, as each came to an end, a successor was elected by procedures which, though not always beyond reproach, at least had greater claims to legality than the series of *coups* and revolutions that characterized so much of Bolivia's earlier history as an independent country.

For the first time, Bolivia seemed to be set upon the right course. Following that course meant adopting many difficult and much-disputed policies, such as nationalizing the mines and carrying out an agrarian reform, but although they shook the nation down to its foundations, they were the only means of rebuilding it on a firmer and more equitable basis. Such measures inevitably aroused violent opposition. Inevitably too, there were mistakes, injustices and oppression. But the first vital steps had been taken towards restoring human dignity to the Indian and recognizing the essential Indianness of Bolivia. So entrenched have these relatively recent and, in their day, extremely radical innovations become that no future government, whatever its complexion, could try to retract them without committing political suicide. The Military Junta which overthrew the MNR in November 1964 was quick to proclaim its adherence to the conquests of the 1952 revolution, such as the nationalization of the mines and the agrarian reform, and described its action in deposing the previous government merely as 'a revolution within the revolution'.

Why was the MNR ousted after twelve years of continuous rule, which was something of a record in modern Bolivia? Clearly somewhere along the route on which it had embarked so confidently it had mistaken its way. Clearly, also, it had lost the original impetus which had carried it to power against all manner of obstacles. Long sojourn in power had a weakening effect and lulled the governing group with a false sense of security. Since the opposition was divided into small fragmented parties and presented no serious challenge, the governing group itself lost sight of the need for unity; rivalries and bickering set in and the old, inherent Bolivian tendency to individualism, personalism and schism began to assert itself. The MNR had never been a very monolithic structure and it was all

245

too easy for factions to break away under the leadership of disgruntled individuals. Then, too, for many years the government had had to contend with an adverse economic situation, partly inherited and partly of its own involuntary making, owing to its lack of administrative experience when it came to power. The cramping stabilization policies introduced in 1956 cured the disease but almost killed the patient, since it put an effective stop to growth as well as to the inflationary spiral. Unrest and dissatisfaction rumbled in the towns where the population was more vociferous in its claims and had greater room for political expression. The main benefits of the revolution, though very real, were not spectacular and they mainly favoured a sector of the population—the peasants—who were only intermittently politically active. The miners, on the other hand, soon became disaffected and obstreperous when attempts were made to retract some of the injudicious concessions made in the first euphoria of the movement.

The realization that something was going very seriously wrong, in spite of the gradual progress towards economic recovery, was brought home to me in 1962 with the abrupt recrudescence of the campaign for an outlet to the sea. Resentment had smouldered against Chile ever since the Pacific war of the last century, but during the past few years this had been latent rather than explicit; relations between the two countries had been superficially cordial while individual Chileans were popular in Bolivia and most Bolivians had some connection with Chile, whether through education, marriage or exile.

The ostensible reason for the renewed outburst of feeling in the early nineteen-sixties was the Chilean Government's action in diverting part of the waters of the river Lauca, which meandered across the joint frontier, watering a remote and sparsely-populated area of the Bolivian *altiplano* and difficult to find on most maps. Somehow, one felt that this was not the whole story. It was not merely a disquieting impression that much of the hullabaloo was meant to distract popular attention from problems at home by 'Marches to the Sea' and by making the unmentionable dictum of Eduardo Abaroa about his opponent's grandmother when he was called upon to surrender at Arica a kind of *leitmotiv* of national dignity. That, after all, is a fairly usual ploy of hard-pressed governments. More ominous was the sensation that Bolivia was losing her way, turning back to the old insubstantial longings to be a maritime state, lifting her eyes above the mountains towards the elusive blue of the ocean.

Certainly, in the early sixties, there seemed to be a general falling-off, a growing lack of confidence in the national ideal, accompanied by the fragmentation of the party in power. Paradoxically, this occurred precisely because the MNR was so firmly settled in the saddle of government. Bolivian history is full of such ironies. Thus the gradually improving physical integration of the country through better systems of communication coincided with the loss of most of the Chaco region. In 1964, when improvement of the economic situation after years of recession and stagnation had just become apparent—the gross national product had achieved a very respectable growth rate of between six and seven per cent in the previous year—the government which had accomplished this feat was violently overthrown. Perhaps this inherently contradictory situation stemmed partly from the fact that, in order to save herself from virtual bankrupty, Bolivia had had to rely to an excessive degree on outside assistance, some of which inevitably involved deviation from the chosen path of the revolution or, at best, compromise. However that may be, the turning point was marked a couple of years earlier by the Lauca controversy. This was the red herring that was drawn across the path of national progress and unification.

The introspective analysis to which Bolivia had to subject herself naturally underlined the importance and potential strength of the Indian and of the indigenous tradition. For the Indian, like his country, was also forged in adversity, the natural adversity of the elements in the high Andes, compounded by the obdurate fate that fell on his race with the advent of the Spaniards. Racialism in the constructive sense of pride of origin, and of the restitution of rights to a downtrodden race,

247

was a central theme of the 1952 revolution. In earlier decades Bolivian writers, thinkers and politicians had oscillated between hispanophobia and indiophobia, in a never-ending search for a national mean. The country finally came to terms with her destiny towards the middle of the twentieth century with the realization that administrative measures to attract immigration had failed and that the indianization of the country was becoming increasingly more rapid.

In this there can be no going back either: the Indian has reconquered his place in the life of the nation and no temporary setbacks can now change that. In this, too, Bolivia, so often condemned or pitied as one of the most backward countries on the South American continent, is well in advance of many of her neighbours whose populations also contain a high proportion of Indian blood, but where there has been less *mestizaje*, so that the most powerful section has managed to keep its Spanish heritage unmixed. There the people of European stock keep mainly to the towns, sometimes exclusively to the capital city, supported perhaps by the produce of some enormous stretch of half-cultivated land away in the *sierra*. The Indians on the other hand, work in the *sierra* as little better than serfs on the *haciendas* of the ruling class or, vainly seeking a better life, huddle in miserable slums tacked together from ancient petrol tins and cardboard boxes, on the fringes of great cities where the lights sparkle as brightly as in Paris and entertainment for the rich is as sophisticated as in the French capital. They live in a reservation as surely as if the government had deliberately adopted a policy to confine them to one. This situation cannot endure indefinitely. Such countries are living on top of a volcano and with every day that passes without a solution being found, the worse the eventual eruption is likely to be. Bolivia at least has tried to face reality.

Recognition alone is not enough, and a restitution of rights to an illiterate people can be no more than formal. Institutions have to be lifted from their obsolete Spanish mould, made more dynamic and adopted more closely to reality. Nowhere is this truer than in education. It is not simply that educational facilities must eventually be provided for the whole population, including the Indian peasants, but the that system itself must be reorganized to serve the country's true needs. In the old Spanish style the universities still turn out far too many lawyer's who cannot find enough clients and so have to turn to other more lucrative occupations, notably politics. Latin American universities have always been a hotbed of political activity, long before the current surge of university protest in Europe. In Bolivia the tendency was intensified not only by the Bolivian's innate inclinations but also because the dull system of teaching mainly by rote caused lively young minds to seek a more stimulating form of intellectual activity on which to sharpen their wits. It was also fostered by the MNR's decision to give the students a say in the administration of the university, a practice which, however laudably rooted in democratic principle, proved as disastrous in its practical effects as the similar decision to give the miners part control of the mines. Youth is even more important in Bolivia than in most countries, mainly because the expectation of life is so short. There is no room, at any rate at the present time, for the elder statesman. It is quite common for an able political leader to be written off in public opinion for no greater crime than that of nearing his sixtieth birthday. For this reason it is essential to modify the educational system so that it can prepare the new generations to face the specifically Bolivian challenges that the future has to offer them, instead of bringing them up in a hidebound and irrelevant academic tradition belonging to another country and another age.

The transformation started by the revolution is, however, continuing all the time. The army is a case in point. Before 1952, the rôle of the army in Bolivia closely followed the pattern that predominates over most of the Latin American continent—a powerful *éminence grise*, perpetually on the watch. That rôle has been gruesomely, and exaggeratedly, portrayed in the post-revolutionary murals on the main staircase of the Presidential Palace in La Paz, where heavily-booted generals, depicted with obscene paunches and features coarse to the point of brutishness, goosestep their way over the supine bodies of the populace. The MNR reversed this situation when they came to power, and as with so many of their innovations, revolutionary exuberance went rather too far. The army was reduced to such an extent that it not only ceased to constitute a danger but could no longer keep public order. Its ineffectualness was increased by the distribution of arms to the miners and the peasants, who became an unpredictable power in the land, a sort of mediaeval citizens' militia reminiscent of the time of the Catholic Kings of Spain. Given the political immaturity of these groups, easily swayed by local leaders whose oratory was not always matched by their probity, it is not surprising that the MNR soon found that it had made another stick with which to beat itself.

From about 1960 on, MNR began to rebuild the army in a new image but once again the counter-emphasis was perhaps too strong. By another of those ironies of Bolivian history, it was the armed forces that the MNR had re-created which overthrew the régime in 1964. It was, of course, a different army from that which had controlled Bolivian politics almost ever since the creation of the republic, and was imbued with revolutionary ideals. All the same, the fact that the armed forces felt obliged or even able, to seize power, instead of operating in the background in support of a civilian government, showed that Bolivia had failed to achieve that very delicately balanced situation in which the function of the armed forces is limited to providing adequate defence and maintaining public order; a balance, it must be admitted, which has eluded most of her sister countries in Latin America.

The MNR showed more circumspection in dealing with the Church, that twin power of the State which holds sway throughout the greater part of South America. It is surprising, indeed, that a régime which, originally at least, had strong Marxist inspiration, should have allowed it to survive. Yet I believe that I have attended more official Catholic Masses in the cathedral of La Paz than in any other South American country and such occasions were always honoured by the presence of the President and of the Cabinet. The church has its formal rôle to play on State occasions but there its influence in Government affairs largely ends. No black surpliced figures eddy down the cobbled streets of La Paz as they do in Quito, or Bogotá or Lima and education is free from the trammels of religious control. Yet religion still has significance, if not an overt social significance, for the middle-class town-dwellers as well as for the Indian peasant and the miner who fuse their Catholic and pagan gods into one unified deity. Bolivia has broken with the stultifying religious bigotry inherited from Spain, but in continuing to recognize a carefully circumscribed rôle for the Church, well removed from active politics, the MNR achieved a synthesis worthy of a people whose intuitive approach to religion is essentially syncretic.

There are still many who consider Bolivia an unruly country, as froward as her landscape. Even Fernando Diez de Medina, one of her most distinguished modern writers—and one with strongly nationalist leanings—admits that '*El boliviano sabe pelear, sabe mandar, pero no sabe obedecer*'—'the Bolivian knows how to fight, knows how to command, but does not know how to obey.' Here again some very persistent Spanish traits emerge, reminiscent of the old Spanish adage: '*Se obedece pero no se cumple*'—'We obey the order but we do not carry it out.' But they have been reinforced by the passive resistance of the Indians throughout the long centuries of oppression so that he too has imperceptibly left his mark on the national character.

In contemplating Bolivian history, one is reminded of Azorín's description of Spanish history: 'The perpetual tumult of opposing passions'. Any Bolivian will describe himself to you with a certain amount of ill-concealed pride as an *eterno revolucionario*—a perpetual revolutionary—and remind you that Bolivia experienced sixty revolutions in the first seventy-three years of her independence. The cachet ascribed to this word, which in most countries would be regarded as dangerously subversive, is reflected in the astonishing number of times with which it appears in the name of the innumerable Bolivian parties which proliferate on the political scene, including one whose intrinsic conservative—some would say reactionary—bent has never been in doubt. Bolívar put it differently, however. 'What is Bolivia?' he asked, and himself gave the answer: 'It is the unbridled love of liberty.'

Countless incidents may be quoted to illustrate the revolutionary addiction of the Bolivian. When I was newly arrived in La Paz I returned to my office one afternoon to find great turmoil in a street that had been perfectly tranquil half-an-hour previously: a well-known politician, who until a few days before had held a high ministerial position, was covering his retreat into a friendly Embassy by firing his pistol into the air, while police and an angry crowd surged in front. Having regained my office by a devious route, I was watching the proceedings from the doorway, well concealed behind the voluminous skirts of two or three *cholitas*, when a Bolivian colleague plucked at my arm.

'Come away,' he hissed. 'Can't you see that they are *barzolas?*' (a very aggressive kind of female militia, named after one of the heroines of the revolution).

And, indeed, when one looked closer, one could see that their fists were full of stones.

In times of stress, it is by no means unusual to go into a Minister's office and trip over a sub-machine-gun propped nonchalantly against a chair or a window-sill as you walk to his desk to shake hands. And no one seemed to think it in the least bit out of the ordinary for a Vice-President of the Republic to be in open and vociferous opposition to the policy of the government to such a degree that he had in the end to be despatched post-haste to an ambassadorial post abroad, though still retaining the nominal title of deputy head of state; or that a successor in this post should rise up in open rebellion against the government and oust it from power.

Being a president is certainly no sinecure in Bolivia. Fortunes are apt to change suddenly as the unfortunate Belzu discovered in 1865. After a triumphal return to La Paz he had successfully defended the city against Melgarejo's troops and was on the Palace balcony being acclaimed by the multitude with cries of

'Long live Belzu'! When Melgarejo arrived at the Palace surrounded by his few remaining officers and apparently a prisoner, Belzu went inside to receive his surrender, but instead a shot rang out and Melgarejo strode on to the balcony.

'Belzu is dead,' he cried. 'Who lives now?'

'Melgarejo,' roared back the prudent crowd. 'Long live Melgarejo!'

Even a triumphal progress is fraught with perils. I can remember one occasion when a President seemed likely to be trampled underfoot by an enthusiastic mob out of control and another when the aged presidential DC–3 seemed in imminent danger of colliding with the military escort planes, equally antique, whose delirious pilots had removed all hands from the controls in order to wave their caps in joyous greeting, as they bounced up and down in the turbulent air only a few feet beneath the wings.

Logically the risks increase in direct proportion to any fall from favour. There was dramatic evidence of this in 1964 when an internationally-sponsored project, near Cochabamba, equipped with those very machines which had been transferred with such alarums and excursions from Cotoca, was to be inaugurated by the President. It was the day after the offending *borro* had been removed from the calf of my leg, so that I was bandaged from knee to ankle but had persuaded the doctors that the occasion was too important to miss. However, a few hours before we were due to fly down to Cochabamba, the President's ADC telephoned to say that the visit had been cancelled, because of the deteriorating political situation in the mining areas. No more than four or five days later, the government fell and the President fled into exile in Lima. Only then did we—and he—learn that the original plan had been to dispose of him with a burst of machine-gun fire at the inauguration of the project on the previous Saturday. I preferred not to reflect how the rest of us standing by his side would have fared, or how far or fast I could have run with my injured leg.

On the whole, however, there is remarkably little danger to the onlooker in a Bolivian revolution, provided you keep your head down, and do not emulate an unfortunate foreign consul some years ago, who looked out at an injudicious moment to see what was going on, only to be picked off by a sniper's bullet. The Bolivians themselves are remarkably casual about the whole business. Once, on the eve of the United Nations Day, ironically enough, there had been a particularly nasty uprising; hostile forces had been entrenched in the surrounding hills and for a while it had been touch and go. A group of us had emerged into the deserted street, after working late on the next day's celebrations, to find a solitary gunman at the corner firing up and down the street at no particular target, and since we were the only moving objects we hastily took shelter on the stairs of a private house of which the door was luckily not shut. Later, we ran half a mile, faster than I would have imagined possible in stiletto heels on cobbles, to the place where the cars had been parked in relative safety. Next day it was learned that a number of people had been killed and I telephoned the Foreign Minister with the suggestion that I should cancel the reception arranged for noon at my house.

'Please don't,' came the surprising reply. 'The Government has announced that everything is normal and to cancel the reception would imply the contrary.' So the reception duly took place, and was attended by three Ministers in token of the normality of the situation, while the rest of the Cabinet sat in emergency session, and by a few other intrepid souls, with a noticeable lack of foreigners and of ladies.

The nonchalance was thrown into greater relief in the context of the 1964 revolution, which was a serious affair. The small hill of Laikakota tucked away in the gully which runs through the centre of the town and divides the university from Miraflores, was bitterly defended by militiamen, who did not seem to know that the President had already flown into exile. They were bombed into submission. Although the bombing was rudimentary by Second World War standards, it was nonetheless horrible, for the defenders of Laikakota were armed only with rifles and protected merely by earthen trenches. Afterwards it was estimated that some two hundred of them were killed.

When at last the noise of the explosions had ceased to reverberate back from the rocky wall on the other side of the valley, I went out cautiously on to the terrace. A few soldiers from the garrison opposite, which had remained loyal to the deposed President until the very last moment, were straggling up the steep escarpment on the other side of the ravine in search of some unknown target. It was two o'clock on a brilliantly sunny afternoon, the sky an unflecked blue, the air sparkling like ice-cold wine. But everything was uncannily still and quiet after the shattering commotion of the last two hours. There was no traffic on the road, and nothing was moving except those few camouflaged figures toiling up to Miraflores and the humming birds flashing blue and green between the geraniums.

Then, suddenly, the unmistakable sound of an engine drifted up from the hidden valley below. Straining our ears, we could hear it chugging up the wickedly steep road, and noisily changing gear on the bends. We waited agog to see what it could be. Some political or military leader, perhaps, driving up to take control of the situation? Certainly this solitary vehicle in a strangely silent city must signify something dramatic. At last it hove into sight, a rather broken-down lorry making heavy going of the last incline, with two or three figures sitting on its open back. It was only when it came right beneath us that we could see that it contained crates of soft drinks and returned empties and that the figures were small boys. Resolutely it chugged on up the Avenida Arce, between intermittent bursts of gunfire, carrying its incongruous cargo into the centre of the fighting area, presumably to disperse refreshments to the contending sides. Later, a solitary soldier came trudging up the same road, in full battle kit, thoughtfully munching a banana, with a bewildered expression on his face as if he was not at all sure on which side he was supposed to be fighting, but was at least intent on getting fed.

It may be that this Olympian unconcern is fostered by the very gentlemanly code which governs the conduct of most Bolivian revolutions. The fate that befell Villaroel is fortunately an exception. Most deposed Presidents are discreetly assisted into exile. Ministers are granted asylum in Embassies and later leave the country with a safe conduct. Even those who are caught and committed to prison are often treated with a certain lenience. On my last Sunday in Bolivia, I visited the prison. I was searched for arms when I went in but afterwards allowed to wander anywhere. There seemed to be no restriction on the prisoners either. The aged jumble of buildings reeked of the open drains, but the more important prisoners were housed in individual cells which they had furnished themselves, some even to the extent of papering the rough walls. It was disconcerting to be warmly greeted on all sides by people whom I had known previously in high office. To my embarrassment one of them insisted on telling me in a penetrating tone and enormous wealth of detail about an abortive escape attempt he had made the previous week. Another, an ex-Minister who was being tried for misdemeanours allegedly committed during the previous administration, barely had time to look up from the typewriter he was busily tapping. He explained apologetically that he was engaged in preparing a study on a subject concerning his former Ministry, for which he was being paid by the present government; this money was contributing to his upkeep in prison and also to the cost of his defence. There cannot be many countries so tolerant that you may be awarded a contract by the government while in prison and under investigation for corrupt practices!

But it is too facile to dismiss Bolivia as an unstable South American state constantly in the throes of an upheaval; there are revolutions and revolutions. The MNR uprising in 1952 was not just another palace revolution, a mere changing of the guard and of the person at its head. It represented a fundamental change in the direction of national life and, although its rule was accompanied by the periodic upheavals endemic in Bolivian politics, there was yet discernible a new thread of stability and continuity running through the nation's affairs. And then, twelve years later, it was suddenly all over, with the 'revolution within the revolution'. One had sensed for months that the tension and the opposition were building up to a point at which a clash was unavoidable and that the armed forces now felt themselves strong enough to act. The ever electric air of La Paz had positively crackled with additional charges. The explosion, then, was expected but when the last crack of gunfire had ceased to crepitate between the opposing hills, lined up themselves in serried ranks as if for battle, an almost disconcerted hush descended on the deep gorge between them. After all those weeks of taut expectancy, the city again lay waiting, but this time under a pall of silence, and for what no one could quite dare to predict.

I had been delegated, with the Yugoslav Ambassador, who was acting as Dean of the Diplomatic Corps, to go to the Palace to seek guarantees for the members of the fallen administration and for the foreign communities. Though it was the middle of a weekday afternoon, nothing stirred. Windows were shuttered, doors bolted and barred, and not even a curious face peered between the closed curtains. Only in the upper reaches of the city a few marauding bands of looters roamed the streets, breaking into the houses of ex-Ministers, now herded in asylum under the roofs of the nearest Latin American Embassies, to steal what was portable and smash the rest. The UN flag, meant to indicate the humanitarian nature of our mission and to protect us from attack, seemed to flutter very wanly as we drove through the strangely silent streets as through a city of the dead. We saw only one other vehicle and that was a UN Land-Rover, commandeered by armed civilians, whom I managed to persuade to return it.

When we reached the street leading up to the Plaza Murillo, a few armed guards stepped forward to ask our business and then waved us on. The Plaza was deserted and bore the slightly abandoned air of a public place that has been the site of some enormous celebration on the previous day. Villaroel's lamp-post was unguarded, its tatterdemalion flowers nodding sadly to themselves. A few wisps of paper and litter blew disconsolately about the square. Before the door of the Palace a man's shoe lay abandoned. Later we learned that the miners' leader, and ex-Vice-President, Juan Lechín Oquendo, who had supported

257

the rebels, had been carried in triumph to the Palace a few minutes earlier on the shoulders of his supporters, only to be met by hostile gunfire. In the ensuing mêlée, he lost his shoe, and some of his comrades their lives.

Luckily we encountered less resistance and were ushered in immediately. The great hall on the ground floor where we had danced and conversed at so many balls and State receptions, and which had at all times been thronged with groups of officials or journalists, was as quiet and cold as the cloister it resembled and as empty as the Plaza outside. There were no more than a dozen men in the whole palace and they seemed to be waiting for the next wave of events to carry them on. A few dishevelled and unshaven characters in civilian clothes lounged on their rifles on the staircase under the wily leer of the caricatured generals in the revolutionary mural. Some of them were obviously the worse for drink. There were few military men about, and no one, either civilian or military, of high rank.

The place was alive with rumours and speculation: the 'communists' were massing at the top of the city and might attack at any moment; the President of the new Military Junta, General Barrientos, was at that moment landing at the airport from Cochabamba, would come early tomorrow morning, or the next day . . . who knew? General Ovando, who had taken over control of the country in the meantime, was nowhere to be found and there seemed some doubt as to whether anyone knew his whereabouts, for a series of conflicting versions were given. We were cordially invited to wait in the Presidential office until he could be located. Inside, we found an American Catholic bishop, also bound on an errand of mercy, prudently standing against a panel of wall between the long windows that ran along one side of the room, for from time to time a few bullets whined aimlessly through the air outside. It seemed very strange to stand in this familiar room where I had been so many hundreds of times over the last five years, talking to the President, introducing visitors, or sitting at large meetings round the Cabinet table discussing the economic development of Bolivia, and to realize that everything was now changed. The room looked remarkably orderly and bore no signs of hasty flight. A few reports lay piled on a small table behind the presidential desk as they always had. The papers on the desk were somewhat more untidily strewn about than usual. The one incongruous note was a crumpled piece of brightly coloured paper flung down on the desk as if a gift had been hurriedly unwrapped before the precipitate departure into exile. Otherwise, there was no echo of the anguished deliberations that must have taken place in this room during the previous night, only a few hours before, as the Cabinet tried to decide whether or not to defend La Paz against the rebel forces. Instead, there was a sense of vacuum, of a gaping pause in the course of history which anyone with decision might leap in to fill. You felt that if you picked up the telephone and snapped out a few orders with sufficient authority people would jump gratefully to attention, glad to be directed again into a well-defined course of action. It was only the mad impression of a moment of course, just as the political hiatus did not last more than twenty-four hours.

They never did find General Ovando for us and when we finally left an hour or two later, accompanied by a supporter of the new régime delegated to 'protect' us, I had great difficulty in preventing my car from being commandeered on the way home by the Rector and students of the University. That we finally emerged unscathed was due entirely to our own efforts and in no way thanks to our supposed protector who was too far advanced in his cups even to be coherent. But next day the President of the new Military Junta arrived in La Paz and within a day or two a surprising degree of normality had been restored.

The vacuum was filled and in 1966 the military régime was succeeded by an elected government headed by General Barrientos. But despite the efforts of this government and its predecessors, many of the fundamental problems remain and, for the historical and geographical reasons already described, these are singularly intractable.

One senses therefore that Bolivia is still seeking the right road to the future. The old dissensions and internal conflicts continue and many of the different parties and factions who combined to overthrow the MNR have since fallen out with one another. And the discovery in 1967 of Ché Guevara's guerrilla contingent hidden away in the thick jungle of the Andean foothills near Camiri seemed to denote yet another departure in Bolivian history, and a rejection of former methods. The link between this movement and similar guerrilla movements in neighbouring countries along the backbone of the Andes and the fact that half the guerrillas were Cubans gave the impression that, in the view of the guerrillas, nationalism was not enough and that Bolivia's problems must be tackled as part of a regional campaign to succour the underprivileged of Latin America by violent means, since others had failed. So far as Bolivia was concerned this was not only alien to the traditional palace revolution; it was contrary, too, to the new kind of progressive revolution introduced by the MNR, which based itself on nationalism.

It was to a certain extent significant that the movement did not obtain the support either of the Communist party or of the peasants in the area in which it was operating—their lack of response is a constant theme in Guevara's diaries and in September 1967 he goes so far as to state that the peasants have become informers. Some observers have deduced from this, and the eventual annihilation of the group, that the new approach was totally rejected. Others have pointed out that the two factors are not necessarily as significant as they seem on the grounds that the area of guerrilla operations was ill-chosen; that the peasants as a whole, and especially in that region, are passive rather than dynamic in their political responses; and that the Communist party, and, indeed, the whole movement of the extreme left in Bolivia, has long been weak and divided.

Someone who has not been back in the country since 1965 and has to rely on the scant information appearing in the press outside is not well-qualified to make any judgment between these two opposing views, but one cannot help wondering whether such extreme situations would have arisen now had the MNR not lost sight of the road along which they had elected to travel somewhere during those twelve years of continuous power.

The root of the problem is that Bolivia is still feeling her way towards a political synthesis, an equivalent in political terms of the synthesis already largely achieved in religion, in culture and in social customs.

14 BOLIVIA is a country to which one cannot remain indifferent. One may love, deplore or pity but, whatever the reaction, it will be as extreme as the characteristics of the country itself. You cannot remain uninvolved. Perhaps it is because the Bolivian people seem to have passed through flames, like the igneous rocks of the *cordillera* beneath whose shadow they live.

It is hard to define this nation, because it sprang from the combination of an ancient, indigenous culture and a superimposed colonial rule, both of which transcended the present-day frontiers of Bolivia, and left well-defined traces which linger on today in an uneasy synthesis. Yet, for all that, there is something unmistakably Bolivian which imposes itself upon the traveller wherever he may wander in that vast and mountain-trammelled land, a way of life, an attitude, a mode of expression that are unique and distinct from their counterparts in other Latin American countries, despite the undeniable similarities. There is, in short, an unmistakable quality of *bolivianidad* which infuses the savour of life and the spirit of the people everywhere, be it on the frosty tundras of the *altiplano*, in the fecund green valleys, or in the jungles and *llanos* which roll away eastwards to the horizons of a more promising tomorrow. It is this quality, this *bolivianidad*, that I have tried to catch, on the wing, as it were, for it is an elusive attribute, flashing out momentarily in a word or a gesture, an encounter, or a landscape.

What perhaps most strikes the traveller is the duality in Bolivian life, a duality expressed in extremes of geography and extremes of temperament, in the antithesis between the aquiline pinnacles of the *cordillera*, chiselling their trenchant identity on an equatorial sky, and the blurred horizons of the steamy savannahs in the east, where aimless rivers curl sleepily round upon themselves and absentmindedly merge into one another; between those sudden, incisive flarings of the Bolivian temper, which resolve themselves in violence and the sharp crack of gunfire, and the gentle, almost somnolent quality of everyday life, full of small courtesies and kindnesses, when even *mañana* does not matter too much, and one may just as well wait until the day after. It is a duality which has its roots deep in history and the bifurcation that occurred with the Spanish conquest, when the Indian, formerly integrated into the fabric of an admittedly hierarchical society, but able to express himself within its highly stylized patterns, was crushed into subjection.

Not that he succumbed easily, however absolute the eclipse of the Inca Empire seemed to be. In defiance of all that has been said to show that his is a primitive and inferior race, he has not only survived against all odds but has left an indelible imprint on the new society that is growing up. The personality of the race was too strong to be obliterated. Even in the worst times of Spanish domination its subtle but pervasive infiltration could be detected: in the baroque carvings and paintings of the colonial period, in which the deft fingers of the Indian artists meticulously followed the artistic instructions of their Spanish masters but smuggled into the European-inspired framework autochthonous motifs, revealed in small animals and flowers of unmistakable American origin, or in the Amerindian cast of feature of some New World Madonna; in their music which trembles between the strange dissonances of the high Andes and melodious Spanish cadences, so that you may find yourself dancing a courtly *cueca*, rich in peninsular memories, to the faintly nostalgic strains of some staunchly indigenous instrument such as a *charango* or a *quena*; and in religion, where the Catholic doctrines, imposed upon the subject peoples in order to save their souls, have undergone many an unexpected transmogrification in order to make them harmonize with the simple pantheism of the Indian cult, which sees spirits enshrined in the natural features of the world around.

Outwardly, the Spanish veneer, thin as it was, remained uncracked for several centuries. Still today there are many traces of the Spanish heritage in public life, even though the bonds of Spanish feudalism have been loosened. You see it in the administration, and in the needlessly complex bureaucracy which entangles itself helplessly in red-tape. You see it too in the personal characteristics of the people, especially in the bigger towns: in the fierce individualism, which collectively becomes an exclusive and often intolerant regionalism; in the political fanaticism which has supplanted the former religious bigotry, now largely superseded; in the deep-seated pride, and sense of the fitness and rightness of things which affects so many aspects of life, from the excessive output of lawyers in the universities to a general distaste for manual work, magnified in certain quarters into an aristocratic disdain for economic and social progress.

But these things you find mostly among the remnants of the *rosca*, the aristocratic upper echelons of former Bolivian society who were ousted from their privileged position by the 1952 revolution. With the recognition of the essential 'Indianness' of Bolivia, and the search for national values rooted in the country's own soil, rather than patterned exclusively on an alien culture only superficially assimilated, the whole texture of Bolivian life has changed. This does not mean the extinction of Spanish influence: four hundred years of history cannot be blotted out. It does mean, however, the perfection of a process that started a decade or two ago, that of weaving together the two strands of Bolivian nationhood, the Indian and the Spanish, into a new and harmonious pattern, so that both aspects are given due expression and Bolivia is able to absorb the best of both sides of her dual heritage. The answer to her essential duality must be a synthesis, such as Mexico has managed to achieve, and Bolivia is considerably nearer to attaining this idiosyncratic blend than many of her apparently more advanced neighbours who also have a strong Indian heritage. Such a synthesis must signify not only complete racial fusion but must also recapture, in a new way, the old, close relationship between man and the land around him. The Andean-Indian has to reconquer his environment in order to regain his lost heritage.

The new synthesis is *bolivianidad,* the quintessential Bolivian quality that one already recognizes today and which is symbolized for me in the valley of Cristina and Juan; in the flying figure of Pablo, clutching his alarum clock; in the wide spaces and steepled skyline of the *altiplano*; in the slag-heaps of the mines and the dour, determined faces of the miners; in the colonists riding on lorries to start a new life in the tumbled eastern valleys and plains; in the bustling go-getting atmosphere of Cochabamba; in Santa Cruz with its self-important, new-frontier air; and even in the grassy streets of Riberalta. You sense it in the wild arabesques and baroque costumes of the devil dancers; in the lilt of a nostalgic serenade heard at night in Camiri, where the jungle and the mountains meet; or in the melancholy strains of a *quena,* floating up from some hidden valley by the shores of Lake Titicaca, where an unknown shepherd whiles away the hours playing to his flock as he gazes over the burnished blue waters of the sacred lake.

It is not a static quality, but one that is evolving all the time, just as the country is developing physically. When Alcides Arguedas published his scathing book, at the beginning of this century, the Uruguayan writer and thinker, Jose Enrique Rodó, wrote to him saying, 'You have given your book the title *A Sick People.* I would call it *A Child People* (*Un Pueblo Niño*).' Many years have passed since those words were written, during which Bolivia has seen many changes and has grown in maturity. One hopes that the development will not be merely material, though increased prosperity is sorely needed by her hard-pressed people, but will conserve and deepen the essential Bolivian qualities enshrined in her customs and way of life, in her folklore, and her music.

The difficulties facing Bolivia both now and in the future are immense, but the great Bolivian writer, Franz Tamayo, was perhaps only illustrating the lessons of Bolivia's own history when he affirmed the creative virtue of adversity:

'People speak of geographical isolation, of mountain obstacles and unconnected waterways. They forget that England was once no more than a gypsum pit and the Netherlands only a swamp, and that it is a fact, frequently confirmed by history, that the greatness of a race is directly proportionate to the difficulties it has overcome in its battle with the environment and the surrounding elements . . .'

KACHARPAYA

It is almost impossible to take leave of anyone in Bolivia. There is always one more stirrup cup to be drunk and farewell has become ritualized in the *kacharpaya*, the dance of farewell. Even when you do manage to break loose, the friends and the *pisco* will follow you down the road. It is no coincidence that the Quechua word for hangover—*ch'aqui*—is synonymous with nostalgia and homesickness.

Alcide d'Orbigny remarked the same trait with affectionate exasperation in 1830. Up at dawn in Cochabamba, before leaving on one of his long exploration trips, he waited all morning for his mule train. And when at last it arrived at one o'clock, he complains, his troubles were not over, for he had not yet managed to leave the town. The muleteers dropped in at every house for a last drink with their relations and friends and even when d'Orbigny hustled them out their friends came running after them with brimming jars of *chicha*.

Yet three years later when he left Bolivia for ever he wrote: 'I brought back from this beautiful and rich region of the American continent not only an immense quantity of materials of all kinds suitable for making it known in all its aspects, but also the most lively gratitude towards its government and people from whom I had always received assistance, marks of esteem and the most refined hospitality.'

Seven months after the events of November 1964, I also

267

left Bolivia in much the same frame of mind and, like d'Orbigny, have been unable to forget. During the last few weeks the *despedidas* multiplied, from official dinners with ministerial speeches, to less formal farewell parties where the '*pisco* sours' and the *yungueños* flowed, the *charangos* and the guitars strummed late into the night and we danced again the *huayño* and the *cueca*. Somehow it was fitting that I spent the last day in Oruro signing an agreement for a new mineral project with confetti spilling out of my hat brim and came back, to the despair of the packers, with a large devil-dancer's mask presented to me by the Prefect along with the freedom of the city.

But the real *despedida* had taken place earlier. Very early on my last Sunday in Bolivia, when the sun was only just warming the frost from the grass, I went alone to the valley of Cristina and Juan. Ovejuyo lay very still beneath the weathered spires of its background cliffs. Outside one thatched adobe hut a *campesino* was cutting the hair of another with intent concentration. Neither looked up as I passed. Then, as I negotiated a difficult rut, a small boy with a scabbed, weatherbeaten face, ran up waving his sling to greet me. The cattle he was watching grazed on nearby.

Higher up there was hardly anyone to be seen: a few women hurrying down from the harvest-yellow fields, their backs laden with bean-haulms, someone standing waist-deep in the ripening barley. For the last time I reached the top of the pass at Las Animas, paused by the dark green waters of the reedy lagoon and felt the same wonder, well-remembered and yet fresh as the first time, at the sudden, dazzling vision of the Illimani and the Mururata, a skyline sculptured in ice above the deep erosion-pillared valley.

I left the car where I had always done and climbed up the steep path to the village on the far side of the valley. It was very still and quiet, so that the sudden honking of a donkey seemed to rend the crystal air. Sometimes without warning a cold wind came soughing up between the wind- and water-worn columns flanking the river-bed, to rattle the sparse stems of the *paja*

268

brava, setting the white plumes of the pampas grass nodding and crackling the dead leaves of shrubs still starred with an occasional purple flower. Small black and yellow birds chattered among the barley stooks and the russet seed-heads of the *quinua*. In sheltered hollows the air was sharp with the acrid smell of wild lupins. Near the tumbledown *hacienda*, with its crumbling chapel and tattered yews, there was more noise and movement. Bowler hats rose above the adobe walls, shielding curious eyes, a boy was flailing a sheaf of barley with a stone, and a flock of sheep suddenly came thudding down the pathway, in a fog of dust, nearly knocking me off my feet.

A little farther on I overtook a wrinkled old woman shuffling along under the weight of a faggot of straw, wrapped in her *aguayo*. Her skirt was of bright orange homespun, and grey plaits straggled from beneath a faded and battered green bowler. When I greeted her in Spanish she replied quaveringly:

'*Buenos días, niñita*'—'Good-day, little girl.'

She stopped for a moment to shift her heavy load.

Then she called me back and asked in Aymara, her rheumy old eyes gazing intently into mine:

'Where are you bound, *niñita*?'

It was almost as if she knew. But looking beyond her at that well-loved landscape I could not give the answer. I simply said, 'I go to the village, mama.'

Addis Ababa 1966–Geneva 1968

GLOSSARY

Sp. – Spanish.   Aym. – Aymara.   Qu. – Quechua.
(Meanings given relate specifically to the context in which the words are used in the book.)

abrazo (Sp.): embrace, greeting
aficionado (Sp.): enthusiast, devotee
aguayo (Aym.): woman's shawl, used for carrying baby, or produce, on back
ají (Sp.): hot pepper
altiplano (Sp.): Andean high plateau
ayllú (Aym.): Aymara community, or extended family

bombo (Sp.): drum
boliche (Sp.): small bar, or café

camba (Sp.): native of lowland area around Santa Cruz
campesinos (Sp.): peasants, country-folk
cañahua (Qu.): cereal native to *altiplano*
cargamento (Sp.): offering of silver plate etc, traditionally carried to the Virgin of the Socavón during the Oruro carnival
caudillo (Sp.): leader, often with charismatic qualities
caudillismo (Sp): political system based on individual *caudillos* rather than parties
cante hondo (Sp.): gypsy music from the South of Spain
ch'allar (Aym.): ancient Aymara custom of pouring libations on the Pachamama, the earth goddess
chasqui (Qu.): fleet relay messengers of the Incas
chacra (Sp.): small-holding
chapaco: native to Tarija, in the south of Bolivia

271

ch'aqui (Qu.): hangover, nostalgia

charango (Qu.): small stringed instrument, traditionally made from carapace of armadillo

chicha (Sp.): beer made of fermented maize

chola (Sp.): woman of mixed Indian and Spanish blood

cholo (Sp.): man of mixed Indian and Spanish blood

chullo (Qu.): pointed woollen cap with earflaps, typical male Indian headwear

chullpa (Aym.): ancient Indian burial turrets

chuño (Aym.): dehydrated potato (black)

chuquisaqueño (Sp.): man born in Sucre (Chuquisaca)

cochabambino (Sp.): man born in Cochabamba

cordillera (Sp.): chain or range of mountains

comparsa (Sp.): group of dancers, or guild, taking part in Oruro carnival

criollos (Sp.): people born in the colonies of pure Spanish blood

criollo (Sp.): anything typical of Spanish colonies

cruceño (Sp.): man born in Santa Cruz

cueca (Sp.): courtship dance (Spanish in origin)

despedida (Sp.): farewell, farewell party

empanada (Sp.): savoury pastry of meat or cheese

fiesta (Sp.): party, celebration

góndola (Sp.): bus (Bolivian and Chilean usage)

gringo (Sp.): foreigner (sometimes specifically a North American)

hacienda (Sp.): farm, estate

huaca (Aym. & Qu.): object of religious or superstitious significance

huayño (Aym.): Indian mountain dance, typical of Bolivian *altiplano* or Peruvian *seirra*

humintas (Aym.): *altiplano* delicacy

jallpja-huaica (Aym.): peppery sauce made of *locoto* (peppers) tomato, and the herb *quilquiña*, usually served as a condiment with meat

jejenes (Sp.): insects with extremely unpleasant bite which lurk in tropical grass

kacharpaya (Qu.): song or dance of farewell

kolla (Qu.): native of highlands

llajhua (Qu.): as *jallpja-huaica* above

llanos (Sp.): plains, prairies
lluchu (Aym.): as *chullo* above
locoto (Sp.): pepper

machismo (Sp.): cult of masculinity, virility
maté de coca (Sp.): infusion made from leaf of coca bush
mujeres (Sp.): women

oca (Sp.): root-vegetable native to *altiplano*
Oriente (Sp.): east, the eastern part of Bolivia

paceño (Sp.): man born in La Paz
paja brava (Sp.): *ichú* grass, the stiff spiky grass native to the *altiplano*
pasantes (Sp.): sponsors of the *comparsas* in the Oruro carnival
pawiche (Guaraní): small temporary wigwam in jungle, made of
  boughs and twigs
paredón (Sp.): execution wall
pelado (Sp.): young person (used in Santa Cruz and Beni)
peón (Sp.): labourer
pinquillo (Sp.): reed pipe
piraña (Sp.): tiny fish, native to tropical rivers in Amazon basin with
  needle-sharp teeth which will strip flesh from bone in a few minutes
plaza (Sp.): square
poncho (Sp.): square woollen garment, with hole for head, typically
  worn by Indian man
pongo (Aym. derivation): serf, labourer formerly tied to his master's
  land
pongueaje (Aym. derivation): the system of holding *pongos*
Prefectura (Sp.): office of the Prefect, the local authority
puna (Qu.): the high Andean plateau (used mainly in Peru)

quena (Qu.): Indian flute
quilquiña: herb, used in making *jallpja-huaica*
quinua (Qu.): millet-like cereal, native to *altiplano*
quipu (Qu.): knot-string records of Incas
quirquincho (Qu.): armadillo

remolque (Sp.): flat-topped barge
rosca (Sp.): local Bolivian word for the wealthy aristocracy

sajta de pollo (Qu. & Sp.): highly-spiced Bolivian dish, made of chicken
salteñas (Sp.): spiced meat pastries, typically eaten in La Paz
sierra (Sp.): mountain, hill
sorojche (Aym.): mountain or altitude sickness

273

supay, supaya (Qu.): evil spirits living in the earth, who have to be appeased

tarijeño (Sp.): man born in Tarija
tarka (Aym.): square, wooden Indian flute.
tío (Sp.): the spirit of the mines, the clay or stone idol at the entrance to the mine to which the miner pays tribute on entering
tola (Sp.): *altiplano* shrub.
totora (Aym.): reed growing in Lake Titicaca
trámites (Sp.): procedures, red-tape
tunta (Aym.): dehydrated potato (white)

varones (Sp.): men

yareta (Sp.): fungus-like growth native to *altiplano*, used as fuel
yatiri (Aym.): Aymara medicine man, or witch-doctor

zampoña (Sp.): reed pipes, resembling pipes of Pan

 INDEX

275

tarka, 274

Tihuanacu, 36, 37, 38, 39, 55, 58, 121

tin, 100, 101, 102, 112

Tipuani, 135–139, 146–151, 160

Tipuani (river), 136, 147, 148

Tiquina Straits, 60, 61

Titicaca (lake), 3, 4, 5, 35, 36, 38, 40, 50, 56–64, 79, 84, 85, 153, 223, 265

Todos Santos, 184

tola, 74, 92, 274

totora, 35, 53, 57, 274

trámites, 22, 219, 238, 274

Trinidad, 211

Tucumán (Argentina), 11, 40

Tunari (mountain), 182

Tunupa, 58, 59

Tupac Amara, 46

Tupaj Catari, 46

Uncía, xiii, 101, 127, 129, 130

Unduavi, 133

United Nations, xi, xvii, 3, 107, 115, 127, 140, 149, 152, 196, 224, 233, 235, 254, 257

United States, xv, 3, 140, 145

Uruguay, xvi, 9, 223, 231

Urus (race), 34, 53

Urus (lake), 112

Uyuni, 58, 164

Valley of Cristina and Juan, 70, 265, 268

Venezuela, 9

Viceroyalty of Lima, 43, 167

vicuña, 67, 153

Villaroel, Colonel Gualberto, 48, 49, 102, 216, 217, 244, 255

Villaroel, Padre Emeterio, 117

Villa Tunari, 184, 187, 188, 189, 190

Villazón, 17, 18, 19, 23, 26, 29

Virajocha, 38, 50

Vírgen de la Candelaria, 117, 118

Vírgen de Copacabana, 63

Vírgen de Guadalupe, 170

Vírgen del Socavón, 117, 118, 121

Wari Wari (Peru—mountain), 156, 157, 159, 161

Yanacocha (Peru), 158

Yapacaní (river), xvi, 196, 198

yareta, 164, 274

yatiri, 80, 244

Yungas, 87, 131, 132, 133, 153, 163, 165, 183, 212, 216

Yupanqui, Inca Tito, 182

Zampoña, 85

Zongo (lake), 108

Zongo Valley, 137